A TIME FOR BOLDNESS

A TIME FOR BOLDNESS

A Story of Institutional Change

NANCY L. ZIMPHER

STEPHEN L. PERCY

MARY JANE BRUKARDT

University of Wisconsin-Milwaukee

ANKER PUBLISHING COMPANY, INC.
Bolton, Massachusetts

A Time for Boldness
A Story of Institutional Change

ISBN 1-882982-54-1

Composition by Deerfoot Studios
Cover design by Nicolazzo Productions

Anker Publishing Company, Inc.
176 Ballville Road
P.O. Box 249
Bolton, MA 01740-0249

www.ankerpub.com

ABOUT THE AUTHORS

Nancy L. Zimpher

In 1998, Nancy L. Zimpher became the sixth chancellor—and first woman chancellor at the University of Wisconsin-Milwaukee (UWM). She previously served as the Executive Dean of the Professional Colleges and Dean of the College of Education at The Ohio State University in Columbus, Ohio.

She is the author and editor of numerous books, monographs, and articles on teacher education, including *Profiles of Preservice Teacher Education: Inquiry into the Nature of Programs,* a book she co-authored with her husband, UWM professor Kenneth Howey.

Dr. Zimpher serves on the Executive Committee of the Great Cities Universities, a coalition of urban public research universities committed to metropolitan renewal. She co-chairs the Urban Metro Joint Task Force on Education of the American Association of State Colleges and Universities/National Association of State Universities and Land-Grant Colleges (AASCU/NASULGC), and is co-chair of the Executive Committee of the Commission on International Programs of NASULGC.

Dr. Zimpher is the recipient of numerous awards including the Edward C. Pomeroy Award for Outstanding Contributions to Teacher Education, American Association of Colleges for Teacher Education; the Public Policy Women of Influence Award, Wisconsin; a recipient of both the Milwaukee, Wisconsin, and Columbus, Ohio, YWCA Women of Achievement Award; and is an inductee in the Ohio Women's Hall of Fame.

Stephen L. Percy

Director of the Center for Urban Initiatives and Research at the University of Wisconsin-Milwaukee, Stephen L. Percy has, since 2000, also served as Chancellor's Deputy for The Milwaukee Idea. No stranger to university engagement, Dr. Percy has been a campus leader in forging community-university partnerships between UWM and Milwaukee communities, including the implementation of a five-year Community Outreach Partnership Center funded by the U.S. Department of Housing and Urban Development.

A member of the UWM faculty since 1988, Dr. Percy currently serves as a professor of political science and professor of urban studies with research interests focused on urban policy, organization of local governance, and policy evaluation. The author of numerous books, textbooks, and articles, his most recent include *American Government: The Political Game* and *Disability,*

Civil Rights and Public Policy: The Politics of Implementation, which received the Outstanding Book Award by the Gustavus Meyers Center of Human Rights in the United States.

Dr. Percy is a member of the Board of Directors of the Nonprofit Center of Milwaukee; a Commissioner for the Social Development Commission, a Milwaukee anti-poverty agency; and in 2000, served on the Governor's Blue Ribbon Commission on State and Local Relations for the 21st Century. He is the recipient of the UWM Alumni Association's Distinguished Public Service Award.

Mary Jane Brukardt

A writer, consultant, and communications professional, Mary Jane Brukardt's career spans two decades in service to higher education, not-for-profit and philanthropic organizations, and Fortune 500 companies. She currently serves as Senior Writer and Editor for the Chancellor at the University of Wisconsin-Milwaukee, as well as consultant to higher education and community organizations across the Pacific Northwest. While at UWM, she also served as Director of Communications for The Milwaukee Idea.

In addition to speech and script-writing, M.J. Brukardt has edited a philanthropic journal and a two-volume history of The Johnson Foundation and Wingspread, recognized by the Public Relations Society of America (PRSA) with an Award of Excellence. She also has received awards from PRSA for script writing and annual reports, as well as recognition from the Council on Foundations for print publications and web site development.

M.J. Brukardt currently serves on the marketing committees for Volunteers of America, the Health Improvement Partnership, and Our Children's Century, Spokane, Washington, organizations committed to serving youth and fostering community.

TABLE OF CONTENTS

APPENDICES

FOREWORD

The LaFollette Institute of Public Affairs at the University of Wisconsin-Madison, in conjunction with our state's sesquicentennial celebrations, recently held several focus groups around the state to find out what citizens thought about Wisconsin. We expected to hear praise of our exceptional parks and recreational areas, enthusiasm for our sports teams—the Packers, the Brewers and, of course, the Badgers—and lots of comments about cheese—and cheeseheads. We weren't disappointed. But we were surprised to hear, repeatedly, how important the University of Wisconsin System is to people's perceptions of what makes this state so unique. As the Institute said in its report, "the state of Wisconsin without the University of Wisconsin would be—well, it wouldn't be Wisconsin."

As president of a System of 26 two- and four-year public colleges and universities, I can think of no higher accolade than for our institutions to be integral to the culture and life of Wisconsin. It's an attitude that goes back to the founding of both this state and the University of Wisconsin, when together they inspired what has been called The Wisconsin Idea: the noble notion that the boundaries of the university are the boundaries of the state.

We are proud stewards of a tradition of partnership with the people of the communities in which we thrive. Our challenge today, just as at our founding, is to find ways in which this tradition can be renewed and made relevant as our institutions mature, our state grows, and the world around us changes. The university partnerships with farmers that marked our first decades quickly evolved to collaborations and innovations in public policy, social development, and economic advances. These accomplishments, in turn, have prepared us to ask critical questions as we face our future: How will we translate The Wisconsin Idea for a new millennium? What does it mean for our scholarship, research, and teaching? What do we have to share with other institutions across the country that are looking anew at their mission to serve their students and communities in creative ways?

These are tough questions, but we must not shrink from finding the answers. Some today are worrying that the academy has sold its soul and is too engaged with the world of business. Others find us too disengaged. I submit, however, that the question is not *whether* to be engaged, but *how*. And the "how" is precisely what this book is all about—and why it is so relevant for all of higher education. We are blazing trails in our changing world of education, and, as in the best of scholarship, we all benefit most when we share our research—failures as well as successes—learn from each other, and move forward.

That is why I am inspired by the efforts of the University of Wisconsin-Milwaukee (UWM) to reshape The Wisconsin Idea for its urban, metropolitan setting. With The Milwaukee Idea, UWM has taken seriously the challenges of community engagement, enhanced research, and student learning to find a meaningful path to concrete action. Faculty, staff, and students have grappled with the tough questions of how the university can be in and of the city and at the same time a sanctuary for thought, reflection, and discovery.

Of all the definitions of engagement, the one I find most relevant to universities and communities underscores relationship. To be engaged is to be committed to a lifetime partnership. The University of Wisconsin System colleges and universities have indeed been partners with Wisconsin since our inception. UWM, in particular, was formed to be "Milwaukee's university" and together—urban community and urban university—will create its future.

The challenge for all of us—land-grant, urban, public, or private institutions of higher education—is to renew our commitment to our lifetime partnerships and, through them, create our own Milwaukee Idea.

Katharine C. Lyall, President
University of Wisconsin System
Madison, Wisconsin

PROLOGUE

It is important at the outset of this volume to be clear about its origins, its purpose, and its perspective. What it is and what it is not. In brief, it represents the reflections and analysis of three individuals who participated in the leadership and implementation of a broad-based initiative to reinvigorate an urban research university. The Milwaukee Idea is the commitment by the University of Wisconsin-Milwaukee (UWM) to embrace partnerships with the greater Milwaukee community. It was launched with the full expectation that community collaboration can enhance and enliven the university's mission of teaching, research, and service.

In this book we tell the story of The Milwaukee Idea—our story—as we worked to envision, plan, communicate, and carry it out. This story is not an objective, third-party assessment; neither is it written by disinterested individuals. It does include a rich array of ideas, perspectives—and yes, critiques—by individuals other than ourselves, yet the description of The Milwaukee Idea that unfolds on these pages is decidedly told from the viewpoint of its three authors.

We recognize that other participants in our change process may have experienced events differently. Outside evaluators may offer different analyses of what took place. We have tried to be objective, but given our roles in The Milwaukee Idea, it is impossible to separate ourselves from the story or be dispassionate about a change effort to which we are deeply committed.

With this disclaimer, it may be useful for the authors to "introduce" ourselves so the reader can understand our role in the story that follows.

Nancy Zimpher came to UWM in the summer of 1998 as the university's new chancellor. Arriving from The Ohio State University where she served as dean of the College of Education, she found Wisconsin's largest public urban research university ready for change but uncertain of its future direction. Believing that our urban research universities have a unique role to play in revitalizing community, she challenged UWM to imagine new ways in which it could partner with Milwaukee. Then she invited students, faculty, staff, and community to work together to create what came to be called "The Milwaukee Idea." As chancellor, Nancy continues to provide the vision, the impetus, and the energy for UWM to dream about and implement change.

In 1998, Steve Percy was entering his tenth year as professor at UWM. After serving as chair of the UWM Department of Political Science, he assumed the leadership of an urban research center on campus, which became an important link between the university and the Milwaukee community.

Steve chaired the Chancellor Search and Screen Committee organized to recruit Nancy Zimpher. As The Milwaukee Idea began to unfold in the fall of 1998, Nancy called on Steve to help organize the administrative apparatus to support the planning and implementation of the university's bold endeavor to link its research and educational missions with the community.

Mary Jane Brukardt arrived at UWM shortly after Chancellor Zimpher, to serve as her senior writer and later director of communications for The Milwaukee Idea. She was tasked with helping to give voice to The Milwaukee Idea, supporting the Chancellor as she took the UWM story throughout Milwaukee, and reinforcing the message that UWM was ready to partner. Her role as newcomer and also behind-the-scenes participant provided her the opportunity to work closely with Nancy and Steve as well as the many people from across campus and community who helped to make The Milwaukee Idea a reality.

That's who we are; now the "why." We wrote this volume for several reasons. First, it was an opportunity to engage in self-reflection. Planning and implementing The Milwaukee Idea has kept us busy, nonstop, leaving precious little time to ponder how we got to this point. Reflection is more than reviewing fond memories, however. It also will inform future efforts to sustain our partnerships, help us assess meaningful results, evaluate outcomes, and measure organizational change.

Second, it is useful to document our effort at institutional strengthening. After more than two years of work we found ourselves occasionally struggling to remember the exact sequence of events, the conversations that informed our work, the processes that created The Milwaukee Idea. In this book we have gone back, purposely, to document the unfolding sequence of events and achievements that culminate in The Milwaukee Idea today and have become an important part of our institution's history.

Third, and most important, we believe our experiences may provide knowledge useful to other institutions and change leaders who are interested in community-university engagement. We say this not out of immodesty, but as colleagues, tested in the ongoing challenge of creating real change at a real institution, eager to share what we've learned.

The idea that universities can play new roles, become more significantly connected to their surrounding communities, and more directly contribute to life quality is not a new one. The idea of engagement, championed by advocates like Ernest Boyer, has stimulated organizations like the U.S. Department of Housing and Urban Development (HUD), the U.S. Department of Education, and the Fannie Mae Foundation to create programs to encourage community-university partnerships. The National Association of State Universities and Land-Grant Colleges has taken up the mantle of engagement as part of the Kellogg Commission on the Future of State and Land-Grant Universities. In its March 2000 report, *Renewing the Covenant: Learning, Discovery, and Engagement in a New Age and Different World,* the Commission argues that:

> It [the transformed university] will be a new kind of public institution, one that is as much a first-rate student university as it is a first-rate research university, one that provides access to success to a much more diverse student population *as easily as it reaches out to engage the larger community* (italics added).[1]

Barbara Holland, former director of the Office of University Partnerships at HUD, makes a similar argument and calls for greater campus commitment to engagement for real collaboration to take place: "There has to be an institutional commitment to engagement and sustainability of campus-community partnerships," she says.[2]

The Milwaukee Idea is UWM's commitment to engagement. And because it is an institutional one—it involves faculty, students, and staff from across our schools and colleges—we believe our experiences are of value to others who are taking up the challenge to create new kinds of universities.

We offer no blueprint, nor do we have all the answers. What we do hope to convey through this story is our sustained enthusiasm for expanding community-university partnerships as a vital component of university life. This is a description of one approach to reaching this goal (warts and all) and our insights (to date) about the challenges and opportunities we face as we move farther out of the ivory tower and into the diverse, even global, communities that comprise our world today.

Finally, we would like to acknowledge our struggle to find the right "voice" for this volume. How do you tell a story that involved so many different participants with such varied perspectives? How do you capture the thoughts and reactions of its leaders and yet also realistically describe the effects of the decisions they made? How do you balance personal insights with narrative that is true to what happened?

Our solution has been to ignore the either/or and present both. We have provided a narrative structure to which we add personal observations and leaders' insights. Where the roles or actions of one of the authors is described, it was the other two authors who provided the description, so that our writing reflects a more balanced look at actions and outcomes. While this device does not achieve total objectivity, it has helped us tell a story whose focus, we hope, is not on its leaders, but on the hundreds of women and men who envisioned the possibilities of The Milwaukee Idea and who continue to make change happen at the University of Wisconsin-Milwaukee.

And so we begin our story.

Endnotes

[1] The Kellogg Commission on the Future of State and Land-Grant Universities. (2000). *Renewing the Covenant: Learning, Discovery, and Engagement in a New Age and Different World.* National Association of State Universities and Land-Grant Colleges, page 10.

[2] As quoted in "Agents of Change," April, 2001, *Matrix,* page 32.

ACKNOWLEDGMENTS

Creating The Milwaukee Idea has been a shared adventure, and we have combined our talents to tell this story. But thanks requires a single voice, a privilege I am honored to claim.

The Milwaukee Idea is a reflection of the vision, hard work, and enthusiastic spirit of the faculty, staff, students, and alumni of the University of Wisconsin-Milwaukee, both past and present. It is they who shaped a modern urban research university and who, when asked to imagine the future, dared to dream large.

That spirit has been echoed and embraced by the many women and men from Milwaukee and throughout Wisconsin who have joined with us in partnerships that have exceeded every expectation. To our friends, I say thank you, for your patience, wisdom, enduring support, and high expectations.

The support of our friends, especially that of the University of Wisconsin System under President Katharine Lyall, has never wavered. Her belief in UWM as a premier institution has helped to guide and inspire us.

All these people have helped create The Milwaukee Idea—but it is Stephen Percy, its director, who has transformed our efforts into a dynamic, energizing force for change at UWM. The genius of his leadership has smoothed our path and lighted our way. He is one of those rare individuals who knows how to create a vision and at the same time take care of the details to make it a reality. He is a treasured colleague and valued friend.

To him, to Mary Jane Brukardt, without whose help the story simply could not have been told, and to all the people of The Milwaukee Idea, I dedicate this book, with every expectation that The Milwaukee Idea holds more—much more—to come.

Nancy L. Zimpher
Chancellor
University of Wisconsin-Milwaukee

MILWAUKEE'S UNIVERSITY

From the *Milwaukee Journal Sentinel*
September 18, 1998

Chancellor Seeks New Role for UWM
By Jack Norman

Proclaiming a new "Milwaukee Idea" as her administration's goal, University of Wisconsin-Milwaukee Chancellor Nancy Zimpher told a huge crowd of faculty, staff and students she is launching a 100-day campaign to redefine UWM's role.

Taking a cue from the so-called Wisconsin Idea of the early 20th century—in which the University of Wisconsin's mission expanded beyond the Madison campus to include the entire state—Zimpher said UWM must become "an idea factory" for the entire Milwaukee area, not just those on campus. Zimpher, in her first campus-wide speech since taking over as chancellor last month, said that a group of "about 100 people, working over the next 100 days," will flesh out the details of what this "Milwaukee Idea" means.

Though her speech was short on specifics . . . the sense of energy and vision she conveyed seemed to be well-received by the standing-room crowd of more than 700 people who packed the Student Union's ballroom . . .

Zimpher's dramatic flair was evident not only in her rhetoric but also the way she staged the event. Wearing a bright red suit while standing in front of a jet-black drapery, she sprayed compliments over a wide variety of university programs, while challenging UWM to "join the urban renaissance of Milwaukee, and the transformation of ourselves as Milwaukee's—and someday, I hope you think this not too immodest—the nation's premier urban university."

Changing the direction of an institution of higher education is, as a former University of Wisconsin Regent once wrote, a lot like trying to move a battleship with your bare hands.[1] It takes strategic leadership—and a lot of people willing to help push.

In 1998, the University of Wisconsin-Milwaukee (UWM) was ready to consider a change in course. The chancellor of the University of Wisconsin System's largest urban public university was ending a seven-year term to return to the classroom. His replacement—Nancy Zimpher, a dean of the

1

College of Education at The Ohio State University—arrived at a pivotal time in the life of the institution and its community.

This is the story of the University of Wisconsin-Milwaukee's change in course, a look at what happened when a public urban institution joined hands with its community—to give the institution a little push. The result was a campus-wide initiative called "The Milwaukee Idea" and a new optimism that change in the academy and in the community is possible.

READY FOR CHANGE

In early 1998 at UWM, things were looking up for an institution that had survived some lean years. Student enrollment—at more than 22,000—was increasing again after five years of decline. Faculty cutbacks, a legacy of reduced state investment, and falling enrollment were stabilizing. UWM's role within the University of Wisconsin System (which includes 25 colleges and universities, and the flagship UW-Madison) also was growing. Historically in Madison's research shadow, UWM had nonetheless attained Research II status in the Carnegie ranking[2] and was determined to grow its extramural funding and programs. New student housing and renovations to major buildings promised to highlight the university's enviable location on 93 acres near the shores of Lake Michigan, just minutes from downtown Milwaukee.

UWM's hometown was also in the midst of a period of renewal. The old image of Milwaukee as the rust-belt home of beer, bowling, and bratwurst was changing as its manufacturing companies retooled, lake and riverfront parks were enhanced, and historic neighborhoods redeveloped. The city that gave the world Harley Davidson motorcycles and Pabst Blue Ribbon beer also offered the soaring extension to the new Milwaukee Art Museum designed by Spanish architect Santiago Calatrava. Professional theater, ballet, and opera companies were thriving, and the Milwaukee Brewers baseball team unveiled plans for the state-of-the-art Miller Park. Strategically located in the center of a four-county region of

UWM at a Glance

- 11 schools and colleges and Continuing Education

Programs

- 81 undergraduate
- 47 masters
- 1 specialist
- 17 doctoral
- One of 148 Public Doctoral/Research Universities-Extensive (Carnegie ranking)

Faculty and Students

- 3,354 faculty and staff
- 23,322 students in credit and 43,000 in non-credit programs
- 75% students work while attending classes

—2000 profile

almost 1.5 million people—about a third of the state's population—the city was a leading commercial, cultural, and manufacturing hub. By the late 1990s, Mayor John Norquist called for Milwaukee to lead "an economic and cultural renaissance for the twenty-first century." [3]

UWM stood ready to contribute to "Milwaukee's renaissance." Home to the state's only School of Architecture and Urban Planning, the university and its graduates were literally helping to shape the city's skyline and its "New Urbanism" approach to livable neighborhoods. UWM's Peck School of the Arts graduates were active in leadership roles in every arts organization in the city, and UWM's School of Education provided more than half the region's teachers. But Milwaukee needed more.

The metropolitan region was not immune to the challenges of major urban centers: a deteriorating core, white flight to the suburbs, failing public schools, and rising minority unemployment. In a state where high-school students consistently ranked in the top five states nationally in performance on ACT and SAT tests, only 40% of African American ninth graders graduated from Milwaukee Public Schools. Milwaukee's infant mortality rate was higher than New York City's and, in 2001, a national study determined that Milwaukee was second only to Detroit in childhood segregation. Despite a decade of prosperity during the 1990s, when metropolitan Milwaukee saw a 32% increase in the number of taxpayers reporting incomes above $100,000 a year, Milwaukee had the dubious distinction of the highest black urban unemployment rate in the Midwest and Northeast. [4]

This was the backdrop against which the University of Wisconsin-Milwaukee began its search for a new chancellor. As faculty, staff, and students looked ahead, there was a growing consensus that UWM needed a leader who could help shape and define its mission as a public, urban, research university. UWM wanted to reassess its relationships with its communities and ways in which its teaching and research could contribute to the challenges and opportunities of a vibrant, yet struggling, metropolitan region. UWM also needed a sharper sense of its unique role within the UW System—not as handmaiden to Madison, but as an urban-focused research institution in its own right. UWM needed to capitalize on and better showcase its advances in research, scholarship, and discovery.

In short, UWM enjoyed an enviable confluence of three important requirements for change: the opportunity for new leadership, a foundation of individuals who recognized the need for change, and growing optimism across the institution—and also throughout the community—that the time and means for change were at hand. The battleship was ready to move.

"Milwaukee's University"

But to understand where UWM was headed, it's also important to know from where it came.[5] The University of Wisconsin-Milwaukee was officially born in 1956 with the merger of the University of Wisconsin Extension Center and Wisconsin State College, Milwaukee (originally Milwaukee State Teachers College). These two institutions, both dating from the turn of the century, shaped the character of UWM.

Academic Primer

System? Governance? Academic staff? For those unfamiliar with the ways of the academy in Wisconsin, here's a brief background. The University of Wisconsin was originally a public land-grant university founded in 1849 in Madison. Today the public system of higher education has expanded to include 26 two- and four-year colleges and universities, all funded through state allocation and administered by a System-wide president and Board of Regents. Each university and most colleges also have their own chancellor and administration.

Faculty at each institution participate in what is called "shared governance"—a right that is written into Wisconsin state law. Tenured faculty members of each department must affirmatively recommend a candidate for hire or promotion. Faculty members elect representatives who serve on Faculty Senate committees to oversee promotion, granting of tenure, campus policy, and the creation or dissolution of new programs, degrees, or schools.

This oversight extends to administration hires as well. When a new chancellor was sought for UWM, for example, the Search and Screen Committee, composed of a majority of faculty members and representatives from all governance groups and major campus constituencies, selected the final list of candidates, from which the Board of Regents named the chancellor. This system instills a

Wisconsin State College, with its long history of teacher training, provided a foundation of innovative education geared to preparing Milwaukee's professionals. Through the UW Extension, UWM was linked to the land-grant traditions of the University of Wisconsin and its commitment to serving the people of Wisconsin. It became part of the statewide University of Wisconsin System with its broad network of students. UWM also benefited from the University of Wisconsin's strong system of shared governance, where faculty and academic staff were, according to Wisconsin statute 36.09 (4), given "primary responsibility for academic and educational activities and faculty personnel matters."

Through UW Extension and Wisconsin State College, UWM also inherited the legacy of thousands of alumni, including, most famously, former Israeli Prime Minister Golda Meir, who had attended the predecessor institution, Milwaukee State Normal School. Most graduates, however, continue to live and work in the region.

The need for a Milwaukee-based comprehensive public university, only 75 miles from the flagship campus of UW-

strong sense of faculty ownership in the university's programs and departments, and also forces a deliberative process that encourages a multi-perspective review of change (although some critics say it also can impede the ability of higher education to respond quickly and flexibly).

Shared governance also extends to "academic staff"—university professional staff members who are not faculty (although they may hold teaching positions) but who serve the university in functions that range from administrative assistants to assistant chancellors. They have separate academic staff committees and representation on faculty committees and the Senate.

Classified staff are non-salaried employees, some of whom are unionized.

Madison, was hotly debated, but by the late 1940s the demand was acute, as the GI Bill flooded the state's institutions of higher education with first-generation students, many from the industrial cities of southeastern Wisconsin.[6] As professor of history and former UWM Chancellor John Schroeder noted in his inaugural address, UWM existed because Milwaukee's civic leaders had demanded it—a "university *for* the people of Milwaukee."[7]

From its inception, UWM sought to answer the call from Milwaukee's business community for skilled engineers, teachers, architects, and artists who would remain to work in the metropolitan area. To this day, nine out of ten students are from the state, three-quarters of UWM graduates remain in Wisconsin, and almost two-thirds of the 100,000-plus alumni continue to live in southeastern Wisconsin after graduation.[8] Programs in the health sciences, nursing, and social welfare have been added to a strong foundation of education, letters and science, engineering, information studies, architecture and urban planning, and business administration.

While serving the education needs of the industrial heartland, UWM was also created to be "Milwaukee's university,"[9] a powerful partner in the life and livelihood of the community. It was to be the urban equivalent of the land-grant institution, using its teaching and research in service to its neighbors. Fred Harvey Harrington, president of the University of Wisconsin during UWM's inception, urged the Milwaukee campus to "move forward along new lines—experiment, generate and try out original ideas and approaches in instruction, research and public service."[10]

This commitment was echoed by J. Martin Klotsche, UWM's first chancellor, who was a strong advocate for the urban university and its potential to "find strength in its urban setting." While he believed that teaching and research must remain central to the university's mission, community outreach had the "unique role" of giving new meaning to the quality of urban life.[11]

And the faculty, staff, and students of the new institution responded. In its early years, for example, Professor Elisabeth Holmes of the English Department

A Walking Tour of UWM

Stroll the tree-lined streets in the heart of one of Milwaukee's oldest neighborhoods and you'll see a 93 acre campus that embraces a mix of architecture, from the stately red-brick Mitchell Hall, built in 1909, and the new wired-for-technology Business Administration Building, completed in 1995. A walk down Hartford Avenue takes you past Holton and Merrill Halls, home at the turn of the century to the original Milwaukee-Downer College, with the Klotsche Athletic Center beyond. Farther down the street, past the 12-story concrete and glass Enderis Hall, home to the College of Health Sciences, School of Education, and Helen Bader School of Social Welfare, you find the Peck School of the Arts and Golda Meir Library, named in 1979 for one of the university's most famous students. Today, more than 18,000 members of the Milwaukee community use the library, in addition to UWM's students and faculty. Your tour next takes you past the tudor-style Chapman Hall, a former library and now home to the chancellor and her administration. Towering above the campus are the four Sandburg Residence Halls, next to the Downer Woods where stray deer occasionally roam. Cross the street, and you're at the glass and steel School of Architecture and Urban Planning Building and its neighbor, the School of Business Administration. Then it's on to the School of Nursing and the brick facades of the Physics Building and the College of Engineering and Applied Science. Look around, and you're back on neighborhood streets.

served as president of the Milwaukee School Board, and Professor Donald Schwartz, a specialist in labor economics, worked with the Milwaukee Federated Trades Council.[12] More recently, the dean of the School of Architecture and Urban Planning serves as chair of the Milwaukee Planning Commission, and the city's African American Ko-Thi Dance Company is resident at UWM's Peck School of the Arts. This pattern of involvement has been repeated by countless individuals who see the university's mission extending beyond the "ivory tower," and shaped by the special needs of an urban setting.[13]

THE QUIET UNIVERSITY

The spirit of invention and originality that marked the inception of the new institution, however, was tested as the years passed. While its professional, arts and science, and graduate programs grew, UWM's hopes for colleges of medicine and law were disappointed, as it was forced to compete with UW-Madison for state dollars and support. Wisconsin's brightest students continued to be wooed to Madison's residential campus, and Milwaukee, the "commuter school," saw its enrollment dip and football team disband.

As William Rayburn, dean of the Graduate School, points out, UWM is surrounded by Big Ten institutions—Northwestern to the south, Madison to the west, and the University of Michigan to the east—all with large endowments and strong reputations to attract students. While UWM has the largest minority undergraduate enrollment of all UW campuses and graduates more than 45% of System's African American students,[14] aggressive and creative outreach programs to Milwaukee's minority communities have only begun to show gains in student diversity.

In 1994, UWM was recognized as a Carnegie Research II Institution (it retained its ranking in the top public doctoral/research institutions when Carnegie revised its categories in 2000). By the mid-1990s, however, falling enrollment and state funding cutbacks reduced faculty numbers and slowed research gains. From 1995 to 1999, Wisconsin state spending on higher education increased by only 3% percent, versus a national average of more than 11%. At UWM, the salary for a full professor ranked 13th among 15 peer institutions.[15]

In 1996, the university administration drafted a formal strategic plan that articulated the institution's commitment to research excellence, quality teaching, and community service. While there was widespread agreement with the three-pronged mission of the university, how best to balance the demands of "town versus gown" remained a sticking point, especially in light of low budget allocations for research funding, faculty reward, and staffing.

> "The people of the greater Milwaukee region are determined to take charge of their future. They see a major doctoral research university as a powerful and necessary resource to help them achieve that future."
>
> —Jack Pelisek, Chair
> Community Task Force
> "UWM and the Future of Metropolitan Milwaukee," 1986

Beyond the campus boundaries, the university's profile in the media with other institutions of higher education, and in the community was, in the words of one prominent businessman, "just not visible." Departments and individuals continued to forge innovative and creative connections with the community (by 2000 UWM's Center for Urban Initiatives and Research, CUIR, had identified more than 200 collaborative projects in operation), but such a focus was less visible at the institutional level.

UWM was sometimes compared to Milwaukee's largest insurance company—Northwestern Mutual, "the quiet company." While that image was right for a company that prided itself on its efficient professionalism, "quiet" was not what Milwaukee wanted—or needed—from its largest university. In a community that proudly calls itself a "City of Colleges," home to more than 16 colleges and universities, including Marquette University, Milwaukee School of Engineering, and Alverno College, UWM needed to turn up the volume to hold its own in a competitive academic market.[16]

The challenge for UWM, in the words of one civic leader, was to become a "player at the table" with fellow institutions and the city's movers and shakers. Community observers believed UWM could become an important force in the community—if it chose to do so. Sheldon Lubar, a prominent business leader and past president of the University of Wisconsin Board of Regents, believed that UWM could become an urban institution that would "attract the best." UWM, he said, "should be and could be the most important institution in this community. It can be the cultural center, a contributor to local and national issues, and provide leadership for the educational and economic challenges we face in Milwaukee."

A CATALYST FOR CHANGE

And so, in 1997 when System President Katharine Lyall met with UWM's University Committee, she found a campus ready to move in new directions and a community that was looking for great things.

"The feeling very much was that the campus needed revitalization," recalled Professor René Gratz, who served on the Chancellor Search and Screen Committee. "The campus needed somebody who could increase our image and visibility and connect with the community. As Jack Welch, former CEO of General Electric, said, 'If there's more change outside than inside the institution, you're in trouble.' I think many of us realized we were headed for trouble if we didn't change."

The first small steps of that change began with the formation of the Chancellor Search and Screen Committee. Chaired by Political Science Professor Stephen Percy, director of CUIR, it included faculty, staff, students, alumni, and community representatives. From the beginning, the process was designed to be open and inclusive, something one student wryly noted was "not typical for UWM." The goal was to give everyone multiple opportunities to contribute ideas and opinions. In the process, key campus leadership was honing collaborative skills and gaining experience that would be required in the months to come.

Campus and community forums were held to develop a list of institutional priorities. A web site recorded comments and progress and, over the weeks of the search, a consensus developed. The new chancellor should be "a strategist, with a genuine vision of where the campus is going"; "a dynamic personality"; "someone with a commitment to diversity and a sense of humor." The chancellor "has to be 'our' chancellor, not System's"; must be able to "see our potential," and "be a catalyst for the entire campus to re-engage."[17]

The University of Wisconsin-Milwaukee was ready for change.

Nancy Zimpher on the Roots of The Milwaukee Idea

How do you tell a story that belongs to literally thousands of individuals and has been experienced in so many different ways? We grappled with that question as I sat down with my co-authors to write about The Milwaukee Idea, struggling for a way to capture the varied perspectives that are important to understanding what has happened at UWM. We decided that we needed more than one voice. We needed more than a narrative, more than a first-person account by leadership, more than interviews with campus and community. And so we decided to use them all.

Throughout this book you will hear from participants, observers, critics and defenders of The Milwaukee Idea. You will read news clips and speeches and references from change leaders. And, in sections like that which follows, you will read personal reflections by Steve Percy and me about why we made the decisions we did, what we did when "Plan A" didn't work, and what we learned about leadership, change, and the power of partnerships.

Imagine the following want ad, one that could have appeared in 1997 in the employment section of a prestigious journal of higher education:

> *Large urban university, committed to research, teaching, and service, located in lovely residential neighborhood, seeks chancellor-wannabe. The successful candidate will help correct university's intermittent mission drift, fix occasional invisibility within culturally diverse urban nexus, and turn urban giant in a direction that will reap long-term gains for students, faculty, staff, and society at large.*

Then, imagine that the Chancellor Search and Screen Committee received a reply from a most unlikely candidate—an academic from the field of teacher education (not the usual pathway to the chancellor's office). Then, imagine that she got the job!

These were the opportunities I faced when I arrived at the University of Wisconsin-Milwaukee in the summer of 1998. I knew then, and am more convinced now, that this urban campus has the potential to be a powerful force in our community and nation. But how to get there? How do you turn an "urban giant" in new directions? How do you transform an institution that, like its peers in higher education, is notable for its ability to resist change? How do you encourage a university, strong in community outreach, to pursue even richer partnerships?

To be candid, I didn't know. Or rather, I didn't have the definitive "Five Steps to Institutional Change" that will transform this campus and other campuses across the country. Michael Fullan, who knows a lot about educational change, has written that there are no cookbooks or silver bullets that can simplify the incredible complexity of the challenges we face today. "The notion that knowledge about change can be packaged and delivered is absurd," he writes in his book Change Forces: The Sequel *and, perhaps more to the point, "Never assume leaders know what they are doing.[18] There were many times I didn't.*

The Wow!

It soon became clear to me that what UWM needed was an elevated idea—something that would get people excited for change. We needed the "wow!" that Tom Peters talks about, the "bold and daring action" that distinguishes organizations on the move.[19]

James Collins and Jerry Porras talk about the BHAG, the Big Hairy Audacious Goal that reaches out and grabs people. It's not the kind of goal you'd expect, like "creating a university dedicated to excellence," but a "huge, daunting challenge—like a big mountain to climb."[20] But it couldn't be just any great notion. It needed to be right for UWM, something that reflected what our university was and believed it could be. Alan Guskin, who has written extensively on change in the academy, says that whatever an institution's vision for its future, it must be grounded in its values or it will have no meaning.[21] To find that idea, we needed to get "closer to the bone" of what an urban university really was all about—what UWM was all about.

What's a BHAG?

A Big Hairy Audacious Goal is clear and compelling, serves as a unifying focal point of effort, and acts as a catalyst for team spirit.... A BHAG engages people—it reaches out and grabs them. It is tangible, energizing, highly focused. People get it right away; it takes little or no explanation ... it could be said 100 different ways yet be easily understood by everyone. ... A vision-level BHAG applies to the entire organization and requires 10 to 30 years of effort to complete ... and it will have perhaps only a 50% to 70% probability of success.... A BHAG should require extraordinary effort and perhaps a little luck.

—*James Collins and Jerry Porras "Building Your Company's Vision" Harvard Business Reeview*

My answer came during a visit to Madison, our state capital, where I learned about Wisconsin's celebration of its sesquicentennial. Part of the festivities included an address by the governor extolling the virtues of The Wisconsin Idea—an idea nearly as old as the state itself—that the boundaries of the university were the boundaries of the state. In The Wisconsin Idea I found the essence of our BHAG—an idea that had stood the test of time, that had widespread recognition around the state, and that held the potential to call the university to renewed action.

What is The Milwaukee Idea?

"Our goal is nothing less than to change forever the quality of our life together, by joining the urban renaissance of Milwaukee and transforming ourselves as Milwaukee's, and someday the nation's, premier urban university."

"It's not us serving the community. It's not the community serving us. It is the notion of together building a community and a university that are the heart of metropolitan Milwaukee. This is the essence of what will become The Milwaukee Idea."

— *Chancellor Nancy Zimpher from a speech given to the UWM Faculty Senate plenary September 1998*

I believe that universities are put on the face of the earth to make both an academic and social contribution. We are to model civic engagement and prepare students for active lives in our democracy. We make our contribution in terms of our teaching, the programs we offer, the lives we enable, the discovery and inquiry we conduct, and through our service. Our links to our community give legs to our mission because our partnerships and connections benefit this community and that, in turn, benefits us. The Wisconsin Idea says that campus and community are intimately connected, a possibility that holds enormous potential for urban universities of the new millennium.

At the heart of The Wisconsin Idea is the idea of partnership—a true collaborative relationship between community and university. What if, we asked, we took that idea of partnership and tried to discover what it might mean for our teaching and our research? What would a transformational change in the way we connected to our community mean for Milwaukee? How would it change the way our students learned, the way we organized our university, the priorities we set? What could a "Milwaukee Idea" mean?

Stay True to Values

And so The Milwaukee Idea became our BHAG, our challenge to think big and act boldly. It did not change our core mission of teaching, research, and service, but provided the framework for a campus- and community-wide conversation about what our future should be. Collins and Porras remind us that while an organization's core mission is the foundation, its vision must be crafted by everyone involved. "Identifying core ideology is a discovery process, but setting the envisioned future is a creative process." [22]

The concept for our Affinity planning and Action Teams essentially came out of a retreat we held late in the summer with the deans and my staff, but its scope and implementation evolved as we went and shaped us as much as we shaped it. Modeled after what many change experts call "complexity theory"—the idea that loosely structured "collaborative diversity" can produce new breakthroughs [23]*—the open process often shifted between chaos and control as we struggled to find new*

What is Change?

It "combines inner shifts in people's values, aspirations, and behaviors with 'outer' shifts in processes, strategies, practices, and systems.

...In profound change there is learning. The organization doesn't just do something new; it builds its capacity for doing things in a new way—indeed it builds capacity for ongoing change."

—Peter Senge
The Dance of Change

ways to interact with ourselves and our community. Madeleine Green talks about "new kinds of conversations"[24] involving all constituent groups that are necessary for creating enduring change. At times we were unsure where these conversations were leading, but we continued to involve as many people as possible in the process. Administrators working with neighbors, staff working with faculty, students with community leaders. That's how you get things done. You open wide the doors.

And then you pay attention to timing. I know there are competing public expectations for the university and skepticism about whether the university can or should play a role in the community. Often, universities are perceived as being very good at coming up with ideas and not as good at making something happen. But the overwhelming issue continues to be: Can you deliver? That's why we created a process for speed with consistently aggressive deadlines to keep ourselves focused on outcomes, not talk. Timing is also part of making good on our promise to ourselves and our community. Our process for creating and implementing new ideas sent the message that we were prepared to change. I'm proud of the fact that it took only 18 months from our first meeting to community launch of the first Milwaukee Idea.

Most important, The Milwaukee Idea process was embedded in guiding values: inclusivity, diversity, openness, a "yes" attitude. We involved students, staff, faculty, unions, and community at every stage, not just at the beginning when it was easy, but later on, when the issues got tougher and the time demands greater. We took our open forum model beyond brainstorming to budget planning and had broad-based funding conversations at UWM for the first time in years.

During the chancellor search process, I'd been cautioned that Wisconsin's faculty governance system—codified in state law—could be a challenge to leadership that wanted change. I come from an academic tradition with great respect for shared governance, and I have found that an active faculty, staff, and secretary of the university are assets for change, not liabilities.

About a year after I arrived at UWM, one of our union leaders came up to me and told me that he'd been watching me. He had been surprised when we first invited the union to the planning table. He didn't think it would last. It has. Union representatives—and deans and students and faculty and administrators—all sit in the Chancellor's Cabinet. As representatives of the various campus constituencies, they have a forum to share their views—and they don't leave our meetings without either being very clear about their views or supporting the action discussed. My goal: No more " them"; just "us."

Early on, one of the faculty asked me how much change The Milwaukee Idea will involve. In all honesty, I estimated that 80% of what we do will stay the same—because we're building on an already strong base. We change at the margins. And, I know that while community engagement offers powerful opportunities for learning, discovery, and institutional growth, it cannot define the work of everyone in the academy all the time.

But as our process unfolded, I'm not sure "the margins" are enough. I better understand Madeleine Green's comment that "change is not an event." She and her colleagues at the American Council on Education studied 26 institutions of higher education and found—as we have—that once you begin a change process, it triggers new change that in turn results in an "unending cycle of reassessment and renewal." There is no point at which you can say "That's it, our work is done, now let's go back to our normal life."²⁵ We've discovered that we can't go back, because we have learned new ways of operating that continue to take us in new directions.

Endnotes

"A Time for Boldness," the title of this book, is taken from a line in Ernest Boyer's 1990 book, *Scholarship Reconsidered: Priorities of the Professoriate* (San Francisco: Jossey-Bass, page 75). It reads: "It is a moment for boldness in higher education and many are now asking: How can the role of the scholar be defined in ways that not only affirm the past but also reflect the present and adequately anticipate the future?"

[1] Laurence A. Weinstein. (1993). *Moving a Battleship with Your Bare Hands: Governing a University System.* Madison, WI: Magna Publications.

[2] The University of Wisconsin-Milwaukee received Research II status in 1994. When the Carnegie ranking was changed in 2000, UWM retained its position among the Doctoral/Research Universities-Extensive classification.

[3] John Norquist. (1998). *The Wealth of Cities: Revitalizing the Centers of American Life.* Reading, MA: Perseus Books, page viii.

[4] Statistics from: *"Investing in Wisconsin's Future: A Report to the Regents" from the University of Wisconsin, Milwaukee;* "Segregation Growing Among U.S. Children," *The New York Times,* Sunday, May 6, 2001; and "The Economic State of Black

Milwaukee" by Marc Levine in *The State of Black Milwaukee*, edited by Stanley F. Battle, published by The Milwaukee Urban League, February 2000, page 173.

[5] Information on the history of UWM drawn from: Frank Cassell, J. Martin Klotsche, and Frederick Olson, with the assistance of Donald Shea and Bea Bourgeois. (1992). *The University of Wisconsin-Milwaukee: A Historical Profile, 1885-1992.* Milwaukee, WI: UWM Foundation, pages 5–31.

[6] Ibid., page 31.

[7] From the Inauguration Address of University of Wisconsin-Milwaukee Chancellor John H. Schroeder, October 4, 1991. Courtesy of the University of Wisconsin-Milwaukee Archives, Golda Meir Library.

[8] Enrollment and alumni information provided by the University of Wisconsin-Milwaukee Enrollment Services and Alumni Relations departments. They are based on 2001 available statistics.

[9] *The University of Wisconsin-Milwaukee: A Historical Profile, 1885–1992,* page 6.

[10] Quoted in *The Urban University and the Future of our Cities* by J. Martin Klotsche (1966). New York: Harper & Row, page 30.

[11] Ibid., page 30.

[12] *The University of Wisconsin-Milwaukee: A Historical Profile, 1885–1992,* page 25.

[13] Ibid., page 11.

[14] In 1999–2000, UWM awarded fewer than 15% of the total number of degrees in the UW System, but 46.8% of those awarded to African Americans (a total of 261 of 557). Excluding advanced professional degrees not available at UWM (law and medicine, for example), UWM awarded almost half (49.7%) of all baccalaureate, master's, and doctoral degrees awarded to African Americans System-wide. Figures courtesy University of Wisconsin-Milwaukee Enrollment Services.

[15] From a presentation to the Wisconsin legislature by The University of Wisconsin System, 1998.

[16] Sharif Durhams. (January 14, 2000). "Milwaukee, a City of Colleges? One Report Says So," *Milwaukee Journal Sentinel.*

[17] Comments on what the new UWM chancellor should be like are taken from several open campus forums, held November 6 and 17, 1997. Notes were compiled by Ellen Murphy, vice chair of the Chancellor Search and Screen Committee.

[18] Michael Fullan. (1999). *Change Forces: The Sequel.* Philadelphia, PA: The Falmer Press, page 67, and *Change Forces.* (1993). New York: The Falmer Press, page viii.

[19] Tom Peters. (1994). *The Pursuit of Wow! Every Person's Guide to Topsy-Turvy Times.* New York: Vintage Books, page xii.

[20] James Collins and Jerry Porras. (1994). *Built to Last: Successful Habits of Visionary Companies.* New York: HarperCollins, page 94.

[21] Ted Marchese. (September 1998). "Restructure?! You Bet! An Interview with Change Expert Alan E. Guskin," *AAHE Bulletin,* published by The American Association for Higher Education, page 1.

Callout, page 10: James Collins and Jerry Porras. (September/October, 1996). "Building Your Company's Vision" in the *Harvard Business Review,* page 73.

[22] Ibid., page 75.

Callout, page 12: Peter Senge, et al. (1999). *The Dance of Change: The Challenges of Sustaining Momentum in Learning Organizations.* New York: Currency/Doubleday, page 15.

[23] Fullan, *Change Forces: The Sequel,* page 22.

[24] Madeleine Green, in *Redefining Success: Education for the Common Good,* an address given at the third annual Urban Initiatives Conference, "Dynamics of Change: The Milwaukee Idea and the New Urban University," at the University of Wisconsin-Milwaukee, June 8, 2000.

[25] Peter Eckel, Madeleine Green, Barbara Hill, and Bill Mallon. (1999). *On Change. Reports from the Road: Insights on Institutional Change.* Washington, DC: American Council on Education, page 1.

2

FROM THE WISCONSIN IDEA
TO THE MILWAUKEE IDEA

From *The Capital Times*, Madison, Wisconsin
January 6, 2000

What's the Big Idea? UWM's New Social Mission
By Samara Kalk

No sooner did University of Wisconsin-Milwaukee Chancellor Nancy Zimpher step foot in the state than she got the idea. The Wisconsin Idea. Zimpher arrived in Wisconsin from Ohio in the summer of 1998 and immediately latched onto The Wisconsin Idea, a partnership between the university and state that has served Wisconsin for a century.

She is interested in renewing that attitude and extending it to Milwaukee. . . . Her goal is to blur the lines between the university and community and build a partnership that will bring a new vitality to the city of Milwaukee and the university. . . .

"It's the right time for renewing our social contract," she said.

No one knows who first coined the term "Wisconsin Idea," but it has shaped the mission of the University of Wisconsin since the turn of the century. Championed by university President Charles Van Hise and Progressive politician and Governor Robert La Follette, it was characterized by the belief that reason could help solve the problems of society, and, as a result, the responsibility of the university was to serve the state. Eventually it was expressed as "the boundaries of the university are the boundaries of the state." Whether this notion is the "great American contribution to higher education" as Ashby seems to think, it has formed the foundation of both the land-grant

> "The great American contribution to higher education has been to dismantle the walls around the campus. When President Van Hise of Wisconsin said that the borders of the campus are the boundaries of the state, he was putting into words one of those rare innovations in the evolution of universities. It is one which has already been vindicated by history."
> —*Sir Eric Ashby*
> *British educator*

mission of the University of Wisconsin-Madison and the urban mission of the University of Wisconsin-Milwaukee (UWM).

GLORIOUS IDEAL

The Wisconsin Idea is the result of a history unique to Wisconsin. The University of Wisconsin (UW) was founded a year after the state came into being in 1848, and the two "grew up together." One of only nine major state universities to share a hometown with its capitol, the University of Wisconsin in Madison is less than a mile's stroll from the legislature. From its earliest years, the university's professors and students were called on to provide policy advice and research to the governor and elected officials. The university, in turn, found the state a strong financial supporter as it grew into an institution with national prominence.

When the Morrill Act of 1862 designated UW a land-grant college, it reinforced the university's existing agricultural research but also encouraged the expansion of its academic inquiry into social and economic issues.[1] From the creation of a milk test that revolutionized the dairy industry to innovative policy work that resulted in the nation's first workers' compensation program, the activities of the university reflected the "glorious ideal"[2] that the state university was "the people's servant."[3]

This notion of service to the people was adopted by the Socialist Party in Milwaukee in 1910 when it was swept into power under Mayor Emil Seidel. Joining with organized labor, the Socialists called for their version of "The Milwaukee Idea," a political agenda of social reforms that included eight-hour work days, the purchase of parkland for public use, and school reform. Mayor Seidel traveled to Madison to seek assistance from the university and was soon working closely with UW economist John Commons, who later helped draft the workers' compensation laws that became the model for Franklin Roosevelt's New Deal. It was the first time—but not the last—that The Milwaukee Idea and The Wisconsin Idea were to converge.[4]

NATIONAL ECHOES

In 1911, another Roosevelt, President Theodore Roosevelt, would write, "In no other state in the Union has any university done the same work for the community that has been done in Wisconsin by the University of Wisconsin."[5] High praise, especially in light of the accomplishments of such early 20th century notables as Seth Low at Columbia, Daniel Coit Gilman at Johns Hopkins, and William Rainey Harper and John Dewey at the University of Chicago. They, too, were sounding the call that universities, in the words of

"The real world is not to be found in books. That [real world] is peopled by men and women of living flesh and blood, and the great city can supply the human quality which the broad-minded man must not suffer himself to lack. There is a variety of life in this city, a vitality about it, and, withal, a sense of power of which, to my thought, are of inestimable value to the student whose desire it is to become a well-rounded man."

—*Seth Low*
President of Columbia 1890–1901

Gilman, "make for less misery among the poor, less ignorance in the schools, less bigotry in the temple, less suffering in the hospital, less fraud in business, less folly in politics."[6]

The academic leaders at the turn of the century believed that research and scholarship could improve society and strengthen democracy. The proper place for learning, they said, was not within ivy-covered walls, but "on the firing line of civilization."[7] As President Low said in his inaugural address, "There is no such thing as the world of letters as apart from the world of men." He went on to assert that the city "will lend itself readily to the encouragement of profound research."[8] Service to the community was not to be a second-class function of scholarship. It was not just "tacked on" as part of a socially responsible vision. It was a vital core of the academy's mission, invigorated by the real-world demands of society.

By focusing on the problems of their community, these leaders believed they would also help build stronger institutions of learning and better prepare their students for life in a democracy. More than that, however, some also believed that the university had much to learn from its community. The greatness of Columbia, Low observed, would be determined not just by the extent that Columbia was part of New York, but by the extent that New York was part of Columbia.[9]

This approach to higher education was short-lived. As Derek Bok notes, the vision of The Wisconsin Idea was not widely shared and "only foreshadowed changes yet to come."[10] The changing political and social landscape, marked by world war and later the Cold War, shifted higher education's priorities to meeting the research needs of a growing superpower. The research mission of the university, epitomized by Johns Hopkins, M.I.T., and Harvard, came to influence higher education across the country at institutions large and small, as academic success began to be measured in terms of published results, rather than teaching and service. As the educator Ernest Boyer observed, that change caused higher education to look inward, shifting the focus "from the student to the professoriate, from general to specialized education, and from loyalty to the campus to loyalty to the profession."[11]

As federal dollars flowed and the GI Bill flooded colleges with new students, universities grew in size and scope, recruiting the best minds for graduate programs and for basic and applied research. The result was a distinguished record of discovery by American education and increasing endowments—at least at the largest institutions. At the same time there was a growing sense—both from within the academy and from society at large—of a widening disconnect between the promised benefits of research and the deteriorating economic, social, and environmental realities of American life. Where were the fruits of America's lavish investment in higher education?[12]

Urban Universities Try New Ways to Reach Out to Their Communities

By emphasizing partnerships with the City of Milwaukee, chancellor [Zimpher] hopes to give the university a niche.... "Students coming here will say, 'I am not only going to school in an urban setting, it will be about the urban setting,'" she predicted. "Students will be told, 'You are certainly going to interact with people very different from yourself.' I think this will become a hallmark of UWM."

The Chronicle of Higher Education
Copyright April 30, 1999
Excerpted with permission

As James Duderstadt, president emeritus of the University of Michigan, has written, the research partnership may have had a negative impact on the higher education enterprise as more institutions adopted the culture and values of the research universities. "To put it bluntly," he writes, "there are many more institutions that claim a research mission, that declare themselves 'research universities' and that make research success a criterion for tenure, than our nation can afford." He predicts a shift in public willingness to support "prestige-driven" institutions to more "market-driven" universities that offer cost-competitive, high-quality services.[13]

In Wisconsin, where its citizens had long prided themselves on their state's financial commitment to education, voices were beginning to ask if dollars spent on the university system were being put to use for the good of the state. There was no shortage of competing causes, from welfare reform to new prison construction. As one state official remarked, "We greatly value The Wisconsin Idea. The bridge between the state and the campus has long been an important one. But there's a sense that a couple of the planks have fallen out of that bridge." [14]

The growing chasm between public expectations and university priorities was mirrored nationally. By the late 1980s, with federal funding for higher education dwindling and public calls for accountability and restructuring increasing, Boyer and others suggested a "New American College," one that had a renewed focus on student learning and would redefine scholarship to "connect thought to action and theory to practice." [15] A campus, Boyer said, "is not an isolated island. It is a staging ground for action.... The more you are engaged beyond, the more you become integrated within." [16] This "practice of engagement," he believed, had the potential to renew both campus and community.

A GROWING CHORUS

This idea of engagement found advocates among those who saw higher education's mission in terms of its social responsibility. Zelda Gamson, director of the New England Resource Center for Higher Education at the University of Massachusetts, Boston, writing in 1997 in *Change* magazine, challenged higher education to rebuild its social capital by reestablishing relationships with the community in order to become a "serious participant in rebuilding the civic life of the United States." To do that, she said, higher education should reward applied as well as pure research and learn new ways of "doing" civic life with a rich array of community partners. [17] Ira Harkavy, of the University of Pennsylvania and an outspoken advocate for community-university partnerships, suggested that higher education will be reinvigorated when it begins to look outward again. Doing good, Harkavy said, may be the best way for universities to do well. [18]

Doing good, especially through the collaborations possible in the urban environment, presents faculty and students alike with rich opportunities to combine discovery with service. In the words of Evan Dobelle, former president of Trinity College, Connecticut, now president of the University of Hawaii, the university has the responsibility to "embrace both the challenges of scholarship and the values of citizenship." It is immoral, Dobelle says, for universities to teach liberal arts on campus while ignoring what happens across the street. "Colleges and universities must do more than comment from the safety of the sidelines. They must enter the battle and they must lead." [19]

For many universities, entering the battle meant literally crossing the street to help revitalize the neighborhoods in which they lived. Trinity College in Hartford, Connecticut, invested $6 million from its endowment under Dobelle's

> "The time has come for fresh ideas and institutional courage. If we are to be a nation truly committed to the quest for civic culture—to respect diversity, responsibility and personal achievement—we are obliged to open a new chapter in the struggle to revitalize our cities. And in that struggle, colleges and universities must do more than comment from the safety of the sidelines. They must enter the battle and they must lead."
>
> —*Evan Dobelle*
> *former president*
> *Trinity College*

leadership to build new schools and a community center near campus. Marquette University, just a few miles away from UWM, spent more than $50 million during the early 1990s to renovate or demolish 115 properties in its central-city neighborhood—many home to drug addicts, prostitutes, and thieves that threatened its ability to attract new students. [20] Former Connecticut College President Claire Gaudiani has called her university's efforts to redevelop the downtown of New London, a project for "social justice."

"We are invited to advance potential," Gaudiani said in 1999 as she issued a challenge for university presidents to engage in a year of deliberation on the topic of social stewardship and an analysis of the role that universities can play in fostering it. [21]

One such deliberation of academic leaders resulted in the release of the "Wingspread Declaration on Renewing the Civic Mission of the American Research University." In it, participants who represented universities as well as foundations, and civic and professional associations, reaffirmed the role of the university as an agent of democracy, a "bridge between individuals' work and the larger world." This happens when students do the work of citizenship on projects of real impact and relevance, when faculty work across disciplines on "public scholarship," and when administrators give voice to the public purpose of the institution.[22]

Such conversations have been happening in universities around the country. In 1996, the National Association of State Universities and Land-Grant Colleges (NASULGC) convened the Kellogg Commission on the Future of State and Land-Grant Universities with the specific task of redefining the future of public universities and reexamining the ideal of public university service to community and nation. Twenty-four presidents and chancellors, under the leadership of NASULGC President Peter Magrath, released six reports over four years under the theme "Returning to Our Roots."

> "By engagement, we refer to institutions that have redesigned their teaching, research and extension and service functions to become even more sympathetically and productively involved with their communities."
>
> —"The Engaged Institution" a report by the Kellogg Commission on the Future of State and Land-Grant Universities

"The irreducible idea is that we exist to advance the common good," [23] concluded the Kellogg Commission. For today's public universities that means "touching base again with the values that shape the public university. The growing democratization of higher education, the great capacity of today's students to shape and guide their own learning, and the burgeoning demands of the modern world require us to think of learning, discovery and engagement." [24]

According to Magrath, engagement is not an "add-on" to the university's mission, a "nice thing to do," but is a mainstream activity, a readaptation of the land-grant philosophy that is "both the right thing for our society's interest and a very smart thing for America's universities who wish to attract the resources and support needed for the fundamental mission of discovering, disseminating and applying knowledge." [25]

Speaking at a conference sponsored by the University of Wisconsin-Milwaukee in celebration of The Milwaukee Idea, Magrath commented on the fact that it is the nation's urban universities that are discovering the value of engagement and leading the way for the rest of higher education.

He cited UWM's School of Nursing and its Institute for Urban Health Partnerships as an example of how engagement benefits community and campus. The Partnership operates four community nursing centers in Milwaukee where students and faculty not only serve thousands of the area's neediest residents, but also help develop public health policy based on health monitoring and research. Literally hundreds of other community collaborations at UWM—from urban brownfield redevelopment partnerships to programs to evaluate lead poisoning in children, from technical training for inner-city teachers to a student volunteer center—all testify to the university's rich history of engagement.

A Closer Look

Leading the Way to Engagement: UWM's School of Nursing
By Sally Peck Lundeen, Dean of the School of Nursing

The Milwaukee Idea is totally consistent with the mission and goals of the UWM School of Nursing. As a practice-based profession, professional nursing must constantly seek to integrate education, research, and practice. In fact, the school has engaged in considerable collaboration with community partners during the past 20 years. This is visible through the four community nursing centers sponsored by the school, our research facilitation contracts with major area hospitals, and joint research chairs at St. Luke's and Children's Hospitals.

The creative vision of Chancellor Zimpher has allowed us to build on this foundation and significantly expand partnership activities while simultaneously meeting the goals of the school and addressing the needs of the community. A recent partnership with Aurora Health Care, funded by the Helene

Fuld Educational Trust, is piloting an innovative, collaborative model of clinical education that is designed to address the current nursing shortage. The community nursing centers provide opportunities to develop new models of health care delivery and interdisciplinary education while providing service to families with limited access to health care.

I believe that the greatest challenge to successful implementation of The Milwaukee Idea is one of attaining a delicate balance between the traditional role of the university and the needs of the community. We must not abandon our traditional foci on education and research, but balance them with direct applications in the community. We must not abandon our search for new knowledge and truth in all areas, but balance this search with the questions of greatest concern to our communities. We must not shift all our attention into the service of broad urban social agendas, but we must seek a balance of resource allocation—fiscal and human—to attend to the social agenda as a part of our mission.

It is my experience that our community partners have embraced The Milwaukee Idea version of the engaged university enthusiastically. They know what a positive influence this kind of partnership can have on the economic stability and quality of life throughout Wisconsin. The real challenge of The Milwaukee Idea lies with those of us in the academy who must embrace and forward a broader vision that values a balance among the multiple missions of the urban university. I am proud that the School of Nursing has responded through the Institute for Urban Health Partnerships, our community nursing centers, and multiple partnerships in instruction and research in order to meet this challenge.

WILL WE LEAD?

The question UWM faced with the arrival of its new chancellor was not whether it should become an engaged campus—it had always been one—but whether it could better use that heritage to transform both city and campus.

There was not, in the fall of 1998, a unanimous consensus at UWM that enhancing university engagement was the best path to institutional prominence. The Milwaukee Idea was not greeted with immediate enthusiasm—by some faculty and staff on campus or some supporters in Milwaukee. With its coveted Research II designation threatened (UWM was ranked in the bottom tier for federal and extramural research funding), many faculty felt that a stronger dedication—in staffing and dollars—to the research mission was the only way to improve the stature of the university, attract the best students,

"Interacting with the community is well and good, but unless it is based on the solid expertise of our research, scholarship and creative activity, we're nothing more than a soup kitchen."

—David Petering
UWM Professor and Director of the National Institute of Environmental Health Sciences Marine and Freshwater Biomedical Sciences Center

and remain competitive with the state's flagship university in Madison. Scholarship and expertise were what the university could bring to the table. Without that strong foundation, some said, its outreach efforts would only be the equivalent of volunteerism.

Others on campus believed that only through an aggressive fund-raising program to restore decimated faculty ranks could the excellence of UWM's academic programs be assured. Many faculty distrusted the administration's ability to support new efforts like The Milwaukee Idea when existing faculty efforts were poorly funded and unrecognized.

"I think a great many of us can and did support the idea of increasing university-community relations," wrote one professor in an email exchange. "We did not expect that the community would be told that it takes an entirely new university to do the job." There were genuine fears that The Milwaukee Idea would be "the urban tail wagging the university dog," as one faculty member described it. History Professor Margo Anderson commented that if The Milwaukee Idea could inspire a multimillion dollar campaign, it would serve a purpose, since the "key to UWM's future is money." The mantra of many skeptics across campus was "show me the money."

Nor was the community entirely prepared to consider a new UWM. While conversations with leading civic and business leaders acknowledged that UWM needed to enhance its standing in the community and become a player in the life of the city, there was ambivalence as to what other effects such change might cause. At community meetings and business breakfasts, support for a new vision, while enthusiastic, was invariably followed by caution.

"Don't abandon your commitment to strong academic programs," was a constant refrain. The message from the community was clear: Try new initiatives and become more involved, but do not sacrifice your academic standing to do so. In other words, "Yes, we support you—if you can do it all."

At the same time, community expectations for university partnerships varied widely, from research collaborations to volunteer student help, from potential new dollars from a funder with perceived deep pockets to instant solutions to intractable problems. Community organizations were eager to define the university's mission in terms of their own needs.

In short, UWM, like hundreds of other institutions of higher education, contemplated its future in the face of conflicting support from within and without. And from within this maelstrom, Chancellor Zimpher announced the beginning of The Milwaukee Idea.

A Closer Look

The Milwaukee Idea as Partnership

By Alan Guskin, consultant to higher education, former chancellor of the University of Wisconsin-Parkside, and former president of Antioch University

When new chancellors and presidents are at their best, they provide their institutions with renewed energy to struggle with their institutions' core missions. This is what occurred at the University of Wisconsin-Milwaukee in the fall of 1998 with Nancy Zimpher. Unencumbered by the struggles of the previous three decades, she adopted the powerful and still meaningful founding idea of the University of Wisconsin and applied it directly to UWM; The Wisconsin Idea that asserts that the boundaries of the university are the boundaries of the state was transformed into The Milwaukee Idea in which the boundaries of the Milwaukee metropolitan area are the boundaries of UWM.

To those not aware of the proud history of The Wisconsin Idea and its acknowledgment throughout the state, it may be hard to explain the instant recognition and symbolic power this new assertion had on the people of Milwaukee and others throughout the state. Symbolically, UWM was vigorously restating its mission to serve the people of Milwaukee. But the new chancellor was not only talking about serving; she stated that UWM was going to enter into a partnership with the people and institutions of Milwaukee. This indeed was good news, and the press and the political, business, and community leaders were enthusiastic in their support for these new directions.

Dealing with symbols is extremely important for a chancellor and something she can accomplish pretty much by herself; implementing university programs to fulfill these commitments requires significant support from key groups of faculty throughout the institution, something that cannot easily be assumed. This may be especially true for UWM, which has struggled for many years to clarify its urban mission while maintaining its aspirations as a doctoral research university. UWM shares these issues with many fellow large urban doctoral institutions that have been struggling to engage deeply with their communities.

In the 1960s, universities located in large urban areas began to think seriously about their mission to serve their surrounding communities, much as their more rural university cousins were created to do in the mid-1800s with the establishment of the land-grant universities. However, dealing with the needs of farmers and rural areas in the late 19th century, and even into the mid-20th century, was quite different from trying to help cities work on issues of poverty, poor schooling, racial strife, new immigrants, urban transportation, and housing. So, too, were the differences in underlying aspirations of the land-grant universities in the 1860s and the urban institutions in the 1960s.

Unlike the creation of the land-grant universities and their mission to serve the agricultural and rural needs of their states, in the 1960s the increasing professionalization of the faculty and the intense growth of research and doctoral missions occurred at the same time these urban universities were growing and developing. The missions of the large urban universities as practiced in their day-to-day life always seemed to be murky and conflicted: Were they to become another version of the flagship research university or were they primarily to serve their urban communities? Or, was the real mission to do both, however difficult that may be?

This difficulty in clarifying its real urban mission-in-practice has been a core issue at UWM since its inception. While numerous faculty have continued to offer their expertise to one or another community or business entity, these activities were, to a great extent, seen as actions of individuals rather than a coordinated effort of the university. Exacerbating this mission confusion were the feelings of many faculty that UWM should be a research university in the tradition of UW-Madison.

The new chancellor of UWM recognized these tensions and realized that the institution's future required it to assert its urban mission without rejecting its other aspirations. If UWM was going to be successful in the long term, it was apparent that it had to clarify its mission-in-practice and assert its distinctiveness within the state, while at the same time developing strong ties to the political power base of Milwaukee. Both these objectives could be reached with the symbolic assertion and practical implementation of The Milwaukee Idea: UWM could be a truly engaged, urban university and at the same time be a major doctoral institution.

The Milwaukee Idea as conceived by Chancellor Zimpher, however, was not a warmed-over concept of an urban university that served the Milwaukee area. Consistent with the underlying implications of The Wisconsin Idea and the new national movement for universities to "engage" in significant ways with their communities, The Milwaukee Idea was conceived of as a *partnership* between UWM and the Milwaukee area.

Furthermore, this new conception of a university engaged with its community was to deal with the national higher education challenges of the beginning of the 21st century: the integration of new forms of student learning environments, new technologies, and new roles for faculty and staff, where appropriate. If successfully implemented, this vision for UWM would transform it into an educational and political powerhouse within the state of Wisconsin.

Reflections

Nancy Zimpher and Steve Percy on The Wisconsin and Milwaukee Ideas

Nancy Zimpher

From the moment I first arrived in this state, I heard reference to The Wisconsin Idea. This mission of mutual service is right for this state and for this institution because it is embedded in the rich traditions of Wisconsin. It has sustainability. At the same time, this idea of connecting the university and the community needs to be reinvented for our time and for our place in an urban center.

UWM is attempting to do nothing less than make The Wisconsin Idea relevant for a new century. The challenge for UWM, and for every institution, is to discover the theory of its life as an institution, to paraphrase Peter Drucker. [26]

Finding that "theory of life" can be tricky, as I discovered when I started talking to business and community leaders about a more engaged UWM. They liked the idea but were concerned that we were changing the core mission of providing basic research and educating Milwaukee's students.

I learned very quickly that transformation must have a "Yes and . . ." strategy. You can never, ever forsake people's fundamental understanding of the role of the university.

It became important that we articulate—clearly and often—our allegiance to the traditional triadic mission of teaching, research, and service. For UWM, however, that vision can be made more alive through the transforming nature of collaboration.

Steve Percy

We should be clear that UWM did not simply begin reaching out to metropolitan Milwaukee with the start of The Milwaukee Idea. Our pattern of partnership spanned decades, from research on minority lending practices in the city of Milwaukee to students providing therapy at area health clinics.

What we had not done before was look at our engagement from a campus-wide perspective and look critically at the nature of our collaborations. Community collaborations can be extremely challenging relationships. More often than we like to admit, universities have not always gotten them right.

I remember attending a meeting many years ago with a community group looking to partner with us for a federal grant for improved educational services. We took a group of deans and had our plans all laid out. We probably sounded as if we were hijacking the agenda and so we were politely shown the door and told not to come back. Fortunately, several of the group's members were willing to work with us to grow a relationship that, over time, did bear fruit. But that experience helped us—as we began to launch The Milwaukee Idea—pay closer attention to how we partnered.

Nancy Zimpher

The heart of The Milwaukee Idea is the centrality of partnership to determining our agenda. This is what will assure our success. And we know we will succeed because our model, The Wisconsin Idea, has stood the test of time. The Wisconsin Idea gives us a firm foundation. The Milwaukee Idea gives us wings.

Endnotes

Callout, page 17, by Sir Eric Ashby, quoted in *Beyond the Ivory Tower: Social Responsibilities of the Modern University* by Derek Bok. (1982). Cambridge, MA: Harvard University Press, page 65.

[1] Jack Stark. (1995). "The Wisconsin Idea: The University's Service to the State," *State of Wisconsin 1995–1996 Blue Book*. Madison, WI: Legislative Reference Bureau, pages 101–179.

[2] Quote by Charles McCarthy, first chief of the Wisconsin Legislative Reference Bureau. Ibid., page 140.

[3] The 1910 platform of the Wisconsin Republican Party. "We are proud of the high eminence attained by our state university. We commend its research work.... We regard the university as the people's servant, carrying knowledge and assistance to the homes and farms and workplaces." Quoted in Stark, "The Wisconsin Idea," page 111.

[4] From email conversation with Gareth Shellman, senior outreach specialist, History, University of Wisconsin-Milwaukee, and based on his paper prepared for the 20th Annual Fromkin Memorial Lecture in 1989. The lecture is printed in Volume II of *The Quest for Social Justice*, Allen Corré, ed., (1992). Madison, WI: University of Wisconsin Press.

[5] Stark, "The Wisconsin Idea" page 101.

[6] Daniel Coit Gilman, as quoted in "School-Community-University Partnerships: Effectively Integrating Community Building and Education Reform" by Ira Harkavy, University of Pennsylvania, a paper presented to a Joint Forum of the U.S. Department of Education and the U.S. Department of Housing and Urban Development in Washington, DC, January 8, 1998, page 3.

Callout page 19: Seth Low quoted in "School-Community-University Partnerships" by Ira Harkavy, page 4.

[7] Wharton School academic Simon Patten, quoted in "Implications of Engagement for University Traditions, Roles and Governance," an address given by Ira Harkavy at the University of Wisconsin-Milwaukee conference "University Engagement in the Community: A Vision of the 21st Century," March 25–26, 1999.

[8] Quoted in "School-Community-University Partnerships" by Ira Harkavy, page 4.

[9] Harkavy. "Implications of Engagement for University Traditions, Roles and Governance."

[10] Derek Bok. (1982). *Beyond the Ivory Tower: Social Responsibilities of the Modern University.* Cambridge, MA: Harvard University Press.

[11] Ernest L. Boyer. (1990). *Scholarship Reconsidered: Priorities of the Professoriate.* San Francisco: Jossey-Bass, pages 12 and 13.

[12] Harkavy. "Implications of Engagement for University Traditions, Roles and Governance."

[13] James Duderstadt. (2000). *A University for the 21st Century.* Ann Arbor, MI: The University of Michigan Press, page 126.

[14] Donald Kettl. "Reinventing The Wisconsin Idea," a February 1999 issue in the La Follette Institute's Sesquicentennial Paper Series, University of Wisconsin-Madison, page 1.

[15] Ernest L. Boyer. (March 9, 1994). "Creating the New American College," *The Chronicle of Higher Education,* page A48.

[16] Ernest Boyer in comments made at a conference, "The New American College," at Wingspread, Racine, WI, 1994. Quoted in *The Wingspread Journal,* edited by Mary Jane Brukardt, Summer 1996, published by The Johnson Foundation, Racine, Wisconsin.

[17] Zelda Gamson. (Jan./Feb. 1997). "Higher Education and Rebuilding Civic Life." *Change* magazine, page 13.

[18] Ira Harkavy, quoted in "It's Not Just Academic: University-Community Partnerships Are Rebuilding Neighborhoods" by James H. Carr, ed., *Housing Facts & Figures,* Spring 1999, published by the Fannie Mae Foundation.

[19] Evan Dobelle. "Stepping Down from the Ivory Tower." Remarks delivered to the National Press Club, Washington, DC, February 18, 1999.

[20] Martin van der Werg. (April 30, 1999). "Urban Universities Try New Ways to Reach Out to Their Communities," *The Chronicle of Higher Education.*

[21] Claire L. Gaudiani. (Winter 1999). "A Call to Social Stewardship," *The Presidency,* a publication of the American Council on Education.

[22] Harry Boyte and Elizabeth Hollander. "The Wingspread Declaration on Renewing the Civic Mission of the American Research University." The declaration was a product of a series of conferences sponsored by The Johnson Foundation at Wingspread, in Racine, WI, in 1998 and 1999.

[23] The Kellogg Commission on the Future of State and Land-Grant Universities. (2000). *Renewing the Covenant: Learning, Discovery, and Engagement in a New Age and Different World.* National Association of State Universities and Land-Grant Colleges, page 11.

[24] The Kellogg Commission on the Future of State and Land-Grant Universities. *Toward a Coherent Campus Culture* (2000) and *The Engaged University* (1999) both from the National Association of State Universities and Land-Grant Colleges, pages 11 and vii, respectively.

The Kellogg Commission reports are available online at www.nasulgc.org/Kellogg/kellogg.htm

[25] C. Peter Magrath. "The Engaged University: It Integrates Teaching, Research and Outreach," an address at the University of Wisconsin-Milwaukee Conference *University Engagement in the Community: A Vision of the 21st Century,* March 25, 1999.

[26] Peter Drucker. (1995). *Managing in a Time of Great Change.* New York: Truman Talley Books/Dutton, Chapter 1: The Theory of the Business.

CAPTURING
PEOPLE'S ATTENTION

From *The Business Journal,* Milwaukee, Wisconsin
Week of September 7, 1998

New Chancellor Gathers Ideas for Change at UWM
By Julie Sneider

Nancy Zimpher has been the chancellor of the University of Wisconsin-Milwaukee for only a few weeks, but she's wasted no time getting to know her new campus, its faculty and students and the community at large.

She's already met with dozens of alumni, and business and community leaders to get their perspectives on UWM, its current mission and future direction.

Zimpher says she's using those sessions to lay the groundwork
for developing a long-range plan for UWM, one that will raise the
university's profile, improve its fund-raising and strengthen its
ties with local businesses. . . .

. . . Given her expertise, some community members view [Zimpher]
as a catalyst for change in public education in Milwaukee.

He shook his head slowly as he left the UWM Union meeting room. The
CEO of a prominent Milwaukee corporate organization had been
invited to help define the University of Wisconsin-Milwaukee's new "Milwaukee Idea," and he had just finished a brainstorming session with about 20
faculty, students, university staff, and community members. "We talked
about everything from campus parking to global warming," he sighed. "How
are you ever going to get there?"

(The irony, of course, was that he considered global warming the more
complex problem. As anyone who visits an American university campus
knows, the most pressing issue in higher education today is where to park the
cars!)

The story does have a happy ending, however. While global warming—
and campus parking—remain concerns, UWM did "get there"—or at least
got moving in a new direction. Through an almost three-year process that
was, by turns, messy, energizing, infuriating, contentious, inspired, and

transforming, the University of Wisconsin-Milwaukee created a vision and, more amazingly (especially for those familiar with the traditional ways of the academy), began implementing a concrete action plan for its future as an engaged university.

FIRST, CAPTURE ATTENTION

As many on campus realized, the arrival of a new chancellor presented the university with a unique opportunity to examine its strengths and continue its decades-long discussion of its role as a growing urban campus. As former Provost and Vice Chancellor Ken Watters, a 31-year veteran professor and administrator, observed, UWM's urban mission had been a focal point of its strategic planning since its founding.

"What we never had—and that's the beauty of The Milwaukee Idea— was a process that engaged such a large and diverse group of people," Watters said. "It wasn't for lack of trying, but we had not quite hit upon the approach that captured people's attention the way this has."

Capture attention it did. Six weeks after Nancy Zimpher began her duties as chancellor of UWM, she stood before a group of more than 700 faculty, students, community leaders, and staff at a faculty-sponsored plenary session. "The time has come to redefine ourselves," she announced to the overflow crowd, ". . . as a centerpiece of metropolitan life . . . and as Milwaukee's, and someday the nation's, premier urban university." And then she asked the university and community to join together to imagine.

Imagine The Milwaukee Idea. She described the visioning process: bringing together 100 people for 100 days to imagine concrete ways in which the city and campus could work together. From those initial 100 people, involvement would grow as ideas were developed and others were recruited to participate. The 100 days would be just a prelude to ongoing creativity and implementation.

Here's how the process worked. The Milwaukee Idea involved five distinct phases: 1) Affinity Groups for visioning, 2) Action Teams for planning, 3) an Evaluation Team to assess plans, 4) Negotiating Teams for final implementation, and 5) the Launch of the Ideas, with ongoing innovation and assessment. Here's what each involved.

The Process

Affinity Groups were large and open to all, and were charged with creating "Big Ideas" that would lead UWM to prominence as an urban research university. They began with a group of 100 people asked to work for 100 days on

The Milwaukee Idea Change Process

Affinity Groups
Visioning
▼
Action Teams
Planning
▼
Evaluation Team
Assessment
▼
Negotiation
Implementation
▼
The First Ideas Launch
Ongoing
Innovation and Partnerships
and Continuing Assessment,
Evaluation, and Accountability

See Appendix B for a detailed outline of The Milwaukee Idea process.

new ideas. They expanded to more than 200 individuals, meeting for five months, and they produced ten "Big Ideas," announced to the community at the chancellor's inauguration. These Ideas would form the core of The Milwaukee Idea efforts: the initial tangible projects around which community and university could rally.

After the Big Ideas (later called "First Ideas" to reflect the ongoing nature of The Milwaukee Idea) were announced, Action Teams were formed to create implementation plans. The Action Teams met for the next five months, were more structured, and limited to less than 20 members. They were assisted by Advisory Groups that were open to all.

When the Action Teams completed their detailed plans, the proposals were assessed by the Evaluation Team, composed of 13 people from campus and community. The group made final recommendations for implementing the First Ideas to campus governance groups and to the chancellor.

The provost and Milwaukee Idea executive director then coordinated the Negotiations for campus implementation. When complete, each Idea decided on the timing and format of the Launch of the Idea. Once launched, the directors of the Ideas continued to assess progress and provide updates to The Milwaukee Idea office. Additional Ideas also were generated, both from the community and from the campus, and implemented as appropriate. The Milwaukee Idea process was headed by the chancellor and managed by administration staff under the direction of Stephen Percy, who continued to oversee ongoing partnerships and assessment of the Ideas.

The community played an active role in all facets of the process except negotiations, which focused on internal university budgets and administration issues.

In addition, a Strategy Team, composed of faculty, staff, administration, students, and community members, provided oversight and support to the entire process.

LEARN BY DOING

While The Milwaukee Idea process appears linear in hindsight, it was not a grand plan outlined at its conception and allowed to run its course. It was developed—often on the fly and through much collaboration—as participants worked together. It was this learning by doing that helped the process succeed. As Michael Shenkman notes in his book on organizational growth, results happen most dynamically when people are immersed in the relationships in which the institution must succeed each and every day. As those vital relationships are strengthened and challenged, energy and new direction result.[1] For UWM, that meant bringing together not just administration and key civic leaders (as had been done in countless strategic planning sessions through the years), but a true cross-section of the campus and the metropolitan community. If UWM was to envision itself as a premier urban research university, each constituent group needed to help create the vision—as equal partners, together.

> "As people talk, try things out, inquire, retry—all of this jointly—people become more skilled, ideas become clearer, shared commitment gets stronger. Productive change is very much a process of mobilization and positive contagion."
>
> —*Michael Fullan*
> *Change Forces*

This collaborative principle is outlined in a recent study of 26 institutions of higher learning that were tackling substantial change. The American Council on Education (ACE) determined there were five key ingredients for successfully engaging a campus:

1) Make a clear and compelling case for change.

2) Craft an agenda that makes sense and doesn't assign blame.

3) Widen the circle of participation.

4) Make connections.

5) Encourage conversations about change.[2]

At UWM, the case for change had been outlined by UW System President Katharine Lyall when she told the Chancellor Search and Screen Committee to find a leader who could transform UWM into a premier institution. It was anticipated by faculty and staff who saw new potential for growth. In The Milwaukee Idea process, the focus on self-directed teams offered the campus the chance to create a vision that truly reflected the institution. Its open, inclusive structure was built on reinforcing networks and getting people to talk.

And The Milwaukee Idea certainly got people talking! As Madeleine Green of ACE notes wryly, "The dangers of talking are over-rated," but crucial to creating the momentum needed for action.[3]

For a campus that some faculty and staff characterized as "disengaged, even with itself," lacking a sense of community, and based on a "caste system" of administration, faculty, and academic and classified staff, such interaction broke new ground. Bob Gleason, a change consultant from the Revere Group who was hired to help facilitate the Affinity Group sessions, observed that UWM wasn't accustomed to "dreaming big, institution-wide dreams." People just didn't know how to participate at first. They would need to learn by doing.

READY, FIRE, AIM

As Michael Fullan has written, people can't think their way into new ways of operating. They must "behave their way into new ideas and skills." He calls this the "ready, fire, aim" sequence of change activity.

> "Complex systems only develop and grow when they are in that special state called 'beyond equilibrium.' Things are crazy."
>
> —Michael Shenkman
> *The Strategic Heart*

"Vision emerges from, more than it precedes, action," says Fullan. "*Shared* vision, which is essential for success, must evolve through the dynamic interaction of organizational members and leaders. This takes time and will not succeed unless the vision-building process is somewhat open-ended."[4]

Just as a new vision for UWM couldn't be mandated from above, so also the visioning process required change first. Learning how to work and dream together was one challenge. Learning how to dream with the community was another. As Jean Tyler, a Milwaukee civic leader and long-time UWM observer, found, too frequently many faculty and staff at UWM waited "until they got everything right" before they would approach the community for input. "It's the old pattern," she said. "UWM will have an idea and they'll say 'This is what we want to do,' and people will say, 'Well, that's not where we are,' and that's the end of the collaboration." With the Affinity process, the community came in at the start to help "figure it out from the beginning."

Learning to dream big dreams was not a smooth process, as many across campus can testify. "This was a *very* new experience for UWM folks," said a department chair who served on one of the Affinity groups. "In the past there have been very few opportunities to cross the divisions of the pecking order at

UWM, and, like most participatory processes, it got a little messy and even testy. It was often painful, but it worked in the end."

Victoria Boswell, past chair of the Academic Staff Committee, welcomed the inclusion of academic staff in the planning process and agreed their participation was crucial to implementing The Milwaukee Idea, even if faculty support for their involvement was less than unanimous. "What academic staff bring to the table is the implementation piece," she said.

Mike Maas, a custodian in the administration building and active participant on two Affinity Groups, said the process began to bring people together in ways he had not seen in years. "We were skeptical," Maas said, describing the attitude of many of the classified staff who participated. "But we were able to speak our mind. Yes, there was a lot of debate and argument, but that's always going to happen." He, like many of those interviewed, agreed that while efforts at involving all constituent groups did not always succeed, the chancellor's practice of inviting everyone to the table set a new pattern for the way things are done at UWM. "I think the very heartbeat of this chancellor is including everybody," Maas said.

INVOLVE DEANS AND CAMPUS LEADERS

While it is safe to say that The Milwaukee Idea process evolved, its seeds were planted at an annual retreat held with the chancellor and deans just a few weeks after Zimpher's arrival. Discussions of how to create a clear vision for the campus soon coalesced around The Milwaukee Idea.

Based on deans' suggestions, initial Milwaukee Idea discussions would focus on five themes:

1) Culture and Education
2) Economic Opportunity
3) Global Perspectives
4) Health and Wellness
5) Urban Environment

As consultant Gleason recalled, the deans responded to the idea of creating a future that built on the concept of The Wisconsin Idea, but had a decidedly urban, UWM focus. They helped Zimpher identify five areas of focus in which UWM might make a difference, both in terms of academic and research growth and community outreach. These included such issues as economic development, improved education, the urban environment, global perspectives and better community health. These were to form the core proposals for The Milwaukee Idea in the chancellor's first speech to the faculty-sponsored plenary and also would define the proposed Affinity Groups.

Involvement of the deans in The Milwaukee Idea process was vital—and also challenging. Their expertise and leadership was essential in the early stages of the process as they helped to articulate areas of focus and motivated their respective faculty and staff to participate. If some of the deans originally thought The Milwaukee Idea was theirs or the chancellor's to implement, they soon realized the process would not be top down. The result was disengagement for some, but creative and enthusiastic support by others.

Some of the deans served as heads of Affinity or Action Teams. Some found their Milwaukee Idea activities spilling over into their administrative duties. Randall Lambrecht, dean of the College of Health Sciences, for example, helped create an interactive and engaged grassroots governance model in his school to address the new opportunities for collaboration raised by The Milwaukee Idea.

Susan Kelly, Associate Provost and Dean of Continuing Education, is a veteran of the change process, having weathered initiatives at three other institutions before coming to UWM from her native Australia. "I'm not starry-eyed about the long, hard road and volume of work," she said, after serving on both Affinity and Action Teams. "But, we have a vision now to which people can attach. And it's a fine one at that."

In addition to enlisting the deans' support, the chancellor also made a point of involving leaders from campus constituent groups—the unions, students, alumni—and, in particular, representatives from the Faculty and Academic Staff Committees. Taking advantage of the "honeymoon" period granted to new leaders, she sought to get them involved quickly, not just as leaders representing particular groups, but as individuals with unique skills and ideas to contribute. By using existing leadership on Affinity and Action Teams, in situations outside their usual frame of reference, she was able to build a "constituency for change" [5] for The Milwaukee Idea.

The support of the deans and campus leadership for The Milwaukee Idea became increasingly important as programs were created that crossed disciplines and reporting structures. More difficult, however, was the task of finding ways to keep the deans meaningfully involved in the face of their existing responsibilities and natural inclination to focus on their own disciplines. Continuity also was disrupted as several key participants had the opportunity to take positions at other institutions and their successors faced the challenge of becoming involved in the middle of the process.

As brainstorming gave way to decision-making on questions such as new programs, staffing, and reporting structures, it also became increasingly difficult for faculty, staff, students, or community members to have an equal voice with the deans in the process. The roles of dean and change agent were at times conflicting ones.

"We did not manage to keep The Milwaukee Idea at the forefront of the deans' priorities," admitted Watters. "We could have designed a steering function for the deans to keep them involved as a group." As the process continued, Percy and Zimpher tried several administrative models to better integrate the deans and to give them a voice. These are outlined in Chapter 7.

USE CONSULTANTS CREATIVELY

The Milwaukee Idea vision, honed at the deans' retreat, gathered momentum. At a follow-on meeting with the chancellor's staff and Cabinet, the outline for The Milwaukee Idea process was created. At consultant Bob Gleason's suggestion, 100 people would be invited to meet for no more than 100 days to create the ideas that would define the future for the university. All ideas would be based on university engagement with the community.

Gleason had been hired by the provost to facilitate the deans' retreat. At that meeting, he introduced the chancellor to management guru Peter Drucker's ideas about the "theory of the business." According to Drucker, successful organizations are clear about the environment in which they operate, have a specific mission, and understand what it takes to fulfill that mission.[6] This notion resonated with the need Zimpher saw at UWM—to create a "theory of the university" that would be right for UWM and its community.

The success of that planning exercise convinced the chancellor to retain Gleason to help guide the next step in the process. Gleason's "bias for action" found a receptive audience in Zimpher and he was able to provide critical help in creating the mechanics of the process. He also suggested the formation of a "Quick Wins" group to champion early victories, and developed the working templates for the visioning groups. His business background brought many useful ideas to a university that, in his words, needed to learn how to dream big dreams, include all constituents, and take action. He also facilitated each plenary session for the first five months of the process, a role that was not warmly received by a campus skeptical of business consultants, but was undertaken with good humor by Gleason.

"Facilitation is not a value-neutral activity," Gleason said wryly. "I found that people typically viewed me as an outsider, or, worse, a mercenary brought in to do the dirty work, whatever that might have been." Many participants found his background in the corporate sector a disadvantage when addressing the needs of higher education and considered his business anecdotes irrelevant. Some faculty, especially those from the sciences, found his approach too "touchy-feely," an attribute they also applied, on occasion, to Zimpher.

Gleason's role as a facilitator also was seen as an infringement on a role many thought should have gone to the chancellor. Several campus emails suggested she would have been the better facilitator, an attitude that reflected the university's general hunger to see and hear more of its new leader. But Gleason graciously served as a lightning rod, deflecting early criticism and concerns from university leadership, and, as the months went by, turning over the reins to the campus as it took ownership of the process. Gleason's early facilitation also gave Zimpher the freedom to observe the process better, comment as needed, and maintain a distance from the operational details.

> "Restructuring will be one of the major activities of many or most of the universities in the country over the next ten years.... Powerful pressures will force major changes in how our colleges and universities are organized. The major issue for those of us in higher education is to face whether we are going to lead these change efforts or be forced into them."
>
> —*Alan Guskin*
> *Restructuring Our Universities*

Gleason was not the only consultant who contributed to the formation of The Milwaukee Idea. Alan Guskin, noted for his work on restructuring universities, was invited to meet with faculty and staff to share ideas on enhancing student learning and integrating change into the structure of the university. He encouraged discussion of ideas that, while not necessarily directly related to the initial stages of The Milwaukee Idea—such as faculty reward, integrating technology, the academic calendar—became increasingly important as the university discovered the impact of the First Ideas on all its operations. He challenged the architects of the First Ideas to design new models for student learning, setting apart the First Ideas to protect the new partnerships until they were strong enough to serve as catalysts for broader institutional change. The Milwaukee Idea, he said, "has enormous potential for partnerships" that should not be tackled through incremental change.

Not all of these suggestions fell on receptive ears or came to fruition. Guskin did, however, provide important ideas throughout the process that sparked new thinking and challenged existing perceptions. He provided ideas for the chancellor and her leadership team as she integrated The Milwaukee Idea into her administrative vision.

SEEK ALIGNMENT, NOT CONSENSUS

Early on, Gleason had cautioned Zimpher and Percy that change at UWM would involve a four-step process, as campus and community moved from awareness to understanding to acceptance and, finally, to commitment. This progress would take time—and continuous, aggressive communication—but it would never result in a 100% commitment level. As was evident from many heated exchanges over the role of faculty, expectations of the community, issues of diversity, and commitment to building the research infrastructure, consensus for the vision from campus and community was an impossible goal. Instead, The Milwaukee Idea process would aim for *alignment* by creating ideas around which people could rally.

So Zimpher created opportunities for individuals to connect across a wide variety of interests. The Milwaukee Idea process allowed individuals from the campus and community to find the niche that appealed to them. They did not need to commit to the entire package before they could contribute to an individual piece.

Biologists call it "flocking"—the pattern that allows birds to fly in a group even while individual members take divergent paths. At UWM, people were given the opportunity to help The Milwaukee Idea fly, even if they supported only some of its goals.

Moving forward drew people into the initiative more powerfully than waiting for everyone to agree. Within the broad framework of community-university engagement and the specific First Ideas of The Milwaukee Idea, there was room for every contribution. As one Affinity Group participant said, "Maybe not everyone will 100% agree with our ideas, but we're working to create something we can all live with."

And so the groundwork was laid for the beginning of The Milwaukee Idea. The Wisconsin Idea provided a concept for the engaged university and The Milwaukee Idea gave it relevance for UWM. The deans helped provide a framework for discussion of key areas of focus, and the broad outlines of an inclusive campus-wide visioning process were sketched. The stage was set for creation of the team that would set it all in motion.

Reflections

Nancy Zimpher on the Beginning of the Change Process
Change doesn't happen by chancellor fiat. It can't be forced. It happens when people perceive that it makes sense for the way they do their work.

I did not intend to go to the campus like Moses with the Ten Commandments and tell people what to do. As Fullan has written, "You can't mandate what matters. The more complex the change, the less you can force it." [7]

But the time was right at UWM. Even though the local paper announced "the honeymoon's over" less than nine months after I'd arrived, I knew I had both the support of the Regents and most of the UWM faculty and staff to do things differently. I do think that part of the success of The Milwaukee Idea was timing: taking advantage of people's goodwill toward a new chancellor. Were I to attempt to launch The Milwaukee Idea today, I don't think I would have the same response—you probably can't do this kind of campus-wide mobilization twice in your tenure, and doing it sooner, rather than later, was the right choice.

That being said, what you tackle during a honeymoon period is important. I did not intend to take on the big, systemic questions—issues of tenure and promotion are for braver souls than I (and respond better to incremental change anyway). With The Milwaukee Idea, we could, instead, focus on our dreams, on what we could all rally around.

Rally is the right term, because I think that Bob Gleason's idea of seeking alignment, rather than consensus, was a breakthrough. When you focus on trying to get consensus, you are asking people to buy the whole package, a package they may not even completely understand or relate to. But they can relate to parts of the vision, and that's the connecting point that gets people on the team.

Finding ways to include everyone on the team was another important step. We made a point of involving campus and community leaders, not in their "official" capacity, but as working, contributing team members. We didn't put together a new university mission, then take it to the deans or the governance groups for adoption. We asked them to help create it and this made a big difference in how The Milwaukee Idea has been accepted.

If all this sounds deliberative, it wasn't. The proposition from Fullan's contemporary change theory—"Ready, Fire, Aim,"—truly applied to what we were doing our first year. We learned from our actions, then took better aim as we went along. If we'd waited until we got our aim right, we'd still be talking.

Endnotes

[1] Michael Shenkman. (1996). *The Strategic Heart: Using the New Science to Lead Growing Organizations.* Westport, CT: Praeger Publishers, page xvii.

[2] Peter Eckel, Madeleine Green, Barbara Hill, and William Mallon. (1999). *On Change III, Taking Charge of Change: A Primer for Colleges and Universities.* Washington, DC: American Council on Education, pages 35–43.

[3] Madeleine Green, in *Redefining Success: Education for the Common Good,* an address given at the third annual Urban Initiatives Conference, "Dynamics of Change: The Milwaukee Idea and the New Urban University," at the University of Wisconsin-Milwaukee, June 8, 2000.

Callout page 37: Michael Shenkman, *The Strategic Heart,* page 13.

[4] Michael Fullan. (1993). *Change Forces.* New York: The Falmer Press, page 28.

[5] David Chrislip and Carl Larson. (1994). *Collaborative Leadership: How Citizens and Civic Leaders Can Make a Difference.* San Francisco: Jossey-Bass, page 108.

[6] Peter Drucker. (1995). *Managing in a Time of Great Change.* New York: Truman Talley Books/Dutton, page 29.

[7] Michael Fullan. *Change Forces,* page 22.

Callout page 41: Alan Guskin. (1996). "Restructuring Our Universities: Focusing on Student Learning," an essay prepared for the 1997 Association of College and Research Libraries Conference.

4

BEHIND THE SCENES
AT THE MILWAUKEE IDEA

From the *UWM Report*
November 5, 1998

Milwaukee Idea Office Going Strong

Whether you prefer your reality virtual or concrete, The Milwaukee Idea has you covered.

Headed by Professor Stephen Percy with assistance from student Sachin Chheda, the staff office is coordinating plenary meetings and providing support to Affinity Groups. They'll also help make sure your ideas and comments get to the right place.

The Milwaukee Idea has both a campus office—complete with phone, fax and e-mail, and a Web site. If you've got a question, comment or idea, that's where to go.

Talking about change is one thing. But what does it take to manage the nitty-gritty task of implementation, day in and day out? If the University of Wisconsin-Milwaukee was to create The Milwaukee Idea, it first needed people and resources to make it happen.

The American Council on Education's study of change in higher education, *On Change,* found that a key factor for successful implementation of new initiatives is the university's ability to put in place people who understand both the institution *and* the change agenda. Understanding and supporting the values behind the process are essential to the leadership team if it is to guide everyone involved through the difficult task of transformation.[1] For UWM, those values included a commitment to encouraging diverse perspectives, a dedication to collaboration, and a belief in the mission of community engagement.

Within a month of the deans' retreat, Zimpher tapped Steve Percy from the Center

Five Attributes of the Ideal Coordination Team

1) Know the territory
2) Be imaginative and see connections
3) Recognize assets and build on strengths
4) Be outside the power structure
5) Be available
   – *Sarason and Lorentz*
   Crossing Boundaries

for Urban Initiatives and Research (CUIR) as executive director of The Milwaukee Idea. Percy had been charged with developing community partnerships by the previous chancellor, John Schroeder, and so he had both the experience and staff in place to take on management of The Milwaukee Idea.

The strong working relationship between Percy and Zimpher began during the search process. As chair of the chancellor search, Percy had the opportunity to get to know Zimpher on both a professional and personal basis, and shared with her a commitment to university engagement.

Percy enlisted student Sachin Chheda and clerical assistant Jessie Weathersby to assist in the countless details of overseeing the Affinity and Action Team processes. And so began The Milwaukee Idea office.

To use the term "office" is probably too lofty a term to describe the two desks stuck in a corner of a classroom in the Physics Building where Chheda and Weathersby began the process of setting up a web site, planning meetings, and building a database of contacts.

Here's how Steve tells the story....

Reflections

Steve Percy on Behind the Scenes at The Milwaukee Idea
I don't think I was ever officially asked to help direct The Milwaukee Idea at UWM. I guess you'd say my position evolved.

As director of UWM's Center for Urban Initiatives and Research, I was one of many individuals at UWM collaborating with the community, generally beneath the institutional radar. CUIR was active in coordinating research around issues of education, economic and community development, and youth. In the fall of 1998, it was one of those projects—a HUD grant to establish a Community Outreach Partnership Center—that brought me to the chancellor's office. I was there to introduce our HUD program officer, Jane Karadbil, and as we talked about the work being done in Milwaukee, Chancellor Zimpher dropped the news that she wanted me to head The Milwaukee Idea. How could I refuse?

It really wasn't a difficult decision. I'd been a professor of political science at UWM since 1989, after six years at the University of Virginia. While I may have started my career following the traditional academic model of teaching, research, and publishing, when I took over direction of CUIR, a whole new range of activities and opportunities became part of my university life. At first it was daunting—who did I know in the community? How could I be helpful? What would be expected of me and UWM? The next few years became an odyssey for me, with a few false starts. Gradually I began to see a wonderful opportunity, the chance to use the skills and talents that I developed as part of my academic career in a whole new way—an enjoyable way—outside the norm, yet informing my traditional work and actually contributing to my teaching and research. Engagement, for me, doesn't mean giving up research or teaching, but using those skills to make a real difference. I've tested the practices of engagement and know they work.

Beyond commitment to the core value of community partnership, however, what UWM needed—what any university seeking change needs—is a richer web of connections, both on and off campus. I've been called a "matchmaker" and I think it's a good term for describing what I do. People and ideas need to be brought together in new—and sometimes pretty creative—ways. It's the networking model of the new economy translated to the academic world.

This kind of networking is often easier to do the farther you are from the chancellor's office. The logical step in creating The Milwaukee Idea office would have been for the chancellor to set up an office next door to hers or give the assignment to a vice chancellor or provost. What Chancellor Zimpher realized is that keeping the initiative outside the administration offices made it more accessible for both campus and community. My office—literally at the other end of the campus from hers—gave The Milwaukee Idea independence and tremendous credibility. That gesture communicated that this was not going to be just another administrative project.

If engagement is to work on campus, it involves coordinating both campus and community priorities. It's essential to have leadership that can speak both languages and that has the trust of both sides.

If I had a campus focus in those first days of The Milwaukee Idea, it was probably involvement. Our goal was to include as many people as possible and get them working together. To do that, we made communicating a priority. You can never do too much and you need to use every vehicle available.

At the same time, we needed to become more credible in the Milwaukee community. I knew from experience there was a lot of distrust. People had been burned before when the university let them down, tried to take over a project or defined success differently. It was important for the community to know we could step up to the plate to be a partner. The Milwaukee Idea office became the figurative and literal place at which university and community could come together.

MOBILIZE RESOURCES

Three Essential Resources for Change:

1) Attention
2) Time
3) Money

And so the work of introducing an institution-wide initiative for community-university engagement began. Acceptance of The Milwaukee Idea on campus would depend on three things: reaching as many people as possible with information about the initiative, providing opportunities for the broadest participation possible, and accessing the funding to make the first two possible. As the American Council on Education report, *On Change III,* notes, a successful change process mobilizes three key resources: attention, time, and money.[2] Campus leadership must focus attention on the change initiative, participants must be encouraged to contribute, and real investment must be made if positive change is to result.

Attention

Drawing attention to The Milwaukee Idea was not difficult, as all eyes on campus (and many in the community) were already on the chancellor, who lost no opportunity to talk about the initiative. The Milwaukee Idea office set about to expand on that foundation, using email, the web, brochures distributed across campus, and regular updates in the university papers and on WUWM, the university's public radio station. Office staff even threatened to find a way to include The Milwaukee Idea in every flu shot being given on campus—if it would help reach more people.

Media Access

Not only did the local newspaper reporter have access to The Milwaukee Idea email forum, he used it, quoting comments by faculty and staff in several articles.

Perhaps the most telling example of The Milwaukee Idea's commitment to open communication was the decision, made early on, to allow a reporter from the local paper access to The Milwaukee Idea email forum. Members of the Affinity Groups were informed that emails sent to the participant groups also would be read by the reporter, because campus leadership believed in the process and wanted to hold UWM accountable to the community for what was happening. While risky, it sent an important message to metropolitan Milwaukee that UWM wanted everyone to know about, and be involved in, the conversations.

Percy also tapped the chancellor's newly hired staff writer, Mary Jane Brukardt, to help with communication efforts. Daily access to the chancellor for last minute fine-tuning helped keep the communication efforts on target and Milwaukee Idea office staff up to speed on the chancellor's latest community outreach activities.

Linking the communication of both administration and The Milwaukee Idea made possible development of a clear "brand" identity for The Milwaukee Idea. Use of consistent colors, graphic design, and message points in all marketing materials increased the impact of The Milwaukee Idea, especially in the broader community.

Time

The Milwaukee Idea asked members of campus and community to invest one of their most precious resources: time. The response was overwhelmingly generous, in part because of the enthusiasm generated by campus leadership and also because people recognized the potential of The Milwaukee Idea and desired to be a part of it.

And the demands were not insignificant. Ellen Murphy, secretary of the university, estimated that it was not uncommon for some faculty and staff to willingly commit more than 20 hours a week to the process, above their regular work requirements. "This overwhelming willingness to invest personal time in The Milwaukee Idea was a key indicator that it would have sustainability," Murphy said.

Several factors helped participants make The Milwaukee Idea a priority. Initial participation was by invitation to a group selected from existing leadership and governance groups. This core had a vested interest in creating a positive process. The chancellor also involved individuals who had served on her search committee, recognizing that they were already vested in her leadership, supportive of her ideas for UWM, and shared her values and goals. Many of these "soul mates" would become key leaders in The Milwaukee Idea process.

The added participation of the entire Deans Council and Chancellor's Cabinet signaled institutional support for involvement by department chairs, faculty, and staff.

From a community perspective, many became involved out of curiosity and because they were inspired by the vision of a renewed and more actively involved university. But in the final analysis, it was the success of the process itself that kept the hundreds of people involved. It worked because people were able to meaningfully contribute to creating change. They understood that The Milwaukee Idea could be relevant for them, their work, and their community.

Money

One reason The Milwaukee Idea office was able to operate successfully was its access to start-up dollars. Funding for new community-supported initiatives was underwritten by new dollars received through revenue growth associated with enrollment increases. In addition, a major commitment from the UW System budget gave The Milwaukee Idea additional dollars to launch the initiatives.

The value of this funding was the autonomy it afforded from the beginning. The Milwaukee Idea was not perceived by most faculty or staff as draining major dollars from existing projects and so they were more supportive of it. Many, in fact, felt that The Milwaukee Idea was key to attracting significant and much-needed outside dollars.

BE OUTSIDE THE POWER STRUCTURE

Sarason and Lorentz's book, *Crossing Boundaries,* notes two of the most important attributes of successful change management: 1) be outside the power structure and 2) be available. The Milwaukee Idea office was both.

"I think that the success of The Milwaukee Idea in part is attributable to creating the free-floating Milwaukee Idea office, putting it outside the box of the administrative structure and putting somebody like Steve in as director," said Gregory Jay, professor of English and an Affinity and Action Team leader. "The office needed to invent itself as it went along."

> "The most freedom you can give anybody, I think, is the freedom to act with the blessing of the chancellor... but without the interference."
> —Nancy Zimpher

Because The Milwaukee Idea was completely new to UWM, its office was shaped by the demands of the process. While formed by the chancellor, it was officially housed in the Graduate School, through its connections to Percy and CUIR. Physically, it was situated outside the locus of power in a building literally across campus from the chancellor's and provost's offices.

While it may have been perceived as working outside the existing UWM administrative structure, continuous communication with the administration forged a strategic link that enabled the office to reflect the chancellor's directions and, at the same time, relay to her the issues and concerns of campus.

Sachin Chheda was a good example of using assets creatively in service to a change mission. Chheda, who was working to complete the last few courses needed for his undergraduate degree, had served with Percy on the chancellor search. A veteran of numerous political campaigns and publisher of the student paper, Chheda brought energy, a sharp organizational sense, and the student perspective to the process. His computer skills, campus contacts, and willingness to speak out on issues he believed in were invaluable. And his logistical skills helped establish The Milwaukee Idea "style."

Chheda knew what it took behind the scenes to make a meeting succeed, details many academics often miss: introducing new people, including the community as equal partners in the discussion, providing hot coffee and cold soda, giving campus visitors directions to unfamiliar buildings.

"I think the fact that I once worked at a fast-food restaurant is what made the difference," Chheda said with a smile. "There has to be a belief in customer service. You have to pay attention to the details, things that the university doesn't always do."

Chheda was deeply committed to the principle of diversity and challenged the Strategy Team to mirror that dedication. "At times, I held their feet to the fire," he said. "When the rest of the team was focused on internal issues, they needed to be reminded, occasionally, to include new voices."

Office staff—not just Percy—were given the autonomy to solve problems, take the lead, and make decisions. Because both Chheda and Brukardt were administration "outsiders"—a student and new hire—they provided an external perspective, the chancellor's "crap detectors," as they were called, who provided candid feedback and integrity to the task.

While connected closely to the chancellor, The Milwaukee Idea office also was able to manage at a variety of levels—working directly with staff in key campus offices such as University Relations, Academic Affairs, Continuing Education, and various centers and departments.

"We could avoid the bureaucracy by keeping the decision-making at the implementation level," Chheda said. "At times this meant an incredible amount of work, so we just pulled in people from across campus as we needed them. It was informal, but created a strong sense of teamwork and creativity." At least in the early months, requests for information or assistance "for the chancellor" opened many doors for office staff.

BE AVAILABLE TO SAY YES

If there is a single attribute that most distinguishes The Milwaukee Idea office, it is its consistent dedication to the possible. This may be a commentary on the negative culture of an academic bureaucracy—to which UWM is certainly not immune—but it is also a powerful blueprint for how to manage change successfully. "Say Yes" was an attitude that began at the top when Zimpher gave the assembled faculty her email address and invited them to use it. They did. It continued with The Milwaukee Idea office, which had an

What does it mean to "Say Yes?"

Comments from participants about The Milwaukee Idea office.

"When I called and asked for a project assistant, they said 'yesterday.'"

"I don't think I ever had to wait for an answer to something."

"They're available."

open-door policy for every Milwaukee Idea participant. And it was carried out daily by a staff who worked late to find ways to connect a community member with an Affinity Group, send out a missing information packet, or track down a meeting location.

It also meant having the funding to say yes, and the flexibility to say it to both community and campus. The dollars allocated for Action Teams allowed team leaders to hire student assistants to handle logistics, host brainstorming sessions, or travel to international conferences for data gathering.

As word about The Milwaukee Idea spread, the office increasingly fielded calls from community leaders and individuals seeking partnerships for new initiatives, several of which were jump-started with a small donation. A query from the city's foundation community grew into an initiative to create a program for nonprofit leadership that developed in tandem with The Milwaukee Idea's economic development Idea (see Chapter 6). A request for student volunteers, channeled through The Milwaukee Idea office, gave rise to the establishment of a student volunteer center. And a funding request from a community collaborator helped launch a neighborhood initiative.

Soon after it opened its doors, The Milwaukee Idea office became the visible symbol of the university's efforts to "Say Yes!" to the community. The Milwaukee Idea was off and running.

Chapter 4 Summary

What We Learned About Making "Behind the Scenes" Work

1) **Find "soul mates."** Zimpher involved members of the Search Committee as leadership because they were already behind her and shared her values and goals.

2) **Choose leadership that knows the campus and knows the community.** Create lots of opportunity for new networks and connections.

3) **Set up an independent office.** The Milwaukee Idea office worked because it was perceived as outside the usual power structures, yet plugged in enough to get results.

4) **Fund it well and fund it right.** Don't be extravagant, but give the process the dollars to do things well. Find ways to give people money without taking it out of their existing budgets—they'll be much more motivated to participate and help the project succeed.

5) **Build connections.** Link leadership at both administrative and implementation levels so that response is flexible and crosses disciplines.

Endnotes

[1] Peter Eckel, Madeleine Green, Barbara Hill, Bill Mallon. (1999). *On Change. Reports from the Road: Insights on Institutional Change.* Washington, DC: American Council on Education, page 6.

Callout on page 45 on "Five Attributes of the Ideal Coordination Team": Seymour Sarason and Elizabeth Lorentz. (1998). *Crossing Boundaries: Collaboration, Coordination, and the Redefinition of Resources.* San Francisco: Jossey-Bass, page 121.

[2] Peter Eckel, Madeleine Green, Barbara Hill, and William Mallon. (1999). *On Change III. Taking Charge of Change: A Primer for Colleges and Universities.* Washington, DC: American Council on Education, pages 45–48.

"IMAGINE":
THE AFFINITY GROUP PROCESS

From the *Milwaukee Journal Sentinel*
November 14, 1998

UWM Wants to Improve Its Ties to Community
By Jack Norman

An early stage of what may become a radical transformation of the University of Wisconsin-Milwaukee played out Friday, when about one hundred people spent the morning trying to give substance to what they call "The Milwaukee Idea."

The Milwaukee Idea—proclaimed two months ago by UWM's new chancellor, Nancy Zimpher—is a more-than-academic exercise whose goal is to make the university directly relevant to every resident of metropolitan Milwaukee.

If Zimpher's goal is achieved, it would make UWM a thoroughly different institution from the sometimes disregarded school it is today.

"We have to increase our presence in the Milwaukee community in very physical and very real ways," said Greg Jay, an English professor who was one of dozens of faculty, staff and civic leaders speaking Friday.

"We have to make this campus be seen as a very friendly place for every kind of person, so when we reach out, they'll feel drawn to us," Jay said.

Seven committees are partway through a several-month process of creating concrete programs to accomplish this. . . . The scope of the committees ranges from the relatively abstract to the very tangible.

THE AFFINITY PROCESS

Two months after Chancellor Zimpher arrived at the University of Wisconsin-Milwaukee, letters went out to about 100 people on campus and throughout metropolitan Milwaukee inviting them to a day-long plenary session to help "create The Milwaukee Idea." The "Committee of 100" would then work for 100 days to develop specific plans for the future direction of the University of Wisconsin-Milwaukee.

Saad Akbar Khan, a UWM junior and Student Association leader, was on the list, and decided, mostly out of curiosity, to check out the chancellor's "crazy idea to get one hundred people in a room to talk." At Milwaukee's Italian Community Center, he found fellow students, union representatives, academic staff as well as the "usual suspects" of faculty, deans, and administrators. About one-third of the invited list were from the community. For six hours they met around circular tables to imagine what the UWM of the future would be like.

Who was the Committee of 100?

To begin the change process, the chancellor and provost invited 100 people to form the core visioning group. One-third were from the community. Campus representatives included leaders from all governance groups, all deans, Chancellor's Cabinet, members of the University and Academic Staff committees, and representatives from major constituent groups, including students, unions, faculty, and staff.

"It was amazing," recalled Akbar Khan, who had transferred to UWM from UW-Madison to take advantage of the diversity the Milwaukee campus offered. "I'd never worked with deans and administration before—as students, we only got to meet them in confrontation and now we had this chance for dialogue. Wow!"

The dialogue got off to a somewhat rocky start, however. Within the hour skeptics were questioning how The Milwaukee Idea could fit into the university's research mission, and some groups—students and community members—were finding it hard to contribute to the conversation.

"At the beginning, the old-guard didn't take us seriously," Akbar Khan said. "I think students and staff felt like we were the 'guests' and the faculty and administration were the 'owners.' But once we got into small groups, we started to talk and then the atmosphere changed."

The Affinity process began with a lot of talk. At the first plenary, the day-long meeting focused on visioning exercises, led by consultant Bob Gleason. Participants, often seated with people they had never met before, began the first steps toward imagining what the university would be like in ten years. They answered questions like "What will learning look like in the next decade?" and "How can we create better economic opportunities for people of all ages?" and "What does it mean to live in a global economy and how, as an international hub, can Milwaukee and UWM broaden the community's horizons?"

The focus, in Gleason's words, was to be on "boulders, not grains of sand." In other words, big concepts, new ideas, around which the campus could agree. At times, some participants may have wanted to throw some boulders themselves, as the discussions over conflicting missions got heated.

By early afternoon the debate had crystallized around the importance of research and teaching versus the engagement focus of The Milwaukee Idea. Faculty from the humanities and sciences voiced concern that too much attention was being paid to the outreach mission of the university and not enough to shoring up the scholarship and research infrastructure. Many faculty felt that years of cutbacks to staff and facilities needed to be addressed before the university could begin looking outward to new community initiatives. They felt that The Milwaukee Idea threatened the strength of UWM's research mission, which should take priority in setting institutional goals. It was a debate that would continue as UWM grappled with the priorities of its mission and sought to find a vision that could speak equally to chemists, urban planners, and 16th century Irish literature scholars.

SELF-SELECT

By the end of the first plenary session, the group adopted the five areas of focus originally suggested by the chancellor for further study: education, the economy, health, international initiatives, and the urban environment. In response to concerns by faculty over the role of research, a sixth focus—Frontiers of Knowledge and Research—also was created. A seventh, Quick Wins, was tasked with creating short-term initiatives that would gather momentum for The Milwaukee Idea.

Seven Affinity Groups

1) Education and Culture
2) Economic Opportunity
3) Health and Welfare
4) Global Perspectives
5) Urban Environment
6) Frontiers of Knowledge and Research
7) Quick Wins

Chancellor Zimpher then asked participants to form Affinity Groups around these seven ideas, and join a group they would commit to work with for the next 100 days. The purpose of each Affinity Group was to "identify the big ideas that give depth and breadth to the UWM vision and to recommend actions that can transcend rhetoric." Enthusiasm for the process was so high, some participants chose to join several Affinity Groups.

"Self-selection was a very important aspect of the overall success of the groups," said Stan Yasaitis, president of the Wisconsin State Employees Union, Local 82, who became co-chair with Dean James Blackburn of the Health and Welfare Affinity Group. "We were able to approach our concerns voluntarily." He believes that his appointment as a co-chair also sent a strong message that The Milwaukee Idea process was campus-wide, inclusive, and open to divergent viewpoints.

The process of self-selection, of course, resulted in groups that varied in size and makeup. Not all groups were representative of campus: The Frontiers of Knowledge group, for example, was composed primarily of faculty, with only one student. Percy quickly recruited a community representative to add some balance.

The self-selection process also worked in reverse. As discussions among groups continued, people chose to leave, preferring not to continue with ideas they could not support. Some moved to other groups. Professor David Petering formed his own group around an issue that he was passionate about—Urban Environmental Health. Others simply dropped out.

Pay Attention to Leadership

Each Affinity Group was asked to choose team leaders, although not every group was able to produce individuals willing to commit to the added responsibility. As needed, Percy, in consultation with the Strategy Team, appointed co-convenors to round out the leadership and a community liaison for each group. Selections were based on availability, leadership ability, and diversity of perspective. The seven leadership teams included students, faculty, deans, union representatives, community members, and academic staff.

In some cases, co-leaders were added to the groups, based on Zimpher and Percy's perceptions of group needs. Deans were seeded throughout the Affinity Groups. With the Frontiers of Knowledge and Research group (formed to safeguard the research concerns of faculty), Peter Watson-Boone, director of the library, was chosen to lead what promised to be a challenging group.

"Peter was a brilliant choice because faculty respected him as an academic, but he wasn't embroiled in the 'research versus The Milwaukee Idea' issue," said community participant and co-chair Jean Tyler. "It's an example of where you look at the challenge for a specific leader and then you go find him or her." With the assistance of then-Provost Watters, who became a participant-observer, the Frontiers group became a creative team that eventually proposed three of the final Ideas.

"You have to have the courage to say 'no' to some people—those who you know do not believe in partnership."
—*Alan Guskin*

In other groups, leadership emerged from within. In Education and Culture, English Professor Gregory Jay helped the group draft its report, and in the process became an articulate spokesman and advocate for the group's Idea. Stan Yasaitis was able to use his meeting planning skills. Student Shannon

McCrory found himself paired with a dean and academic staff member in chairing the Urban Environment group.

There were downsides as well. The Quick Wins group included three assistant chancellors, in part because their operational functions were natural fits for a group tasked with short-term, campus-based change. It was hard for the administrators to be as objective as needed, however, and the group struggled with implementation.

USE THE INTERNET

Within a week of the first plenary, The Milwaukee Idea office had created a web site listing membership on all Affinity Groups and a schedule of their meetings. The web site would become a community meeting place as participants checked updates, scheduled meetings, and reviewed Ideas. Within three weeks, the web site would log almost 1,500 hits.

Visit The Milwaukee Idea Web Site:

www.uwm.edu/MilwaukeeIdea

KEEP PEOPLE INVOLVED

Recruitment of campus and community members continued throughout the Affinity process (which eventually stretched to almost 200 days). People were encouraged to contribute by virtual correspondence or in person. Many did, doubling the membership of the Committee of 100 to more than 200 within months of its formation. Involving students, however, was a challenge. Inconvenient meeting times, the demands of coursework, and limited recruitment efforts to students meant few beyond top leadership actively participated.

Many community participants gave liberally of their time, attending meetings built around an academic—not business—schedule, held at a campus with limited parking. While efforts were made to include community representatives on every Affinity Group, there was significant attrition as corporate, industry, and government leaders used to making quick decisions ran up against the university penchant for exhaustive discussion. And it soon became apparent that university and community people

The Affinity Process

The Affinity process ran from October through February. Five large-group plenary sessions were held, one approximately every month, supplemented by small-group meetings arranged by each group. Each plenary was facilitated by Gleason, with Zimpher and Percy providing encouragement, troubleshooting and answering group questions. Only the first and final plenaries were held off site. The rest were held during the day on campus, with free parking (a perk of infinite value) offered to all community participants.

didn't know how to talk to one another. Faculty were more comfortable talking with their peers. Civic leaders didn't understand what faculty do. "There is literally a translation problem," noted Tyler, who helped broker discussions between faculty and community leaders.

Affinity Group meetings varied in number and make-up, dependent on the needs of the group. One Affinity Group logged almost 25 meetings, in addition to the five plenary sessions over a five-month period. Two groups had more than 30 members, including several deans. Most used email extensively to debate Ideas, announce meetings, and provide follow-up. Many sent their opinions and comments directly to the chancellor as well.

Email worked well for the campus community, but many community members without email were unable to participate fully. Affinity Group convenors were encouraged to contact those members directly with meeting announcements and updates, and The Milwaukee Idea office sent hardcopy information to community members as needed, but the delay often meant some individuals were left outside the discussion.

AVOID "INFINITY" GROUPS

The largest challenge during the Affinity process was keeping the groups on target and progressing toward concrete proposals for new Ideas. The Education and Culture group once listed more than 18 major Ideas, any one of which would have involved a significant institutional commitment. The Global Perspectives team joked that their Ideas were so big that world peace was an action step.

To avoid having the Affinity Groups become "infinity groups," Percy and Gleason prepared a packet of information for group members and leaders that included role descriptions, a meeting template, and a detailed timeline outlining key tasks (see Appendix C). Percy also met formally and informally with co-convenors to monitor progress and provide assistance.

STAY ONE STEP AHEAD

Early on, Zimpher formed a Strategy Team—a tactical group to help monitor the process, troubleshoot, and attempt to stay one step ahead of an initiative that was taking on a life of its own. Initially made up of Provost Watters, Percy, and Gleason, it soon included Chheda, Brukardt, and then-Assistant Chancellor of University Relations Sandra Hoeh. The group remained flexible and included whoever was needed to address current challenges, from helping to plan the chancellor's inauguration to a Milwaukee Idea conference.

What's the #1 Requirement for Strategy Team Members?

"Be honest." Two words from the chancellor's "chief idea critic," Ken Howey, professor of curriculum and instruction at UWM—and husband to the chancellor. "In a strategy group like this, it is absolutely critical that there are no holds barred about what's going on in the process."

When Zimpher mobilized a "Reading Group" to help assess Affinity Group proposals, its members—including community members Jean Tyler and Carl Mueller, an alumnus and business consultant, and campus representatives Dean Greenstreet and Assistant Vice Chancellor Sona Andrews—stayed on as Strategy Team members. The evolving group's key strength was that it represented, in Watters' words, "true believers"—trusted people who understood The Milwaukee Idea, believed in it, and were committed to its success.

Zimpher also found the Strategy Team meetings gave her the opportunity to focus on the process. Meetings were chaired by Percy, which freed Zimpher to "just sit back and think about the Ideas and what we were doing"—a luxury other university presidents and chief executives will appreciate.

Milwaukee Idea Connectors

1) **Diversity and Multiculturalism**
The Milwaukee Idea will reflect and encourage the richness of cultures in our community and on our campus.

2) **Partnerships and Collaboration**
Each idea will be based on partnerships with the community and will involve new collaborations within the university and in the metropolitan community.

3) **Interdisciplinarity**
The word may be made up, but the practice of linking across disciplines, departments, and colleges will be a hallmark of The Milwaukee Idea.

4) **Campus Life and Culture**
The Milwaukee Idea will strengthen our traditions and identity and enhance student life.

5) **Communication and Support**
Each Milwaukee Idea will include detailed descriptions of how it will be implemented and shared with the campus and community.

IDENTIFY THE CORE

It was the Strategy Team, working with Gleason, who helped to develop what came to be called "Connectors"—five cross-cutting themes that participants repeatedly identified as important to their visioning. These Connectors became the backbone of the First Ideas, elements that helped the Affinity Group assess whether they were on target. If the Idea did not incorporate the five Connectors, it didn't fit The Milwaukee Idea. The Connectors were developed initially to help structure the Affinity Group discussions. They became integral hallmarks of The Milwaukee Idea and the values that guide decisions.

Also critical to the development of The Milwaukee Idea was a paper produced early in the process by Professor

Ken Howey. A member of the Education and Culture group, he drafted an outline for a "Big Idea" to help his group focus the many divergent ideas that were floated. Key in the draft was the concept of a curriculum component for The Milwaukee Idea—anchoring community relationships in student learning, as well as in research and outreach projects.

His belief, echoed by the chancellor, was that the teaching and learning environment for students needed to change if UWM was to truly become a new kind of university. Students must be encouraged to see the university as more than a means to a better paycheck, to also see it as a place that could help them enrich the lives of those in the community.[1] The paper eventually evolved into a proposal for an alternative general education program and, more importantly, it influenced all the Affinity Groups to consider ways in which new approaches to student learning could be incorporated into their Ideas—including community-based and service-learning.

"The way I look at it, The Milwaukee Idea is really a strategic plan for what an urban university should be about, not wholly, but centrally. And enhanced student learning is central," Howey said.

New UWM Chancellor should prepare to negotiate educational minefields.

Though there are few who have levied any criticism against [Zimpher], it's obvious that the honeymoon may soon be over, and the realities of wheeling and dealing not only in what some call a man's world (make that a White Man's World) may soon hit home.... [T]here are many land mines outside her door.....

Zimpher will soon discover that Milwaukee is known as much for sexism as it is for racism and the media isn't particularly easy on out-of-towners who disrupt the status quo with bright notions.... Race relations and institutional racism continue to be a cancerous growth at UWM.

—*Mikel Kwaku Osei Holt*
Milwaukee Community Journal

A Closer Look

Race: The Affinity Group That Wasn't

"What do I expect of UWM?"

Jeannette Mitchell, program officer for the Helen Bader Foundation, a leader in Milwaukee's African American community, and a long-time observer of the university, asked the question and paused. "I expect you to *do* something with all your research. You're an urban institution and it's time to begin looking at issues of race in this community. Who else can do this better than UWM?"

Metropolitan Milwaukee has the dubious distinction of being called one of America's most segregated communities. A recent study by the Lewis Mumford Center for Comparative Urban and Regional

Research found that metropolitan Milwaukee was the second most-segregated region in the nation for black and non-Hispanic white children under age 18. The 2000 census revealed that Milwaukee had become a "minority-majority" city, with 55% of its population people of color and a Hispanic community that had doubled since the previous decade. The city's suburbs, however, remained largely white.[2] Despite the appointment of special commissions and town meetings, in Milwaukee, race continues to be the subject "no one wants to talk about."

UWM always has sought to be Milwaukee's urban university, but it is only slowly beginning to look like the region it serves, with growing Native American, Hmong, Hispanic, and African American populations. Despite aggressive recruitment and pre-college programs, students of color make up about 14% of the student body compared to an 18% minority presence in the four-county region, and their drop-out rate continues to be higher than that of their white counterparts. Only one in 20 UWM faculty members is black.[3]

The need to begin talking about race and its impact on both the campus and community was raised at the first plenary session. Because it was so important—and so contentious—the decision was made by the Strategy Group to make diversity a common concern of all the groups, rather than "marginalize" it in a single Affinity Group. Diversity became one of the "Connectors," although some groups had a difficult time translating that into tangible proposals.

The Milwaukee Commitment

The Milwaukee Commitment is UWM's plan for diversity, developed separately from The Milwaukee Idea and in conjunction with a System-wide effort to encourage and support minority recruitment and retention of faculty and students. The plan was commissioned by Chancellor Zimpher and has set aggressive targets for minority scholarships, pre-college programs, and faculty development.

Beverly Cross is associate professor of curriculum and instruction at UWM and served as a Milwaukee Idea Action Team leader. She's also outspoken about the need for UWM to take seriously the issue of race if the change process is to succeed. "There is an illusion fooling many of us on university campuses. It is so convincing, so intricately woven that we will literally have to shred apart the lie to see the truth," she writes in a campus publication. "The illusion is we can soundly and honestly build community partnerships without challenging racism. This illusion carries high stakes for all of us."

Cross warns about "drive-by" relationships where the university takes what it needs from the community without reciprocal engagement—or effort to work toward real change. "It seems obvious to me that in a hyper-segregated, hyper-racist city like Milwaukee we would have to place racism squarely in the center of our work around collaborating with the city," Cross writes.[4]

And so, as The Milwaukee Idea has moved forward, the spotlight has been focused on involving a diverse range of partners and on working with minority groups to address issues that directly impact persons of color: small-business support for minority business, improving graduating rates for urban schools, and addressing health concerns for the economically disadvantaged, such as lead poisoning and water contamination.

Campus and community agree that issues of race need continued and deeper attention. "We probably needed to prove to ourselves that racism is too difficult in Milwaukee to be handled only through The Milwaukee Idea," said Jean Tyler, who had helped moderate an unsuccessful discussion on race with civic leaders in the early 1980s. "This discussion is going to have to have a very defined, strong leadership of its own, and it's going to have to be forcefully a part of agenda after agenda. We need to get it out there and then start dealing with it."

TAKE IT PUBLIC—EARLY

At each of the plenary sessions, Affinity Groups presented their Ideas to each other for vetting, and then moved into individual sessions to refine the Ideas further. But laying the Ideas open for public criticism was not limited to the Affinity Group sessions. Zimpher and Percy took The Milwaukee Idea on the road.

Why Go Public?

Get public reaction back to the Affinity Groups to help fine-tune their ideas.

Signal to the community that UWM values its input and partnership

Generate public excitement for The Milwaukee Idea.

Make UWM accountable for results.

Using handouts and low-tech overheads so they could present "The Milwaukee Idea show" anywhere, Zimpher and Percy outlined the emerging Ideas—as unfinished as they were—at a series of ten special community meetings held throughout January and February. Alumni, business leaders, neighbors, media, elected officials, and funders all were invited to hear about progress and respond with their opinions and concerns. A parallel series of campus meetings was held, targeting faculty, academic and classified staff, and students. Three meetings for classified staff, including an early-morning meeting for third shift, drew more than 600 participants. Representatives from the Affinity Groups, as available, helped with the presentations (usually about three or four co-convenors joined Zimpher and Percy) to answer specific questions. Notes were taken at each and shared at the plenary sessions.

This public vetting so early in the change process was a risky decision. The Affinity Group proposals were still fluid and practical implementation questions had yet to be addressed. It raised expectations—higher than many people at Milwaukee's quiet university were used to.

But the vetting made all participants feel accountable. They knew they were being watched and what they did really mattered. At the same time, it reinforced the self-imposed deadlines. It was hard to fall behind when the community knew when people were supposed to finish. Most important, the vetting provided vital community feedback for the Affinity Groups. As the meetings progressed, groups began to hear consistent messages: improve community access to UWM, communicate strengths better, address issues of race and diversity squarely, and keep the focus on student learning. Clearly, Milwaukee was supportive but waiting for results.

A Closer Look

Quick Wins: The Process Stumbles

From the beginning, one of the key components of The Milwaukee Idea process was "Quick Wins"—a concerted effort to create immediate, visible change in support of the overall vision. First articulated by Bob Gleason, Quick Wins would help get people's attention and, through its success, provide energy to the longer process.

Quick Wins was set up as an Affinity Group, although it soon became obvious that its focus would be less on ideas than on process. Led by Assistant Vice Chancellor Sona Andrews and classified staff member Berthina Joseph, the group included mostly academic and classified staff and administrators. The first weeks were spent developing a process for soliciting and processing ideas that could be inexpensively completed within six months. Hundreds of suggestions poured in: a farmers market on weekends, new picnic tables for summer lunches, service awards for classified staff, neighbor appreciation day.

Soliciting ideas went well; determining which ideas qualified—and getting buy-in from supervisors—proved the bigger challenge. Some on the Affinity Group felt that the assistant chancellors were too quick to reject ideas that fell under their jurisdiction. They, in turn, felt they provided the group with a "reality check" on what was possible. The bottom line was that of the almost 100 suggestions that the Quick Wins team forwarded to supervisors for implementation, only about a quarter were completed within the six-month timeframe. Then, after the Affinity Process ended, Quick Wins was given to The Milwaukee Idea office to continue, without provision for additional staff to manage the requests. What could have given energy to The Milwaukee Idea faded when momentum was lost. "There just wasn't any bang at the end of the process," said Victoria Boswell, a group member.

"Ironically, the Quick Wins was the slowest thing to finish," said Andrews, who acknowledged that the 100-day time frame allotted to the Affinity Groups wasn't long enough (even when extended to 200 days), both to create a campus-wide process *and* implement Quick Wins. "It may have worked better to have had the Quick Wins process in place *before* the Affinity Group was formed. Then the group could have focused on the ideas, pushing them through quickly, and building excitement," Andrews said.

Nevertheless, there were victories. An idea for more picnic tables around campus prompted new black-and-gold umbrellas in the student plaza. A "neighborhood appreciation day" became a university-sponsored "Block Party." And plans for improved campus signage resulted in bold new signs and maps that helped put a new face on the university.

If the beginnings of Quick Wins represented the first halting steps of The Milwaukee Idea, the process would soon regain its balance. After the First Ideas were launched, Quick Wins was reorganized. But that story will have to wait until later.

GATHER SUPPORT

By early 1999, the results of the months of brainstorming were well on their way to being finalized. Reports for each Idea were posted on the web site, revised, and reposted. Affinity Group members got a boost when, at the monthly plenary, Katharine Lyall, president of the University of Wisconsin System, joined them to express her support for The Milwaukee Idea and to promise additional funding from System. She made good on that promise later that spring at the UWM Faculty Senate meeting when she announced a $1.5 million System pledge in support of The Milwaukee Idea.

UW System's pledge was an important public vote of confidence and the first step toward what many on campus saw as an opportunity for UWM to make an unprecedented request to the Regents and legislature for major funding in the state's next biennial funding cycle.

That The Milwaukee Idea would be a cornerstone of future financial resources support was expected, although some faculty voiced concern that initiatives outside The Milwaukee Idea would be left out of new funding. As one faculty email noted, this was troubling in light of the university's recent history of budget cuts and staff reductions. "I think I and others would be more comfortable letting the chancellor get on with the business of enhancing our external reputation if we had been living in an atmosphere that was otherwise supportive." Restore our infrastructure first, some faculty said, before The Milwaukee Idea leads us in new directions.

Mindful that creating new Ideas is one thing, but integrating them into the fabric of the university quite another, Percy and Zimpher met with campus governance groups such as the University Committee to update them on the progress of The Milwaukee Idea and to discuss ways to involve them in the development of the Ideas. Conversations on the role of governance would increase during the Action phase of the process.

ALLOW PEOPLE TO FINISH

Meanwhile, the academic tendency for interminable revision was a real temptation for the Affinity Groups, who continued to debate and refine their Ideas. Fortunately, The Milwaukee Idea schedule was firm: On March 26 the chancellor would be inaugurated. The First Ideas would be ready and announced on that day. Just as the public vetting helped to keep the process on target, the public deadline of the March inauguration also helped to keep the process on track. Because final reports and concrete ideas would be announced by the chancellor at the event, very real deadlines inspired The Milwaukee Idea results.

It was important that those involved in the process—which was demanding of time and energy—knew their responsibilities would not outlast their commitment. It is a testament to the energy generated by The Milwaukee Idea that many Affinity Group participants voluntarily remained involved in the Action phase as well.

Professor Laurie Glass was surprised that involvement was sustained. "We all know that to involve more people takes time and energy, and frankly, I'm surprised that it has kept up at the level that it has," she said. "Nancy has been successful in keeping everybody informed and around the same table."

ASSESS THE RESULTS

To meet the looming deadline for final reports from all Affinity Groups, Zimpher appointed a Reading Group of 11 members. Priority was given to assembling a diverse team that included a dean, faculty member, a student, Milwaukee Idea staff, administrators, and two community members. Several four-hour meetings were spent discussing each proposed Idea, assessing strengths and weaknesses, and responding to the Affinity Groups with questions and encouragement.

In some cases, the Reading Group determined that the details of the Ideas needed refinement; for others, the Idea itself needed overhauling. A wide-ranging proposal to launch a city-wide sustainable development initiative, for example, was scaled back, and a culture and education plan was divided into two proposals to address campus and community needs separately. The Frontiers of Knowledge group, which had come up with several ideas, was encouraged to develop three of them further.

Not everyone appreciated the work of the Reading Group. One of the participants in the Frontiers of Knowledge group felt that the inclusiveness of the Affinity process was undercut by the small size of the Reading Group. Because the Affinity Groups hadn't been told a separate group would evaluate their proposals, they felt caught off-guard and dismayed by the lack of members with research backgrounds.

"Suddenly all the real decisions would be made by a group of people who weren't even identified—and who didn't include any researchers," one faculty participant said. "I understand the chancellor can't sit around talking with two hundred people, but there must be a better way." At the core of the discontent was the fear that The Milwaukee Idea was abandoning the university's research mission and the sense that communication had been less than open.

In reality, the very real need for Percy and Zimpher to keep the process moving quickly put implementation ahead of communication and undermined credibility. Reaction to the Reading Group also underscored the need for continued leadership support for UWM's core mission of research, teaching, and outreach.

The conflicting demands of keeping The Milwaukee Idea process moving would continue to bump up against the need to be open.

"I believe that when we stick to our values in the process, it works. It was at the times we didn't that we ended up in trouble," staffer Chheda said.

A Closer Look

Face the Issues: The Milwaukee Idea Conference

Six months after the start of The Milwaukee Idea, attitudes across campus were, as could be expected, mixed. A small percentage of faculty, staff, and students—primarily those active on Affinity Groups—was involved and supportive. A similar percentage determined that university engagement was at odds with its goals for scholarship, research, and teaching, and openly criticized it. As one email correspondent noted sarcastically, "Scholarship? Well I guess that's just not 'engaging' enough these days!" By far the largest group of people had only a general idea of what was happening and was waiting to see how it would all turn out. As one critic of higher education has observed, "passive resistance" is still the weapon of choice with most faculty.[5]

Community engagement was not a new idea at UWM, but how a renewed focus on this mission would play out in the everyday life of faculty and staff was not clear. It was time to have a discussion about how The Milwaukee Idea fit into UWM traditions and culture, what the campus was already doing, and how it could do more, as well as how engagement affects tenure and reward, teaching, and research.

In conjunction with the chancellor's inauguration, a two-day conference on "University Engagement in the Community" was held to begin the discussion. It drew several hundred faculty, students, and community and business leaders. Peter Magrath, president of the National Association of State Universities and Land-Grant Colleges, which had commissioned the Kellogg report on university engagement, was joined by Ira Harkavy, a national spokesman for community-university partnerships. Panels of former UWM chancellors helped to put the movement in the context of UWM's traditions.

The national speakers put the ideas of engagement in perspective, a valuable exercise for the UWM community. The conference was the beginning of a frank discussion about engagement and the challenges the university faced. It also gave UWM a chance to discuss generally the fundamental attitudes and philosophy of The Milwaukee Idea. Community, student, and faculty panels spoke honestly about their expectations, experiences, and concerns.

"I don't think our reward system has anything to do with real community service," said Frederick Jules, professor of architecture and member of the conference's Implications for Research panel. "It's publishing, teaching and then service, and you can publish much more easily without engaging in the community."

His comment sparked a heated debate among members of the conference audience. One participant, who had served on a UWM promotion review committee, took issue with the notion that only publishing was the route to tenure. Faculty who were able to provide evidence of what they'd accomplished in the community *were* credited for their efforts, he said. "There have been people who have made it through the process," he said. "But in every case they produced some evidence of their [community] activity—reports, media coverage." Others in the audience disagreed that such service was recognized over publishing. "Let's be brutally honest," said another participant. "Until the structure of the university reward and promotion system changes, and engagement becomes more valued in the culture of the university, it's still pretty much of an add-on. If you're doing great things in the community and haven't published, I don't think you're going to get tenured."

Gregory Squires, a panelist and then UWM professor of sociology, agreed that engagement alone is not enough for the university or the community. Faculty need to have something to offer the community before they can contribute meaningfully.

"If you have something to offer, they'll find you," Squires, an active leader in community service, told the conference, "But it has to be mutual engagement. It's not the university telling the group what to do. You need to learn to think about being part of a team." At the same time, Squires warned, the university needs to maintain its integrity as a critical, independent source of knowledge. "It's a delicate balancing act to play," he said. The results, however, are worth the struggle. "My involvement has enabled me to learn a whole lot more about the nature of what I claim to have as my academic specialty. You broaden your expertise and your network."

CELEBRATE

Almost 200 people returned to the Italian Community Center in February for the final "Committee of 100" plenary session. After five months of hard work, the seven Affinity Groups proposed ten "First Ideas" that would help UWM become more engaged and more responsive to its urban community. The Affinity Groups were ready to turn their Ideas over to the next phase of the process to begin the implementation. But before they did, participants shared what they'd learned from their intensive months of meeting, debating, and dreaming.

"In twelve years at UWM I had talked with precious few people outside my discipline or building—much less from off campus. Now I was in dialogue with occupational therapists, sociologists of race, elementary education specialists, book store owners, dancers, librarians, community organizers and a whole host of others who became my friends and allies."
—*Greg Jay, Affinity Group participant*

The most valuable aspect of the process was the opportunity participants had to meet and work with others outside their disciplines and life experiences. Affinity Group members said their discussions had, for the most part, been open, creative, and supportive of divergent views. Repeatedly faculty and staff cited the important contributions made by community members and their desire to continue and expand "feedback from the community." Use of email and the web "kept the process open" and helped the teams respond quickly. One participant said that the most successful part of the process was coming to believe that real change was possible. That belief was tempered by the knowledge that "we can't move forward without reaching out to a lot more people."

The stage was set for the official unveiling of The Milwaukee Idea and the results of the visioning work. With the pomp and circumstance that only a university can muster, Chancellor Zimpher was inaugurated and, in the presence of the governor, mayor, county executive, alumni, and System president, announced the ten First Ideas.

"It is a time for boldness," said Zimpher in her inaugural address, the 200 members of The Milwaukee Idea Affinity Groups seated proudly together. "We have the Ideas. Now, we need to get to work!"

Reflections

Nancy Zimpher and Steve Percy on the Affinity Process

Nancy Zimpher
The first phase of The Milwaukee Idea was bookended by two public events: our initial plenary session and the inauguration. The plenary, held off campus, included both faculty and community people and was the chance for us to announce that UWM was ready to change, and we were going to create our new vision together with the community. The inauguration was the public ceremony celebrating that joint vision.

In some ways, making the inauguration the culminating event of our visioning process was tactically important. We gave ourselves a very real and very public deadline. And, as is so often the case, when people have a deadline, they meet it. Had we only had some arbitrary publishing deadline to meet for an internal audience, I'm not sure we would have produced as quickly or as creatively as we did.

We also deliberately chose the inauguration—not some media event in the community—as the place to announce The Milwaukee Idea because we wanted to anchor our announcement in the university, weaving it into the majesty of our traditions. The Milwaukee Idea is very much UWM and it was important that ownership begin here.

Of course, no matter where we would have announced it, The Milwaukee Idea wasn't really news. We'd been talking about it for months with anyone who would listen. What was news was that the university had actually done what it promised. We'd come up with new ideas for community engagement and we were continuing to move ahead. It doesn't always happen that way in higher education!

Steve Percy
Going public early helped to keep us honest. I often felt we were out there, working without a net, but our public promises—made in person and broadcast over radio and television and in the newspaper—kept us focused on delivering concrete action.

And I think the community was pleased to be involved. We had almost 50 people come to a neighborhood briefing, for example, and not one person complained about parking or noisy students! They wanted to be a part of what we were doing. It made a difference to our Ideas and to our partnerships.

Nancy Zimpher
Early in the process, someone came up to me and said, "Surely you have a plan, Nancy." I think that many people thought that The Milwaukee Idea process was just a creative exercise in team building and that meanwhile, somewhere in my desk drawer, was the "Zimpher Strategic Plan for UWM" that I would haul out when the dust settled.

I'll admit that the 100 people, 100 days" was a shameless way to get people's attention. But it succeeded because I did NOT have a plan tucked away somewhere. Was I part of the process? You bet. Did I manipulate it so results would conform to what I thought UWM should be doing? No way. If I was instrumental at all, it was, I hope, in helping to keep participants focused on the values that are core to engagement: genuine partnership and the belief that across the university we do our best research and teaching when we work together to serve our urban communities. We want authentic partnerships that respect the integrity of all participants, and that kind of relationship building was far more important to me than any final Affinity Group report.

Chapter 5 Summary

What We Learned About Visioning

1) **It's not easy.** There are tough questions to address and relationships must be nurtured. Don't expect to get everything right the first time.

2) **Make values explicit.** The "Connectors" became the milestones against which everything was measured and helped to give structure and purpose to The Milwaukee Idea.

3) **Set real deadlines.** Setting challenging deadlines is possible when the need is real, not arbitrary. Make the conclusion public for added impact.

4) **Inclusiveness pays off in new ideas.** The final UWM vision was stronger because all constituents were invited, and the process encouraged new leaders.

5) **Community vetting keeps you honest and on schedule.** Taking ideas public early signaled UWM's willingness to partner and generated important community support.

Endnotes

[1] Jon Wergin and Jane Grassadonia. (May, 2001). "The Milwaukee Idea: A Study of Transformative Change," a paper prepared for the Office of University Partnerships, U.S. Department of Housing and Urban Development, page 19.

[2] Statistics on Milwaukee from: "Metro Milwaukee Statistical Profile, 1999" published by the Metropolitan Milwaukee Association of Commerce; "Segregation Growing Among U.S. Children," a *New York Times* May 6, 2001 article by Eric Schmitt; and reports on the 2000 Census from the *Journal Sentinel,* available at www.jsonline.com/news/census2000.

[3] UWM statistics from *The Milwaukee Commitment,* a UWM strategic plan for racial and ethnic diversity, available at www.uwm.edu/Dept/DSAD/milwcomm/.

[4] Beverly Cross. (Fall, 1999). "High-Stakes Illusion of Community," *Myriad,* published by the University of Wisconsin-Milwaukee, page 2.

[5] Peter Eckel, Madeleine Green, Barbara Hill, Bill Mallon. (1999). *On Change. Reports from the Road: Insights on Institutional Change.* Washington, DC: American Council on Education, page 9.

ACTION!
THE ACTION TEAM PROCESS

From the *Milwaukee Journal Sentinel*
March 25, 1999

She Has Its Attention: Now UWM Hopes Zimpher Delivers
By Jack Norman

The University of Wisconsin-Milwaukee chancellor has excited people on campus—faculty, staff and students alike—with her energy, inclusiveness and widely appreciated willingness to listen.

The question is whether the next year will see her begin to deliver on the early promise. . . .

With her Milwaukee Idea project—10 initiatives for university-community collaboration—Zimpher is pushing UWM to become a trailblazer in an emerging national movement called "the engaged university," in which schools embrace new kinds of community partnerships.

The Milwaukee Idea is "a big experiment, to move our research and teaching into issues that matter for the community," Zimpher said. "It's a real metamorphosis of this institution."

The 10 projects range over topics such as education, substance abuse, job development, environmental health and fresh-water resources. . . .

"The acid test in a year will be when big issues come up on the greater Milwaukee table and people ask, 'Is UWM there?' We're going to invite the community to advise and assess with us the best use of our resources. That's risky business. . . ."

"It's too early to judge her," said one professor who insisted on anonymity. "But she hasn't done anything that's alienated large numbers of people, which is an accomplishment in itself. . . ."

It was a crisp, sunny day and Chancellor Zimpher, dressed in the University of Wisconsin-Milwaukee black and gold, was crossing the university's Spaights Plaza, the open-air quad between the Golda Meir Library and UWM Union. As usual, it was filled with students, lounging on the lawn, listening to music, eating a quick lunch, hurrying to finish lab work. As she picked up her pace to enter the Union, a student approached and introduced himself. Pumping her hand, he told her how pleased he was with everything the new chancellor was doing. And then he paused, and added, "So far!"

A Good Job, so Far

Six months after The Milwaukee Idea was first described at the faculty plenary meeting, much had been accomplished. An unprecedented groundswell of excitement, curiosity, and interest had been generated. People were talking about what The Milwaukee Idea was about and what it meant for their work and for funding their projects. Community people were asking about the initiative, curious for the first time in many years about what was happening on campus. And ten "First Ideas," produced by the seven Affinity Groups, had been announced, to great fanfare.

The Ideas were indeed big ones, tantalizing in their potential. They embraced major initiatives in education, the economy, and the environment and held potential to enhance both UWM's research and teaching mission and the quality of life of the metropolitan region. The First Ideas included:

• An alternative university general education requirement that would celebrate the city's multicultural assets and involve UWM students more directly in the urban community and its issues.

• An international program of study linking Wisconsin's major industrial city to the world.

• New partnerships with the public schools to enhance K–16 learning.

The Milwaukee Idea's Ten "First Ideas"

Education
Cultures and Communities
A new core curriculum emphasizing multiculturalism, service-learning, and public arts.
International Affairs Initiative
Programs in international studies with expanded study abroad opportunities.
Partnerships for Education
Expanded partnerships with Milwaukee Public Schools.

Economy
Consortium for Economic Opportunity
A community-based consortium to provide technical assistance and research on economic development.
Technology Center
A clearinghouse for technology transfer, linking area business and UWM expertise and research.
Knowledge Fest
An open house celebrating UWM research.

Environment
Partnerships for Environmental Health
A collaboration with health and social agencies to address urban health issues.
Healthy Choices
An initiative to study substance use on campus and in the community.
Fresh Water Initiative
A world-class institute for research on the science, politics, economics, and ecology of fresh water.
Campus Design Solutions
A statewide network to create alternatives for improving campus buildings, spaces, and neighborhoods.

- A consortium for economic opportunity, linking university expertise with small businesses and entrepreneurs, especially those from the minority communities.

- A technology center to transfer the discoveries and creative scholarship of the university to the needs of business and industry.

- A celebratory festival of research and knowledge.

- An international center for freshwater research, housed on the shores of Lake Michigan.

- New partnerships of community health agencies, researchers, communication, and outreach experts to address urban health problems.

- A "healthy choices" program, targeting issues of substance use on campus and in the community.

- Neighborhood and community collaborations to enhance the campus environment.

The Ideas, while visionary, were secondary to their implementation. As productive as the Affinity process had been in unleashing a creative vision, what came next was crucial: moving idea to action. And so, the second phase of the process began as dreams were cast in the concrete reality of budgets, staffing, timetables, and the nitty-gritty of internal reporting structures.

CHOOSE YOUR LEADERS—CAREFULLY

The demands of implementation are different from visioning. Instead of big-picture creativity, you need individuals with experience, expertise, and leadership to set priorities, build new infrastructures, grapple with the details of budgets and headcount, in short, to "bring the idea to scale." As Graduate School Dean William Rayburn said, the Affinity Groups mirrored focus groups and the Action Teams were task forces.

But how to create a task force that would be true to the inclusive values of The Milwaukee Idea, yet still be balanced, focused, and able to make hard choices? The Milwaukee Idea Strategy Team gathered in the chancellor's office to mull the second phase of the process. The team began by selecting leaders to head each of the ten First Ideas. Criteria included commitment to The Milwaukee Idea, expertise in the subject matter of the Idea, leadership ability, knowledge of campus infrastructure, and—last but certainly not least—a willingness to work through the summer on a tight five-month deadline.

It was decided to select co-chairs, preferably representing different constituencies (such as students, union, academic and classified staff, and faculty)
and diverse disciplines or backgrounds. In addition to the campus chairs, each
group also would have a community liaison, a member from metropolitan
Milwaukee, who could connect the group to community networks and provide an important outside perspective.

The selection of the team leaders successfully fulfilled the requirement for
university diversity. Leaders included students, deans, faculty, and academic
staff. Some had not been involved in the Affinity process, but were keenly
interested in The Milwaukee Idea. Others continued with the work they'd
started in an Affinity Group; still others switched to different Ideas.

A Closer Look

The Milwaukee Idea and Students
By Ajita Talwalker, former president of the UWM Student Association

As a student at the University of Wisconsin-Milwaukee, I had the unique
opportunity to co-lead an Action Team on the International Affairs Initiative.
I was able to help our team develop a more comprehensive and global education for this university and the Milwaukee community. The team was unique
and inclusive of students, faculty, academic staff, deans, and business and
community leaders. Together we were able to develop a student-centered
Action Plan that talked frankly about access to a global education. With
strong components in curricular development, service-learning, and scholarship opportunities for students who otherwise would not have the opportunity to have an experience abroad, the plan reaches out to every student at this
university.

As president of the Student Association, the parts of The Milwaukee Idea
that are most significant to me are the concrete programs and scholarship
opportunities that will open the doors of this university to those students
from underrepresented constituencies that have traditionally been shut out of
institutions of higher education. As an urban university, UWM in particular
has an obligation to recruit and retain a diverse student body that is reflective
of the community at large. Milwaukee Idea projects involving partnerships
with the Milwaukee Public Schools, investments in pre-college programs such
as GEAR UP, student scholarships for study abroad, and low-income and
underrepresented students are all critical in addressing the needs at the heart
of Milwaukee's communities.

The link between The Milwaukee Idea and the Milwaukee Commitment (UWM's plan to expand the diversity of its student body, faculty, and staff) is also an important part of the success and appeal of The Milwaukee Idea. When we talk about programs that get traditionally underrepresented students to this university, we also now talk about what measures we can take as an institution to keep students here. By reaching out to underrepresented communities in Milwaukee, we are talking about breaking the cycles of poverty and oppression that have kept students from institutions of higher education.

Both The Milwaukee Idea and the Milwaukee Commitment force us to reexamine what we want our community and our university to look like and redefine the mission of what an urban university should be.

SUPPORTING LEADERS

Selecting Action Team leadership was not without its challenges. The Strategy Team was under pressure to appoint leaders so they could be announced at the chancellor's inauguration. The time constraints may have resulted in several less-than-optimal selections. As Strategy Team member Jean Tyler recalled, there were many intelligent and able people selected, yet without the right fit of leader to task, "They tend to squander all those gifts."

Other factors conspired to disrupt the Action Teams. Soon after their appointment, two group leaders left to take jobs at other universities and one community liaison left Milwaukee. Replacements were found, but experience proved to be important to continuing the group's momentum. In one case, the leader brought in had not been involved in the process, and this slowed down the group's ability to move forward as quickly as the others.

Students who were selected to head Action Teams also provided important perspectives, but were most successful when the student shared tasks with staff or faculty. The one group in which a student and dean shared leadership resulted in an unequal distribution of duties.

There were many successful pairings, however. While most Action Team leaders had never worked together before—and some had never even met—those who met regularly developed strong professional relationships and personal friendships. Action Team leader René Gratz joked that after the Action Team phase was completed she suffered withdrawal from her daily meetings with co-chair Diane Reddy. English Professor Gregory Jay and Dance Professor Marcia Parsons, who co-chaired the Cultures and Communities group, continue to partner and, when they're together, still finish each other's sentences.

Associate Professor of History Marc Levine and Lucy Holifield, director of the Small Business Development Center, co-chaired both the Economic Opportunity Affinity and Action Teams and continue to lead the Consortium for Economic Opportunity.

Supporting Leaders

One Action Team that had facilitation support was the Nonprofit Management Education Project—a community-based team. A facilitator was hired to help the team through its planning process and the result was a cohesive group with ongoing momentum.

While leaders may have been chosen for their expertise or commitment to The Milwaukee Idea, not all possessed equal skills in running meetings. Some community participants even hinted that team members with more corporate experience might have been better choices than faculty to head the teams. "I think the chairs could have benefited from a day's retreat on how to facilitate a meeting," said one Action Team participant, frustrated by her team leader's inability to manage the diverging views of her group.

ACTION TEAM STRUCTURE

With the leadership on board, the Strategy Team turned to selecting Action Team members. The Affinity model with its open invitation for participation was replaced by smaller groups of selected individuals who would be able to deal with the challenges of creating workable plans. The selection process began with an open invitation to campus and community to submit qualified names for consideration.

Action Team Structure

Team Leaders
Two to three people; a mix of faculty, staff, and students.

Community Liaison
Community representative with relevant expertise.

Action Team
12 to 15 people, with 1/3 from community.

Advisory Council
Open to anyone interested. Met at discretion of team leaders.

The Action Team process reflected the values of the Affinity process: inclusive and diverse. Campus and community members were invited to nominate themselves to one of ten Action Teams. From that pool about 12 to 15 people were selected for each group. This kept the groups small enough and yet assured diversity. The Strategy Team, poring over lists of nominees, tried to balance campus and community membership; assure a variety of disciplines and departments were represented; include students, union, and academic staff; connect to members of the Chancellor's Cabinet and campus leadership; and assure a variety of voices, opinions, and expertise.

Did UWM get it right for every group? Probably not. The Strategy Team was limited by the people who chose to nominate themselves. Some members conceded that the group may not have done enough to communicate the process. "Either people didn't know we were forming groups, or they didn't know it really mattered," one member said.

Membership did matter. As had happened with the Affinity process, the voices of community and students were limited on some teams. One participant characterized her team as "void of student input," reflecting the small number of students who had nominated themselves. This was understandable, given the summer schedule the groups were to follow and students' work commitments off campus.

Hector Cruz-Feliciano, a student leader of the Healthy Choices group, provided an important perspective to his team. He became involved only when he was actively recruited by The Milwaukee Idea office. "More effort should have gone into reaching out to students," Cruz-Feliciano said.

Other Action Teams ended up with a majority of members from a particular school, college, or discipline, which may have influenced the direction of the team's work. "There was no place for other disciplines," an Action Team participant said, frustrated with her team's engineering focus and at her inability to broaden the discussion to other academic fields. Others felt that the groups had been formed for "political purposes," rather than selecting the right kinds of people. The groups were seen as too large to work quickly and well under the tight deadlines and didn't include a good mix of "experts, the people who are stakeholders in the process."

"I think all of the Action Teams suffered from some special interest," noted Dean Rayburn, who also chaired the Technology Center Action Team. "But that's part of the nature of the institution. And, if you don't involve people who are influential and who speak their mind, you won't have choices. It's when it becomes one-sided that it doesn't work."

Every effort was made to assure that the teams had the right mix of expertise and experience. Team leaders were given the lists of nominees to review before final decisions were made, and many used the opportunity to veto suggestions or recruit people they felt would be positive additions. Healthy Choices Team leaders Joan Wilk, associate professor of nursing, and Allen Zweben, professor of social work, had never met before the first team leader meeting, but their shared response to the list of candidates (they vetoed one of the chancellor's suggestions) signaled the start of what became a strong partnership.

Because the number of nominees exceeded the number of slots available, the decision was made to form Advisory Councils for each Idea. The Councils included people who did not make the Action Team as well as individuals who indicated interest in continuing to be involved, but in a limited role. Team leaders were encouraged to use their Advisory Councils to provide feedback on their progress, fill in with expertise as needed, and serve on appropriate subcommittees. How the different groups used their Councils is explored further in this chapter.

A Closer Look

An Education in Partnerships

Timing is everything. As UWM learned shortly after the new Partnerships for Education Action Team was formed, it takes the right people at the right time to make a partnership work. The Milwaukee Idea had a process that was neat and straightforward, but as Chancellor Zimpher observed, "Sometimes the real world takes over and you adjust accordingly."

Grants Aim to Help Schools Use Technology

$3.2 million to pay for training teachers, preparing future teachers

Two Federal grants aimed at helping Milwaukee Public Schools and the University of Wisconsin-Milwaukee... were unveiled Wednesday.... [MPS Superintendent] Spence Korté said one of the best aspects of the grants was the high degree of cooperation between UWM and MPS in designing the programs to be funded.

— *Alan Borsuk*
Milwaukee Journal Sentinel
September 2, 1999

As Chancellor Zimpher announced the Action Team to address new Partnerships for Education in Milwaukee, the community part of the collaboration evaporated. A citizen-led initiative ousted the existing board of the Milwaukee Public Schools (MPS), and the superintendent resigned. Recognizing that it would be futile to move ahead with UWM's new ideas about ways to address the challenges of the state's largest (and most troubled) school system until its leadership was in place, Action Team leaders Beverly Cross and Joseph Douglas waited to convene their group. The challenge was further complicated by the fact that UWM had been charged by the state legislature to oversee proposals for charter schools in Milwaukee, a fact that strained relations with MPS.

So as the Action Team waited for better timing, UWM, through the chancellor's office and the School of Education, continued meeting with MPS leadership, building trust and exploring mutual interests. One of those interests was a series of grant proposals to the U.S. Department of Education to enhance urban teacher training. The proposals had all the hallmarks of a Milwaukee Idea: creative, collaborative, involving several schools and colleges as well as multiple community partners. Only trouble was, the grants weren't part of The Milwaukee Idea plan.

A problem? Not if partnerships and results are what really matter. With the new grants in hand, and relationships with MPS leadership growing, Percy and Zimpher reconstructed the original Action Team. Armed with more than $3 million in funding, and a renewed focus on teacher training, UWM organized some of its efforts as the Milwaukee Partnership Academy for Teacher Training. In addition, the dean of the School of Education was given the title of chancellor's deputy for partnerships for education, tasked with exploring additional collaborations.

The lesson? The Milwaukee Idea is a strategic plan for what an urban university should be about. Its goal, as Bob Gleason articulated early on, was not consensus, but alignment. With educational partnerships, new and existing projects could become part of the university's ongoing efforts. There's a lot of room for creative approaches under The Milwaukee Idea's big tent.

SET A DEADLINE

As with the Affinity process, deadlines were vital to both motivating participants and keeping the groups accountable. By the time the Action Teams were formed, it was May. The Milwaukee Idea did the unthinkable and asked the Action Teams to work through the summer to avoid losing precious momentum. Milwaukee was waiting to see what would come of all the Ideas; the teams had to keep moving. "This is not a 'do-it-if-you-feel-like-it' effort," Zimpher said. "It's very mainstream to the future of the university and its role in the community."

Meeting the deadline proved to be a challenge. Several groups, due to leadership changes, last-minute budget concerns, and group dynamics, were late by a few weeks. One community member joked that he was surprised when his group missed the deadline. "Where were these professors when I was in school and had a paper due?" he quipped.

KICK IT OFF

While the Affinity process involved monthly plenary meetings to give the Committee of 100 ample time to meet as a large group, the Action Teams would need less structure, since the template for The Milwaukee Idea was now ingrained. A kick-off session that brought members of all ten teams together was important, however, to set the tone, establish the parameters, and start to create a feeling of purpose. Over a light meal in the UWM Union as about 150 people gathered to receive their charge, Zimpher reviewed the progress of The Milwaukee Idea and challenged the group to think creatively about how to integrate the First Ideas into the life of the campus and community. She asked them to think beyond existing organizational structures and, if necessary, create new ways to encourage partnerships and cross-disciplinary teams.

Specifically, the Action Teams were responsible for proposing a comprehensive organizational structure and a detailed funding outline for each Idea. They were to keep in mind the Affinity Group Connectors, the values of The Milwaukee Idea: diversity, collaboration, interdisciplinary work, student life.

Some teams found the charge too vague and the emphasis on the Connectors a diversion from focusing on the practicalities of implementing the Idea. "What I didn't see was content [in the Action Team Charge] and that was a little scary to me," said Professor David Petering, who headed the Urban Environmental Health team.

Action Team Charge

Each Action Team was to create an implementation plan that included the following elements:

- Vision statement
- Launch strategy
- Organizational and staffing structure
- Community partners
- Diversity plan
- Interdisciplinary collaborations
- Resource needs (over five years)
- Funding sources (over five years)
- Outcomes
  —See Appendix D for the full Charge

"The fundamental things we were asked to satisfy were not content, but things like diversity and interdisciplinarity. Of course, we included them in the final report, but I felt the university should have centered more on content," Petering said.

To aid the teams with their plans, Percy drafted a template for the final report that also included a worksheet for a detailed budget (see Appendix D for a sample.) Assigning concrete dollar figures and projecting salaries and headcount proved to be a challenging task. Some of the groups, especially those not headed by deans, felt that they didn't have the authority to recommend structures or new hires that cut across established school or departmental boundaries.

"We were mandated to come up with a plan that had concrete steps," said Professor Marc Levine, who co-chaired the Consortium for Economic Opportunity Action Team. "But we didn't quite have the power to make some of the changes we'd have liked." His solution, one followed by several of the groups, was to propose a structure but leave the final decisions to the

Negotiation phase of the process. Other teams ran into obstacles when they tried to get dollar figures from various departments or institutes to help create their budget. Dean support and involvement with the teams would have made the budget process more manageable, especially for team members unfamiliar with budgeting details.

CREATE A PROCESS

At the first Action Team plenary, the teams received their charge from Zimpher and Percy, then the groups broke out to discuss their Idea and set future meetings. Unlike the Affinity process, there were no large-group discussions, visioning questions, or detailed agenda. Each Action Team was on its own when it came to deciding how it would do its work. For many, the first meetings proved interesting.

"Diane and I went into our first Action Team meeting ready to get to work," recalled René Gratz, who co-chaired the Knowledge Fest Idea with Diane Reddy. Neither Gratz nor Reddy had been actively involved in the Affinity process, but both were excited about The Milwaukee Idea and asked to become more involved. "We had mapped out a course of action, based on the Affinity Group proposal, had some preliminary ideas, even picked some dates to launch our Idea," said Gratz. What they'd neglected to do was factor in their Action Team. "By the end of the first meeting, we walked out and said, 'What hit us?'" Gratz recalled.

"We realized very quickly that our people didn't want to take their roles on the team as one of merely producing what the Affinity Group had done. They wanted to take a crack at the concept," Gratz said. "Our group didn't just want to do product, they wanted to do process."

The desire to "take a crack at the concept" wasn't limited to the Knowledge Fest team, as other group leaders soon discovered. Because Action Teams were formed from lists of nominated individuals, and because many Affinity team members needed a much-deserved break from the process, several of the Action Teams had few carry-over members from the Affinity Groups that developed their Idea. "No memory" was a problem for teams who soon found they needed to spend several meetings just getting up to speed on the Idea or rehashing some of the conceptual work.

"We should have had key people from the Affinity Group on each Action Team," said Rayburn, who was the only person on his team who had participated at the Affinity level. What the teams gained in new ideas and enthusiasm was mitigated by lost continuity.

Gratz and Reddy, once they'd recovered from the battering they received at their first meeting, opened up their meetings for creative brainstorming. They spent several weeks helping the group get to know each other by building in social opportunities, like pizza suppers and refreshments before meetings. "And then we just started talking and ideas were flowing and it was very exciting," Gratz said. "Once people had a chance to think about the concept and be part of the process, we could move ahead." Because Gratz and Reddy had not had a vested interest in the original Affinity proposal, the plan that resulted from their Action Team, while rooted in it, was considerably different.

Marc Levine and his co-chair, Lucy Holifield, unlike Gratz and Reddy, had both moved from the Affinity process directly into the Action Team. Both had participated in creating the idea for the Consortium for Economic Opportunity and both were professionally involved through their respective centers, Holifield's Small Business Development Center and Levine's Center for Economic Development. While they had not worked together before, they found they were "on the same page from day one" about their Idea and were able to keep their group focused on the plan as outlined by the Affinity team.

"We went in clearly stating the mission for this project," Holifield said. "People on the team wanted to advance the agenda and needed strong leadership to stay focused and find consensus." Both admitted they found it frustrating to work with a large group that at times wanted to "start all over" and repeat the visioning process rather than stay focused on creating an Action Plan.

Joan Wilk, Allen Zweben, and Hector Cruz-Feliciano found the tension between their perceptions as leaders and the group's needs a source of strength for their Healthy Choices Action Team. This tension was also an opportunity for creative work. As Fullan writes in his sequel to *Change Forces,* "Conflict and diversity are our friends." It is out of tension (the "edge of chaos" as he calls it) that learning is possible. One of the secrets to balancing on this edge is to keep activities loosely structured around a more rigid core of deadlines and expected outcomes.[1] This was a model several of the teams followed.

"Allen, Joan, and I had an idea of how things should be done, and when we brought it to the meeting people didn't respond as we expected, so we had to make concessions," Cruz-Feliciano said. The bargaining helped build consensus, especially in a team that was evenly divided between campus and community members.

"We had a great process," added Zweben, who is director of UWM's Center for Addiction and Behavioral Health Research. "This was a real community project. The group took over ownership early in the process."

Like Gratz and Reddy, the Healthy Choices leadership used meetings to build their team, but also relied heavily on email. They began by having every member respond by email about why they were involved and what they hoped to gain. From the responses, they hammered out their group priorities. "We started with what the group wanted and where they wanted to go," Wilk said. "Our agenda as leaders was to get the group to feel like equal participants in the process, and I think that was effective because everyone's response had equal weight."

The unity created by the push and pull of the group was such that, early on, the leaders decided to limit participation to the original members. When the chancellor asked them to add another community leader, they refused, not willing to sacrifice the hard-won unity of the group.

> "The process is as important as the product, and we knew that if we were going to talk about teaching about community (the core of the Idea), we had to have one first. Our group had to become a community."
>
> —*Greg Jay*
> *Action Team Leader*

Marcia Parsons and Gregory Jay, co-chairs of the Cultures and Communities Action Team, took the opposite approach. They opened up their group, which grew and changed with each meeting. "We adopted a 'Say Yes' attitude, which I think we got partly from Nancy and partly from the process," Jay said. By August, they had almost 30 people attending their meetings. "We created a grassroots effort," said Jay.

A member of the Committee of 100, he had reservations about how The Milwaukee Idea would impact research and scholarship at UWM, but, after helping to create the Cultures and Communities Idea, became a passionate advocate of the new opportunities community engagement offered his teaching and scholarship. "I became involved because I was convinced that humanities and arts people have to step forward or the engagement train is going to leave the station without us."

Most of the Action Groups also involved experts or encouraged research on related topics to add depth to their work. Members of the Fresh Water team traveled to Europe to attend a conference to help them as they formulated ideas for their international research program. David Petering met with Milwaukee's Health Department to discover ways to better relate the plan to the needs of the city. Dean Rayburn enlisted the help of local businessman and entrepreneur Sheldon Lubar to talk to his group about venture capital and how it might relate to technology transfer.

The Community in the Classroom
By Gregory Jay, UWM professor of English and Action Team Leader

The full text of this article was published in the July/August 2000 issue of Academe, the magazine of the American Association of University Professors

What was the deconstructionist doing at the Social Development Commission, anyway?

As I sat in the office of the commission's executive director, Deborah Blanks, listening to her discuss race, education, and public service, I felt both inadequate and inspired. That appointment was one of a series of meetings with community leaders that I had begun to attend off campus as part of my commitment to The Milwaukee Idea, the University of Wisconsin–Milwaukee's new effort to build bridges between the ivory tower and the city street. Blanks, an articulate African American community activist, clearly had much to teach me, though this was hardly the kind of seminar table I had been accustomed to after 20 years as a professor. My place at this table was not at the head, and the syllabus was not of my devising. There were no students in the room, except perhaps for me.

I am probably not alone in feeling disorientation at the kind of experience I had that afternoon. As institutions of higher education increase their efforts at community engagement and civic participation, more and more faculty members find themselves going through an awkward transition. The walls dividing the campus from the world that surrounds it are falling fast, sometimes for good reasons, sometimes for reasons that should alarm us. Community engagement for the purpose of enriching education is exciting; community engagement for the purpose of enriching corporations and endowment accounts is suspect. Yet the problems faced by contemporary institutions of higher education make it increasingly difficult to discern the fine line between these two purposes. My decision to get involved in my university's new initiatives stemmed largely from my conviction that faculty had better draw that line before someone else does it for them....

Clearly, the mandate lay in turning the university's attention toward addressing worldly concerns. But what, I wondered, could the place of the arts and humanities be in a redesigned "engaged university," especially one known as a "commuter school" in a hypersegregated, working-class town with a public school system known nationally for its crises? I accepted the invitation [to participate in the Chancellor's year-long brainstorming session] partly because I feared that the trend toward seeing universities primarily as job-training centers would only be accelerated if arts and humanities faculty gave up in advance. But the 1960s idealist in me also became excited about the possibility of really transforming the curriculum by mainstreaming much of the best progressive scholarship and pedagogy developed over the last thirty years. . . .

At the start, the process did not look promising. Only one of the project's ten working groups was to discuss "culture and education," the others being more pragmatically focused on health, technology, international affairs, and the like. But our culture and education group was large and varied; it included state legislators and community activists as well as students, faculty, and administrators. The first payoff was almost immediate: liberation from isolation in our separate universes. Large metropolitan universities are notoriously fragmented places, and in 12 years at UWM I had talked with precious few people outside my discipline or building—much less from off campus. Now I was in dialogue with occupational therapists, sociologists of race, elementary education specialists, bookstore owners, dancers, librarians, community organizers, and a whole host of others who became my friends and allies in the months to follow. . . .

Our idea, then, was this: Why not propose a new, optional core curriculum focused on "cultures and communities"? [Informally called "CC".] This curriculum could be an engine for innovation and experimentation, a place to test the principles of The Milwaukee Idea and of much of the scholarly and pedagogical thinking upon which it is based. . . . If the University of Wisconsin–Milwaukee intends to engage its region, it must recognize the plurality of cultures and communities around it and the need to create productive dialogues among them. If we are to educate the future citizens of our region (and statistics show that a large majority of UWM students remain here), then we are well advised to design a curriculum that intentionally addresses these issues and provides the knowledge and skill to negotiate the challenges they offer.

The work of the cultures and communities group blossomed as campus and community involvement increased. Each meeting drew new, enthusiastic members until we ran out of chairs and lunches. Usually these monthly sessions drew from 15 to 30 people, about a third of whom came from off campus. Discussions were wide ranging and intellectually challenging. We invited people to think and speculate, so that the sessions often resembled a combination of graduate seminar and town-hall meeting. We discovered that we were becoming a community, and that the culture of listening, dialogue, and respect developed in these sessions would be essential to the vision of the new curriculum.

Working groups on specific subjects (community partnerships, teaching and learning, student recruitment and retention, and so on) met separately, sometimes off campus, and generated reports for the final "action plan." After almost eight months of work, we produced a 50-page proposal, which, after four months of campus and community review, received the chancellor's endorsement for implementation. . . .

To build the network for [our] collaborations, CC has begun arranging meetings in the community with potential partners, such as Deborah Blanks's office. We have talked with the staff at Public Allies (an AmeriCorps agency), visited with the history curator at the Milwaukee Public Museum, and met with a local foundation officer who specializes in youth development initiatives. What I find most interesting about these meetings is their intellectual, even scholarly, content. Our off-campus neighbors include many people we have come to call "community scholars," individuals who are deeply learned in their fields through real world as well as academic experience. They articulate sophisticated analyses of their work and concerns, give us bibliographies, and treat us to seminars.

When we approach them with the respect due to colleagues, they respond in kind. This approach helps prevent the notorious tendency of university-community relations to degenerate into cynical pragmatism or institutional condescension, which happens when universities concoct "solutions" that they then attempt to sell or impose without first listening to the community partner (often wrongly thought of as a "client" rather than as a colleague). In the long run, we hope to involve these community scholars in the design, preparation, and teaching of our curriculum, and to get our students out of the classroom and into community learning sites. . . .

It is way too soon to say exactly what the curriculum will look like, though principles and goals are beginning to take shape. . . . I don't intend to become a career administrator or to give up my writing and teaching. For now, I have made changes in my time commitments and daily work life, not only because I believe in our project, but also because I don't think we really have a choice at this time. Higher education in the 21st century will not much resemble education in previous centuries. History reminds us that the norm we defend today bears little likeness to the accepted practice of 30, 50, or 100 years ago. Urbanization, globalization, technology, multiculturalism, feminism, the culture wars, the science wars—all around us, the forces uprooting academic practices grow stronger. Certain core ideals of higher education—the nurturance of independent and free thinkers, the uses of knowledge for social justice and equality, the responsibility to improve the material lives of people, the strengthening of democratic citizenship—must still guide how we grow in the future. Community engagement should mean that the university and its partners join together in building new ways to realize these core ideals. Compromising or abandoning them would damage both the campus and the community, and in the process squander a great opportunity for revitalizing both. As long as there's a chance we can keep these ideals central, I'll stay engaged.

INVOLVE THE ADVISORY COUNCIL

While community membership varied from group to group (Knowledge Fest had only one regular community member, while Healthy Choices had eight), the Advisory Council was one way in which the Action Teams could involve more individuals from outside the campus. How Action Teams used their Councils varied, depending on the needs and style of the group.

Parsons and Jay "dissolved the boundary" between the Action Team and Advisory Council from the beginning, creating a single large group. Environmental Health, on the other hand, had only one meeting with its Council to review the final report and provide feedback. Levine and Holifield met twice with their group, which they used to "reality test" the work of the Action Team. "If we had left it an open-ended process, we would have had essentially a second Action Team," Levine said. "We got good advice, especially from UWM people who helped us on the internal structure proposal."

INVOLVE THE COMMUNITY

Without exception, every Action Team leader praised the contributions of their community participants. Michael Morgan, then executive director of the nonprofit Spirit of Milwaukee and member of the Knowledge Fest Action Team, found he could provide a valuable outside perspective. "The team really relied on my relationships in the private sector in trying to understand what types of initiatives would be attractive and what would motivate them," Morgan said. "Many times after our meetings I would

Action Team Leaders comment on community contributions:

"The community contribution was invaluable—it gave us a clear sense of the needs of the community and their perception of what they thought the university should be doing."

"Our community member was very helpful in giving us a perspective that we, the campus, faculty, staff, and students, didn't have."

come back to my office and call others in the community and kind of bounce ideas off them to make sure my perspective was accurate."

Keeping the community involved on the Action Teams was difficult, however. "One of my frustrations was trying to figure out how to sustain a level of community involvement," Jay said. "It's hard for them to figure out exactly what their relationship is to The Milwaukee Idea. And there are real distances between our cultures."

This perception was echoed by Steve Holt, executive director of the Milwaukee Jobs Initiative and an Action Team participant. "It's a cultural divide, so people are talking past each other." He saw community enthusiasm for creative proposals colliding with academic issues of research, tenure, and teaching responsibilities. Architect Jeff Hanewall agreed. He was surprised when he observed faculty unable to see beyond the interests of their discipline. "I thought they would be interested in what was good for the entire school or community," he said. "It was not a major stumbling block, but I do think the sentiment hindered our vision."

Morgan felt that some orientation to the university might have helped community members better understand the university perspective. "It would have been good on the front end to talk to the non-university members of the team about how the university works and the various relationships among the departments. Sometimes during the course of our discussion we would talk about some things that, to me, felt like a highly bureaucratic way to go about it. After you understand the institution, though, you understand why the process is important," Morgan said.

The disjoint between university and community perceptions also laid bare some issues only the university could tackle. Conversations about campus structures revealed long-standing conflicts between academic staff and faculty and among departments, institutes, or colleges—conflicts that could only be addressed internally. "There are some things The Milwaukee Idea can't accomplish," said past chair of the Academic Staff Committee Victoria Boswell, who served on both Affinity and Action Teams. "The community can't fix our working relationships. That's up to us."

The rewards, for those Action teams that tried to bridge the "cultural divide," included strengthened community networks. "It's helped me already," Zweben said. "I have contacts and people referring other community people to me. They feel free to call me now, so it's benefited me."

A Closer Look

A Prototypical Milwaukee Idea: Nonprofit Management Education

Ironically, one of the Ideas that most successfully illustrated the collaborative, interdisciplinary nature of The Milwaukee Idea was not one of the ten First Ideas. The Nonprofit Management Education Project, or NME, began at the instigation of three Milwaukee foundations that saw a need in the community for more extensive training opportunities for nonprofit leadership. They believed the health of the nonprofit sector in Milwaukee was seriously compromised by the lack of training and educational programs specifically targeted to not-for-profit leaders.

Aware of The Milwaukee Idea, and familiar with Steve Percy's work, they contacted him to see if The Milwaukee Idea was interested in helping them explore the possibilities. The fit was a natural, and so, in the fall of 1999, well after the first ten Action Teams had wrapped up their work, Percy and the nonprofit community convened a 13-member NME Steering Group to explore next steps. They formed an Affinity Group that eventually numbered 85 people drawn from area colleges and universities, funding organizations, nonprofits and, of course, UWM.

> "It was necessary for us to address diversity issues, for nonprofits, for board development as well as recruitment and retention. It was a priority."
> —*Michael Dudley Pastor of Capital Christian Center and NME Steering Group member*

With the Affinity and Action process of The Milwaukee Idea completed, NME was able to learn from what had come before. They hired a facilitator, Jean Tyler, who not only was familiar with the process, but also knew the community well. They paid close attention to keeping the group diverse, open, and representative. They set a time limit of six months. And they dreamed big.

"We were, at times, heavy with process," admitted Kathleen Pritchard, community impact director for the United Way of Greater Milwaukee and Steering Group member. "But the process was important to getting the relationships off the ground. We put a great deal of effort into bringing people together. It was an effective model because we had good facilitation, leadership at the top with The Milwaukee Idea and the chancellor, as well as involvement of the nonprofit groups."

Robyn Mayrl agreed that the process was necessary to create trust among the partners. As vice president for program development at the Helen Bader

Foundation, she helped initiate the idea and solicit financial and program support.

"I think it took time for the university folks to understand a little bit where we, the nonprofits, were coming from. [The process] gave us the opportunity to be heard and to begin to look at the universities, and UWM in particular, as potentially a very credible partner that had a lot of resources that could be mobilized. It was a long process we probably needed to go through."

The Affinity Group broke into work groups to gather information, analyze needs, and make recommendations. By the final months, the work groups met together to hammer out a plan for a broad initiative that would include new degree programs, nondegree certificates, technical assistance, and research in service to nonprofit management training.

As a next step, the group formed an Interim Board (much like an Action Team) to oversee development and implementation of the proposal for the first year. The 15-member board (which purposely included substantial representation by people who served on the Affinity Group) included four representatives from UWM as well as funders and nonprofit organizations. Thanks to significant donations from the original foundations, NME has hired a director and opened its doors as the Helen Bader Institute for Nonprofit Management at UWM.

"This is a fascinating project because it's almost a prototypical Milwaukee Idea—that came from the outside," Stephen Percy said. "While not one of the ten First Ideas, it's a great example of an Idea finding us because of the accessibility The Milwaukee Idea brings to our university. We've now made it our '11th First Idea.' The Institute for Nonprofit Management illustrates how the process can work, how The Milwaukee Idea can respond to community needs and serve as an incubator for new opportunities that hold great promise for both UWM and Milwaukee."

GET IT FUNDED

When UW System President Katharine Lyall first met with the Affinity Groups to encourage their efforts, she promised support for The Milwaukee Idea. In May, as the Action Teams began their work, she returned to UWM to announce $1.5 million in new dollars for the initiative. It was an important signal of continuing support for UWM's urban mission and the first step in a four-part funding strategy. Linking System, state, UWM, and private dollars, Zimpher created $4.5 million of "bridge funding"—a plan to finance the launch and implementation of the first 11 Ideas until a comprehensive multiple-year request could be made to the state and a campus-wide campaign launched. Part of the strategy included using dollars generated by increased enrollment to match funds invested by individual schools and colleges for The Milwaukee Idea.

As budgets for The Milwaukee Idea were developed, it was important that funding discussions be held in the context of the entire university, a process begun at the university's first budget retreat, called "Investing in UWM's Future." Administration, faculty, staff, and students met for two days to "make sure we can afford our aspirations," as Zimpher told the group.

Prominent on the agenda was a discussion of how to create a long-term funding plan that would balance the overlapping financial demands of improving research, student services, faculty salaries and, of course, funding The Milwaukee Idea. Talking about a campus-wide financial plan across colleges and administrative offices had never been done before, and the discussions opened up the budgeting process to involve faculty, students, and staff in the decisions. As the conversation continued in the months that followed, it forced people to begin looking at the totality of the university's mission, not just at research, diversity programs, or even The Milwaukee Idea.

"'Investing in UWM's Future' has served to kind of put us all on the same page about where we're going as an institution," said Ruth Williams, assistant vice chancellor for Academic Affairs and coordinator of the campus-wide group that continued the budgeting discussions. Her group produced a paper that called for "new initiatives in research, student learning and outreach based on broad community partnerships" through The Milwaukee Idea.[2] It also helped people begin to see creative opportunities to fund campus priorities.

From the beginning it was understood that, among other things, The Milwaukee Idea was key to increasing fund-raising efforts at UWM. "The Milwaukee Idea is, in some sense, academic branding," said Victoria Boswell, who served on both Affinity and Action Teams. "We can't have a capital campaign unless we brand it." And The Milwaukee Idea was a popular brand for local funders. Corporate leaders understood The Milwaukee Idea and liked the focus on economic development, international initiatives, and technology transfer.

The potential for new dollars through Milwaukee Idea initiatives was not lost on deans who had their own interpretations of what the initiative could mean for their school or college, on faculty eager to fund their pet research projects, or on those whose interests fell outside the First Ideas. "Our department has been told by a dean that we cannot expect any support from the university since we are not part of The Milwaukee Idea," said one professor who, despite his participation on an Action Team, was not able to directly link his research with a First Idea.

"The fact that The Milwaukee Idea has resources *is* important," said Professor David Petering, who was a vocal faculty advocate for increased research funding. "But frankly, to me it's like anything else. I wouldn't do it just for the money. There's a lot that's attractive about the [Idea]. And generally, the process of getting people together and thinking and working together in and of itself, whether it brought in any dollars or not, was a really good one."

GET IT IN WRITING

As the Affinity Teams had faced a ruthless deadline, so also Action Teams found the summer fading and their September 15 deadline approaching. Knowledge Fest leaders Gratz and Reddy pulled all-nighters, writing the report in tandem. Cultures and Communities created a report from the contributions of its large and diverse membership. The Fresh Water Initiative formed a writing team that labored for days to create a detailed, illustrated plan. The International Affairs Initiative produced several versions as its deeply divided Action Team struggled with how best to present and define its report. The Technology Center, hobbled by changes in leadership, submitted its plan past the deadline.

Regardless of how—or how late—the Action Teams crossed the finish line, cross it they did. The plans, following Percy's template and packed with recommendations for new hires, multiple-reporting structures, and creative accounting, were submitted, ready for the next stage: Evaluation.

Reflections

Nancy Zimpher and Steve Percy talk about the Action process

Nancy Zimpher
The Affinity Group process had given us some really dynamic ideas with tremendous potential. We'd purposely kept the process open to get the campus and community working together, to signal that we were serious about wanting every voice. But taking an idea and figuring out how to budget for it or which dean should manage it needs a different dynamic.

We knew that the sizes of the Action Teams would need to be smaller than the Affinity Groups—to get the work done quickly and effectively. But we didn't want to shut out the "X" factor—that unexpected person who walks in the door and brings an incredible new idea or energy. And we especially wanted to find ways to keep the community involved. The temptation to fall back on the "usual campus suspects" was always a real one. So we used the nomination process to narrow our participants, but kept the door open by making our Advisory Groups open to anyone—no limits.

And that paid off. Cultures and Communities is a great example. Greg Jay dissolved the lines between his team and Advisory Group. People kept joining and he kept using them, and in the process he built a team of 30 or 40 people that actually got things done. We succeeded, I think, in providing structure for those who needed it, but enough freedom that the Action Teams could make the process their own.

Steve Percy

One lesson that we did learn throughout the Action Team process was the importance of leadership. We selected many of our team leaders for their scholarly background—their knowledge of freshwater or urban health research, for example. Our teams may have been better served had we thought more broadly.

We also were deliberative about inclusivity and that also may have led us to compromise somewhat on who we selected. That was an important value for The Milwaukee Idea, and I believe that it was important to do that. We made a symbolic statement to the campus and the community, for example, when we named a student—Ajita Talwalker—as leader of an Action Team.

What we did not do—and would do later with groups that followed the initial ten Ideas—was provide facilitation support to the leaders. That would have helped some of the groups move forward faster, especially those that faced internal conflicts.

Looking back now, we know that many of the Action Teams struggled with creating administrative structures for their Ideas. They weren't used to thinking outside the traditional academic structures because there are few models for cross-disciplinary projects on campus. Some of the teams solved this by providing different options or operating principles that guided formation of new entities. More details by the teams would have helped in the evaluation and negotiation phase that followed. As we discovered, not all teams were able to finish at the same time. What was more important was that they were able to give thoughtful attention to making implementation possible. Flexible deadlines paid off.

CHAPTER 6 SUMMARY

What We Learned About the Planning Process

1) **Selecting leaders and team members is an art.** Celebrate when it works but be prepared to offer facilitation support or intervention when it doesn't.

2) **Pay attention to the balance of power.** Student leaders were most effective when partnered with faculty or staff, not with deans.

3) **Stay flexible.** The process works, but be open to new opportunities and new partnerships. When parallel initiatives develop, welcome them. When new ideas come from outside, support them.

4) **Details are more important than deadlines.** With visioning, deadlines keep people focused. With planning, it's important to get the details right. Give people time to find the right process and allow them to finish.

Endnotes

[1] Michael Fullan. (1999). *Change Forces: The Sequel.* Philadelphia, PA: The Falmer Press, page 22.

[2] From the Preamble to "Investing in UWM's Future," a report of the Chancellor's Budget Advisory Committee, January 12, 2000 draft.

WEAVING NEW STRUCTURES: THE EVALUATION AND NEGOTIATION PROCESS

From the *Milwaukee Journal Sentinel*
July 5, 1999

UWM Chief Looking at Administrative Reform
Staffers reportedly uneasy about
how changes would affect them
By Jack Norman

Having made a big start in the last year at changing the University of Wisconsin-Milwaukee's community image, Chancellor Nancy Zimpher is now in the early stages of what may be major overhauls of the university's internal structure.

The process went public last month, with an open forum for faculty and staff to voice their thoughts. . . .

Through her Milwaukee Idea project, Zimpher has been pushing expanded interdisciplinary work and community outreach.

UWM is also planning for 10% growth in the student body in the next five years.

"Do we have the administrative structure that can carry that out?" [Zimpher] asked. . . .

Two weeks after the Action Teams first met to begin their work in the summer of 1999, The Milwaukee Idea Strategy Team gathered in downtown Milwaukee. Meeting at the University of Wisconsin-Milwaukee's Continuing Education campus, in a renovated 19th century building in the heart of the city's retail center, the group spent the day planning next steps. It was the first time the Strategy Team had had the luxury to look at the big picture; leadership and staff had been busy coordinating Affinity and Action phases—not to mention the inauguration—and it was finally time to take a big breath and take stock.

The Milwaukee Idea had unleashed a wave of creative activity and excitement as hundreds of people became involved in planning a new future. The challenge ahead—as the Strategy Group saw it—was to take the "outside-the-box" creativity of the First Ideas and begin moving it into the mainstream of the university. As Zimpher had often said, The Milwaukee Idea would not succeed if it was perceived by faculty, staff, and students as a separate, one-time-only program. It needed to be woven into the fabric of the university.

Integrating The Milwaukee Idea would depend on a critical assessment of the viability of the Action Team proposals and buy-in from administration and governance on new ways of operating. It would involve tough decision-making by a relatively small group of administrators, deans, faculty, and staff—decisions about who could hire new people, who would administer new institutes, and who would report to whom. From Affinity to Action to Evaluation to Negotiation Teams, the decisions were funneled into smaller and smaller groups of individuals. The challenge was to keep the process open at all levels or risk loss of credibility in the entire process. This could not become a "back-room decision."

The solution was to create a two-pronged approach. After the Action Teams submitted their written reports on how to implement the First Ideas, an Evaluation Team, composed of campus and community members, would assess each proposal and determine feasibility. If the plan was on target, the team would recommend to the chancellor that the Idea proceed as proposed. If the Evaluation Team had questions or concerns about the viability of the Action Plan, it would recommend that additional planning work be done before implementation.

Based on the recommendations of the Evaluation Team, Percy and the provost would meet with relevant deans and Action Team leaders to negotiate the funding and reporting structures proposed by the Idea. And finally, the First Idea would be launched. At least that's what everyone hoped would happen. As the Strategy Group mapped out the final phase, members were confident evaluation and negotiations would be complete within five months. They were optimistic that the First Ideas would be launched just a year from the beginning of the first Milwaukee Idea meeting.

It was not to be. While some Ideas met the schedule, others hit snags. Evaluating the Action Plans would take a lot longer.

EVALUATION

Keep Everybody at the Table

To keep the Evaluation and Negotiation processes as inclusive as the Affinity and Action phases, the Evaluation Team was formed by putting out the call to campus and community leadership to nominate participants.

Member expertise was an important criterion for the Evaluation Team. Practical implementers with a critical eye for detail—not visionary dreamers—were sought. The governance groups were asked specifically to nominate

Evaluation Team Membership

Representatives from:
- University Committee
- Academic Staff Committee
- Student Association
- Classified Staff
- Academic Deans Council
- Milwaukee Idea Strategy Team
- Community Groups

individuals who were familiar with The Milwaukee Idea and the university's budget process. Generally, the group succeeded, although some of the Action Team leaders felt that the Evaluation Team did not have the depth needed to adequately assess individual Action Team proposals. Some faculty, used to the rigors of the grant process, felt that the group was able "at best to give the proposals a surface review." They questioned whether the Evaluation Team was knowledgeable enough about UWM and the technicalities of the proposals to assess their feasibility.

Community participation was limited to three people to keep the Evaluation Team a workable size. Zimpher had hoped to include more, especially as the demands of the process meant not all members participated in evaluating every proposal. But even when the meeting schedule got heavy, the community participation was loyal.

One of the representatives was Jose Olivieri, a Milwaukee attorney who also served as a member of the UW System Board of Regents. His involvement provided The Milwaukee Idea with a litmus test for community understanding.

Define the Mission

More important than finding the right mix for the Evaluation Team was defining its mission. From the beginning, Percy had told the Action Teams that they were not in competition. There was no plan to whittle the ten First Ideas down to a more manageable number. Implementation would depend entirely on the feasibility of the plan. If the Action Plan was workable, the Idea would be launched. The expectation was that the Ideas would be implemented over a period of months, as they were ready. The spirit of The Milwaukee Idea would continue to be "Yes!"

Evaluation Team Charge

Review
each plan individually and as a group

Clarify
details with group leaders

Assess
viability for immediate launch

Recommend
action for each Idea to the chancellor

For the Evaluation Team members, it meant that their charge was to assess how well the Action Team plans fulfilled the mandate to embrace collaboration; interdisciplinarity, community partnerships; and diversity. As well, the plans needed to be financially realistic and provide solid strategies for generating additional funding. The Evaluation Team's goal was to recommend to the chancellor whether each Idea should move forward or whether it needed more planning. (See Appendix E for The Evaluation Team charge.)

It soon became obvious to the Evaluation Team that several of the Action Plans were not yet ready for implementation. Some proposals were too broad and didn't provide the detailed specifics needed for implementation. Others were delayed as the Action Teams struggled to meet deadlines. Still others had failed to create community partnerships. Then the dilemma the evaluators faced was how much guidance they should give to the Action Team in steering it toward the next steps. Should they just tell the Action Team "not ready," or take a more proactive role and say "ready if you do this and this...."

"Our struggle was how much do we tell the Action Teams what we think they should do as opposed to just taking what they propose and making a judgment," Olivieri said. As discussions proceeded, the Evaluation Team decided to outline its concerns about each plan, provide clarification and focus as needed, but let the Action Teams and the chancellor determine the next steps.

Keep It Moving

Initial plans for the Evaluation Team called for three full-day meetings where it was anticipated the 18-member group would discuss the proposals, provide feedback to the Action Teams, then, after a response by each Action Team, make final recommendations. As Action Plans trickled in late, and as discussions with the Action Teams and among the Evaluation members became more involved, the meetings multiplied. What began as a one-month process soon stretched to four as scheduling conflicts slowed the process and the Evaluation Team discovered it needed more time for adequate assessment.

A workable pattern soon emerged. Evaluation Team members would review two or three Action plans (typically each was between 50 and 100 pages in length), then discuss them as a group at a half-day meeting. Percy would draft a summary of the group's comments and

Evaluation Process

Evaluation Team reviews report; formulates questions for Action Team

▼

Percy drafts summary and gives to Action Team leaders

▼

Percy and Action Team leaders meet to discuss response

▼

Percy drafts summary of Action Team response

▼

Evaluation Team reviews response; formulates recommendation

▼

Evaluation report on web to governance groups for input

▼

Percy drafts final recommendation for chancellor

concerns and forward it to the Action Team leaders. They, in turn, would often confer with their group members (usually by email), then meet in person with Percy to discuss further. Percy would draft a summary of the discussion with the Action Team for the entire Evaluation Team to review before making a final decision. Once made, Percy would write a final recommendation to the chancellor regarding the status of the First Idea.

The demands on both Evaluation Team members and Percy were extensive. Every Team member interviewed commented on the time commitment. "It was personally a challenge for me to read all the Action Team and evaluation reports within the very short turnaround time and to juggle the long meetings with my other responsibilities," said academic staff member Linda Huang. Professor Joseph Rodriguez, who found the team's meetings "awfully long," appreciated the few concise Action Team reports. Those that numbered more than 100 pages, he felt, were not necessarily more detailed or coherent, but rather "reflected disagreements among committee members."

Ellen Murphy, secretary of the university and member of the Evaluation Team, praised Percy's role in providing continuity for the Team as it sifted through reports. "Steve was pivotal in how he presented the feedback and elicited response," Murphy said. "He was masterful at conveying our concerns without deflating the Action Team." What could have been a confrontational discussion between Action and Evaluation Teams became a productive forum for refining the proposals.

Community representative Michael Morgan believes that the process succeeded in part because tension was largely avoided between Evaluation and Action teams. "The process could have broken down at the Evaluation stage, but Steve took the time necessary to try to understand what was being proposed by the Action Teams and the kernel of concerns of the Evaluation Team. The result has been good refinement of the plans."

Find Balance

Keeping the Evaluation Team on task and moving forward had to be countered with the need to give the Action Teams adequate time to respond to concerns and questions. Because of scheduling constraints, most Evaluation members did not meet with individual Action Team leaders, relying instead on Percy, Milwaukee Idea office staff, and one or two interested evaluators to have the conversation and report back.

Most of the Action Team leaders found this frustrating because they wanted the opportunity to discuss their proposals in depth. "We had no dialogue with any new partners from the Evaluation Team," said Cultures and Communities leader Gregory Jay. "So it didn't increase the circle of conversation. Nor did we meet with the chancellor or provost. We kept asking to meet with the people who would be making the decisions. We all felt a lot of frustration."

Some Action Team members felt that some concerns raised by the Evaluation Team could have been cleared up quickly by a face-to-face meeting held before the team began its assessment. "That would have shortened the process a lot," Marcia Parsons said.

> "We have everybody all fired up to get our report done and now we're all just sitting around. It drains creditability and is by far the weakest part of this whole process."
>
> —Greg Jay
> Action Team leader

Moving beyond the planning to launch was foremost on the minds of the Action Team leaders. Having spent the summer planning, they were eager to begin work. Many community members also were impatient with the slow pace of the university. Zimpher recalled a conversation with a member of the Healthy Choices Action Team who buttonholed her at a civic dinner, asking, "How is my Healthy Choices doing? You do understand how many of us in the community have been engaged and that really support this, don't you?"

The reality of the process, however, was that serious evaluation of ten detailed, institution-changing proposals takes time. As Percy noted, expectations for The Milwaukee Idea were so high that anything less than full steam ahead was frustrating. Indeed, having 11 major initiatives in the final planning stage within one year's time was "incredible for a university," said Consortium for Economic Opportunity Co-chair Marc Levine. "Sometimes it takes years for programs to get going, but if there is excitement about The Milwaukee Idea and people start saying nothing is happening, that is not a good thing."

Ready—Or Not

As the Evaluation Team reviewed the proposals, members found themselves sorting the plans into three piles: 1) ready to go, 2) needs tweaking, and 3) needs work.

The Freshwater proposal, for example, held enormous potential, but—as even the Action Team members admitted—it needed more work. The Idea involved the establishment of a major international research facility to study issues of fresh water, from aquaculture to international water rights. The Freshwater Action Team had worked hard to overcome existing institutional conflicts, but had not been able to identify strong community partners or resolve interdisciplinary challenges.

Rather than push for immediate launch, the Evaluation Team asked for more study. In response, the chancellor formed a coordinating committee to continue the planning work on the Freshwater proposal. To give members of the Action Team a well-deserved reprieve, the coordinating committee included some original members but was primarily formed with new appointees.

Other Action Team proposals, like Campus Design Solutions, had enough start-up possibilities to be put on the fast track. Most proposals, however, needed fine tuning—budgets scaled back, reporting structures creatively addressed, timelines finalized—and so the next step was negotiation.

NEGOTIATION

Negotiate Early and Often

Evaluation recommendations in hand, Percy began the next phase: Negotiation. For each of the First Ideas deemed ready, a Negotiating team was formed that included the Action Team leaders, Percy, the provost, relevant deans, and any campus people who would be involved in heading up the Idea. Their charge: Work out the details to make it happen.

The "details" included such topics as reporting structure, new hires, budget, space allocations, and governance procedures. To say the discussions got interesting is an understatement. Deans who had put The Milwaukee Idea on the back burner suddenly refocused when proposed centers or institutes were shifted to other colleges. Several deans felt that decisions they had previously made were being shifted outside their school or college, along with significant dollars. Faculty were being asked to lead initiatives that deans thought should be under their purview. As The Milwaukee Idea tried to keep the process moving forward, the deans demanded greater consultation.

At the same time, faculty leaders who had invested hours in helping to create and plan their Idea balked when other candidates were suggested to head up the initiative. They questioned the fairness of how leadership opportunities were being assigned and asked for a more formal selection process, one that was within the traditional governance structures. Governance groups were concerned about the range of new programs and positions being created outside of the established process. Proposals that had involved hiring five new faculty now needed to be restructured to work with three. Budgets needed to be divided across schools and colleges using forms that didn't yet exist. Reporting issues that had festered for years "came home to roost." Structures proposed by the Action Team took on new importance when people discovered they might really happen.

The challenge to "think in new ways" proved a daunting one, especially when it also involved acting in new ways. As one observer commented, "People

who have territorial boundaries will not try to work across those boundaries
when they have little incentive beyond money for a few positions."

The meetings multiplied and the months passed. While community
members chafed and Action Team leaders waited anxiously for the signal to
begin, the Negotiation phase was critical and demanded a consultative, measured approach.

As Healthy Choices Co-chair Allen Zweben noted, he got a lot of calls
from community partners impatient with the university's perceived foot drag-
ging. But he defended it. "I think we ought to be very careful about how we
work through the budgetary issues. We are talking about power, structure,
and territory with ideas that are outside the box. I believe the chancellor is
wanting to have that box arranged in new and innovative ways."

Leaders were selected to manage each of the First Ideas. In many cases,
they were those individuals who had been involved in the Action Team
process or who emerged when interdisciplinary collaborations were formed.
Marc Levine and Lucy Holifield, for example, were Action Team leaders who
agreed to head up the Consortium for Economic Development. Greg Jay, the
leader of the Cultures and Communities team (CC), was soon set up in an
office to manage the new CC program.

For the International initiative, now called the Global Passport Project,
new leadership was found when two international programs from across campus were consolidated under the banner of Global Passports.

Who the new leaders would report to remained the next question to be
resolved. A primary tenet of The Milwaukee Idea had been that all Ideas, by
their nature, had to be interdisciplinary. But UWM had no systems for programs that involved people across colleges. It would need to be created—with
the assistance of UWM's governance system.

Involve Governance

One strength UWM had was the involvement of the faculty and academic
staff in The Milwaukee Idea. Leaders from both the University Committee
and Academic Staff Committee were active participants and also served on
the Chancellor's Cabinet. Throughout the year the chancellor had provided
the Faculty Senate with regular updates on the progress of the Idea. But as the
Ideas moved closer to implementation, it became increasingly important to
involve the governance groups more directly.

As mentioned earlier, the tradition of faculty governance is alive and well
at UWM, where both faculty and academic staff are involved in academic
decisions from tenure to new course development. Their participation in
assessing the new Milwaukee Idea proposals was essential. Ideas like Cultures

and Communities, Healthy Choices, and Global Passports involved development of new curricula. Nontraditional learning and service-learning options were part of most of the Ideas and needed faculty input. Funding for new faculty and proposed structures that would affect existing systems needed review by governance. "We've got to get The Milwaukee Idea back into the system," warned Laurie Glass, then chair of the University Committee.

So, early in the Evaluation process, Percy met with Glass, Academic Staff Committee Chair Steve Atkinson, and Secretary of the University Murphy to design a system. Since most faculty committees did not meet more than once a month, there was a real concern that governance would slow the process. The goal, according to Glass, was to find a system that would work efficiently, yet keep governance involved.

The solution was to make the Evaluation Team reports available on the web and in hard copy in the library when they were final. The University and Academic Staff Committees, which met weekly, then divided the reports among their members, commented on them, and returned them to the Evaluation Team before the final recommendations were made to the chancellor. But that was only the beginning.

The Art of Finding Balance
By Ellen Murphy, Secretary of the University

When Chancellor Zimpher announced The Milwaukee Idea at her inauguration, she talked about weaving it into the fabric of the university, "like threads through a cloth." The warp of that rich tapestry, through which the initiative was woven, was the strong cloth of university governance. And the weaving process, it turned out, required both skill and art.

UWM's system of shared governance instills a strong sense of faculty ownership for the nature and quality of the university's programs and departments. Faculty and staff expect to play a major role in vetting proposals for the academic programs. And so, as The Milwaukee Idea's proposals for First Ideas were evaluated, faculty and staff committees became active participants.

The Milwaukee Idea was not an unfamiliar concept to campus leaders. Chancellor Zimpher had articulated her vision of The Milwaukee Idea within the context of existing values and plans that predated her arrival (e.g., The Wisconsin Idea and UWM's own strategic plans). She had also—perhaps wisely—defined her vision in only the broadest of strokes. She had involved both internal and external constituencies to define and refine the detail in that vision. This purposeful ambiguity cut both ways. Embraced by some as an opportunity to shape the future, it also was criticized by others as symptomatic of a lack of commitment to more traditional research and scholarship and respect for pre-existing shared governance structures.

The existence of the tradition and values of UWM's shared governance served many purposes during the emergence of The Milwaukee Idea. It was invoked by some as a reason the chancellor's broad-based community agenda for engagement could not be viewed as legitimate; on the other hand, it was reassuring to many—especially those skeptical but willing to give the initiative a chance—because, ultimately, changes in programming, curricula, merit, and tenure/promotion criteria would have to be brought through the existing faculty-controlled governance processes.

A major point of tension along the way was how to balance the roles of the administration-selected Affinity Groups, Action Teams, and other task-force "adhocracies" that first incubated Milwaukee Idea initiatives, and the elected faculty standing committee structures that shared responsibilities for academic programming. Therein lay opportunity and the need for an artful approach.

Some of the concerns were addressed when Senate executive committees were incorporated into the Idea evaluation process; others when many of the members of the various ad hoc groups were appointed by the governance groups themselves.

The role of The Milwaukee Idea office was also a critical one. Although the public position of the office was not to create parallel programming, and efforts were directed to launching initiatives into existing schools, colleges, departments, and other governance units, this was not always accomplished as smoothly or rapidly as hoped. The perceived outside authority of The Milwaukee Idea office, particularly with regard to budget and human resource deployment, precipitated a coalition between the Academic Deans Council and the Executive Committee of the Faculty Senate. Deans felt negotiations with faculty in their units for buyouts or other Milwaukee Idea activities without the dean's knowledge or consent undermined their ability to lead their schools or colleges. Faculty and academic staff governance leaders felt the extra governance adhocracy was eroding authority previously vested in elected rather than administratively selected faculty.

Rather than break down negotiations, a new design was created. The result was a Milwaukee Idea Trustee Council—with four members appointed by the deans, four members appointed by the Executive Committee of the

Faculty Senate, and two members appointed by the Executive Committee of the Academic Staff. The solution was found both in anchoring implementation within existing tradition and creating a new way of operating.

Ultimately, governance processes will make the difference between a chancellor-dependent initiative and transformational organizational change. It will be the journey through governance processes that will either make an initiative a more permanent part of the institutional fabric, reject it completely, or change it and make the more permanent change look quite different from the original.

Of course, form follows function, and it may well be that if/when The Milwaukee Idea (writ large) mindsets permeate the university, so, too, may the supporting governance structure change. But, in the meantime, these structures provide the mechanism for initiative, refinement, support, and ownership from the faculty and academic staff upon whom successful implementation depends.

And so the Negotiation phase, despite its bumps and setbacks, proved to be the testing ground for new relationships across the university and a new way of institutional organization. True to form for The Milwaukee Idea, the solution to reinventing UWM lay, not in going back to old structures, but to opening up the process and inventing new ones. The new infrastructure, still being tested, involved creating new Dean and Trustee Councils, designed to encourage interdisciplinary networks and funding.

A New Infrastructure

The First Idea

Administrator
▼
Lead Dean
▼
Deans Council
▼
Trustee Council

Each First Idea was given a Deans Council made up of the deans whose colleges or schools were involved in the Idea. For example, the Center for Healthy Living Choices, headed by Allen Zweben, would report to a Council made up of deans from Social Welfare, Letters and Science, Education, Health Sciences, and Nursing.

A Lead Dean, in this case Dean Blackburn from Social Welfare, would handle the direct reporting duties. This structure not only gave the deans opportunity to participate in the decision-making process, it also helped The Milwaukee Idea connect with the schools and colleges that would be important partners. (See *Principles for Administration,* an outline of the new structure, in Appendix F).

Marshall Goodman, former dean of Letters and Science at UWM and currently provost at San Jose State University, was an Action Team leader and participated in The Milwaukee Idea from its beginning. He saw firsthand how The Milwaukee Idea changed relationships on campus. "The level of collaboration by the deans in my five years [at UWM was] at an all-time high," he said. "It's very hard to reengineer a university because people are committed to the status quo, but The Milwaukee Idea has the imprimatur of the chancellor and President Lyall's support, and that sends a signal to people that if UWM is ever going to do it, it needs to happen now."

Get Help Rearranging the Box

While the Deans Councils helped smooth interdisciplinary issues, there was no formal mechanism for general oversight of The Milwaukee Idea. The solu-

Trustee Council

Five Deans
Four Faculty
Two Academic Staff
Milwaukee Idea Office

Provides advice and decision-making to facilitate cross-disciplinary partnerships and Milwaukee Idea initiatives

tion was to form a Trustee Council to oversee the initiatives and make cross-disciplinary partnerships easier. The new Council gave the governance groups the opportunity to help shape the outcomes, provided deans with a forum for shared administration, and kept the implementation process open and transparent. It's important to note that each governance group—University Committee, Academic Staff Committee, and Academic Deans Council—appointed its own members to the Trustee Council. The Milwaukee Idea office did not help to shape the Council.

Questions of budget also required lengthy negotiation as proposals ground on for new staff and space needs (always an issue on a campus some called "space-challenged"). How do you allocate staff costs for faculty who are involved in a grant project as well as The Milwaukee Idea? How do you coordinate compensation when one college talks about "replacement costs" but another uses a "percentage charge" system? All these questions and more needed to be addressed. In fact, a completely new budget form needed to be developed for The Milwaukee Idea.

Meanwhile, to meet immediate financial needs until a major funding request could be submitted to the state legislature, The Milwaukee Idea announced a Matching Fund program that offered half a million dollars to First Ideas that could match their request with financial resources from a school or college. The dollars were offered in two cycles and were administered by members of the Trustee Council. The funding was for ongoing support, as long as the position continued to support The Milwaukee Idea.

In essence, this approach helped loosen the purse strings of the individual schools and colleges, leveraging dollars that already had been provided from UW System, the chancellor's office, and private funding.

While steps were taken to involve the campus and governance in the budget process, less attention was paid to questions of funding in relation to community partners. While all Action Plans carefully laid out plans for hiring faculty and staff on campus, many Action Teams did not address ways in which community partners would be funded—an essential component to successful engagement, in the eyes of some campus leaders.

Dean of Nursing Sally Lundeen, for example, expressed concerns that unless community partnerships also were supported with dollars, community members would continue to be perceived as sources of volunteer labor, not equal partners. Money, as she observed, is a great equalizer.

"The community is important in so many ways," she said. "They have a commodity worth our investment, if you will, and we need to acknowledge our truly reciprocal relationship."

Translating community partnerships into the currency of dollars and cents was not a primary focus of the Negotiation process, and so each First Idea approached community funding in different ways. Cultures and Communities, for example, immediately set up a mini-grant program that encouraged—and funded—community-initiated projects. Other First Ideas focused on creating a campus infrastructure for the launch of their initiatives, with community funding yet to be addressed.

Take Another Look Inside the Box

While the administrative structure of The Milwaukee Idea was being hammered out, the chancellor also was reexamining her staff with an eye to creating a more flexible and responsive team. The current model of assistant chancellors and provost's office reporting in a hierarchical pattern could not respond quickly enough to campus or community needs.

> "As the essence of The Milwaukee Idea is partnership and collaboration, we need a bona fide member of the community serving on our internal leadership team."
> —Nancy Zimpher
> at Faculty Senate plenary

And so in a faculty plenary meeting in the fall of 1999, the chancellor announced an administrative reorganization around "functions that are needed to attend to our mission and our goals." This included a new vice chancellor position for "Partnerships and Innovation," a role that recognized the importance of community participation in setting the university's agenda. It was filled by Joan Prince, a community leader. In addition, three "Chancellor's Deputies" were created to address functions that cut across the university. These included education partnerships, campus and urban design, and The Milwaukee Idea.

UWM has chosen to create new structures from within—although they are, as the chancellor has often said, "subject to change."

Steve Percy on the Evaluation and Negotiation Process

Coming off the Affinity and Action Team phases of The Milwaukee Idea, I can truthfully say the demands of Evaluation and Negotiation were unexpected. I just didn't anticipate the amount of time needed to coordinate the Evaluation Team, communicate with the Action Teams, and keep the whole process moving.

We'd hoped to have one or two full-day meetings with the evaluators to review proposals, but the level of dedication they brought to the task saw that time grow exponentially. We also needed to be mindful of the schedules of our community members, who don't often have whole days available for what was a volunteer effort.

But it truly was an exciting and extraordinary process. Working through all the different perspectives and issues and points of view, yet always focusing on finding ways to be broad and inclusive and creative, then finding the resources and matching them to the people and the authority to make it all happen. What a challenge!

The role of The Milwaukee Idea office as communication link and coordinator was essential, and our position outside the main administration building continued to be a strength. But it also showed me that the office needed to expand its mission, or there was a danger we would become administrators for the individual Ideas. Our goal was never to be the implementer of The Milwaukee Idea, but the facilitator for it.

I remember one of the Evaluation Team members taking me aside one day concerned about my ability to run all 11 of the First Ideas. I said, "Whoa!" The Milwaukee Idea office was not going to be the administrator of every Idea. Each would have to find its own place. They need the freedom to develop in their own ways. We'll provide the support.

If the Evaluation phase was time-consuming, Negotiations were challenging. And they should have been: We were talking real dollars and new lines of authority. I think the deans felt that decisions about staffing and budgets were being made arbitrarily—although, in fact, The Milwaukee Idea staff had been working with administration for months to determine budget parameters.

That's when we realized we had to return to our values of inclusiveness and openness and find new ways to keep everyone—especially the deans—part of the process. So we stopped the process, but just long enough to figure out a way to work together. I learned that when a problem reaches a certain level of magnitude, you can't just talk to people about it individually. You need to get everyone together, directly confront the issues, give people a forum to discuss their concerns, find solutions together, and then move on. The Deans Councils and the Trustee Council came out of that. As difficult as that process was, it is a mark of the flexibility of The Milwaukee Idea and of UWM. When things didn't work, when we hit the wall, we adjusted what we were doing and kept moving.

We also needed to find ways to expand the impact of the dollars available to The Milwaukee Idea. If the campus saw all the new money coming from The Milwaukee Idea, it would give a wrong impression about our role and it would fail to get additional campus support. Instead of mandating that the schools and colleges "kick in" their own funding for The Milwaukee Idea, we provided an incentive, the Matching Grant program. Carrots work much better than sticks. The result was overwhelming. In the first round, we received proposals for more than $600,000, more than double our $250,000 target.

In looking back at the Negotiation process and how, with the help of the provost, the deans, and governance, we were able to introduce new structures into our university, I am impressed by the flexibility of our institution.

With our interdisciplinary Ideas, we have augmented the traditional line authority of our deans and department chairs. We have had students and community members serving on committees that are making decisions that directly affect how our university operates. We had the provost working with The Milwaukee Idea, not managing it, as you might expect. We had a Regent evaluating our Ideas. And, in the Trustee Council, we have added a governance body that evolved in response to the concerns of the University Committee and Deans Council. These are significant changes—many involving the redistribution of academic responsibility—and UWM has responded. How these new relationships and structures will play out remains to be seen, but I am confident that the entrepreneurial spirit of The Milwaukee Idea will continue.

CHAPTER 7 SUMMARY

What We Learned About Evaluation and Negotiation

1) **It takes much longer than you expect.** But don't rush it. This is the critical stage at which the institution creates the structures and relationships that will help it move forward.

2) **Involve everyone.** You need every voice—community, faculty, students, and staff. This is not the time to abandon your commitment to collaboration.

3) **When things break down, stop to fix them. But don't stop long.** At some point negotiations will get heated. Listen to concerns, address them openly when they reach critical mass, but keep the process moving.

4) **Go outside the box.** You don't solve new problems by using old solutions. Involve creative risk-takers and support new ideas, no matter where they come from. Help the institution stretch.

8
ARE YOU READY?
THE COMMUNITY PERSPECTIVE

From *The Business Journal,* Milwaukee, Wisconsin
Week of January 3, 2000

Many Old Challenges Extend into New Year
Editorial

The final chapters have yet to be written for several important news stories and editorials covered by The Business Journal. . . Here are a few plot lines to watch in the next millennium: . . .

Will University of Wisconsin-Milwaukee Chancellor Nancy Zimpher transform her Milwaukee Idea into a Milwaukee reality, forever linking the community and the school? . . .

I t is only a short bus ride from the University of Wisconsin-Milwaukee to the corner of Locust Street and Humboldt Boulevard in the heart of Milwaukee's Riverwest neighborhood. A racially diverse area in a steadfastly segregated city, it's located across the river that separates the comfortable suburbs along the northeast shore from the working-class neighborhoods and factories of the city to the west. Known for its tree-lined streets and "Milwaukee bungalows"—small clapboard homes with big front porches—Riverwest is where you'll find Woodland Pattern Book Center, across the street from a coin laundry, just a few steps from a storefront with a faded Tai Chi sign.

But the front of Woodland Pattern isn't faded. Its façade throbs with color and shapes, patterns that reflect and amplify its surroundings. Step inside and you'll find row upon row of books, binders, and soft-cover pamphlets, walls covered with unfamiliar titles. A maze of rooms opens, each one filled with a plethora of literary choices. Two children giggle in a corner, three teenagers with interesting piercings study a photograph in the gallery at the back of the building, and an elderly man quietly reads by the front door. In the center—the still center—is Anne Kingsbury, a small woman with long graying braids, who has run Woodland Pattern since the late 1970s.

The brochure at the front desk says Woodland Pattern exists to bridge the gap "between the creation of art and its communication, revealing and celebrating the contemporary." In practical terms it is a nonprofit center for small-press contemporary literature and poetry. (It has more than 15,000 titles, including special sections of works by African American, Asian, feminist, gay, Hispanic, and Native American writers.) Early on, Woodland Pattern discovered that offering new works by unknown writers wasn't enough to bring readers in. People need to learn more about contemporary culture, and so partnerships with the public library, schools, community groups, and ethnic centers, combined with public readings, workshops, and art exhibits, created an enterprise that now employs half a dozen people to coordinate the more than 50 events held every year.

A veteran of community collaboration—including partnerships with many faculty at UWM—Kingsbury knows how challenging, and how rewarding, it can be. When she read about the new chancellor and her Milwaukee Idea in the local paper, she decided she wanted to become involved, to help strengthen ties with the university, and to help "institutionalize" a pattern of engagement she believed could benefit the university and the community. She signed on as community liaison for the Cultures and Communities Action Team.

A Case Study in Partnership

One of Kingsbury's creative university partnerships was with Professor Lane Hall, then chair of the Art Department at UWM, and Lisa Moline, the person behind Woodland Pattern's striking façade. Hall had been researching large computer-generated murals and found Woodland Pattern a willing canvas. A class he offered on creating 40-foot murals from a standard desktop computer soon began meeting at the center because "just the shift in architecture forces students to get out into the community," Hall said. "When you're dealing with the aesthetics of neighborhoods—of different cultural groups—it brings up issues of patience, of listening, of not imposing points of view."

The partnership took off and soon Hall and Moline's students, with help from Kingsbury and her staff, had connected with the local elementary school and adults from Woodland Pattern's weekend workshops to use their new graphic skills to create community histories. Local businesses were approached to help with upgrading the printing equipment, and a grant from Microsoft helped the partnership create a public art project for Milwaukee.

For Hall, the relationship succeeded because it worked for everyone. "I see research, service and teaching as a very malleable triangle where one thing flows into another," he said. "Approaching all of these with open questions..."

and trying to figure out where the points of connection and power are. . . . I think really exciting things can happen with that."

THE COMMUNITY RESPONDS

Kingsbury was not the only community member inspired to join The Milwaukee Idea. Affinity Groups, community vetting sessions, Action and Evaluation Teams, Advisory Councils—all attracted literally hundreds of community members eager to work with the university. Many heard about the initiative through reports in the local newspapers, everything from the *Business Journal* to the weekly *Milwaukee Community Journal.* "Chancellor Seeks New Role for UWM" read the headline in the daily *Milwaukee Journal Sentinel.* Reading about UWM was indeed news because for so long local coverage of the university had been minimal. When Chancellor Zimpher arrived and was pictured on the front page wearing a Wisconsin cheesehead hat at a university event, press interest was piqued. Six months into her tenure, and countless newspaper, radio, and television interviews later, UWM, Nancy Zimpher, and The Milwaukee Idea were linked in the minds of both the campus and community.

And so when UWM invited the community to participate, people responded. For some, like Kingsbury, it was an opportunity to help the university create ways to form valuable partnerships that would help metropolitan Milwaukee. For others, like Johna Rogovin, then director of the Southeastern Wisconsin Community Health Charities, it was an opportunity to think creatively about community challenges as a member of an Action Team, and link her own organization more closely with

> "I returned to Milwaukee in late 1994 after living in California for ten years. To me, Milwaukee is on the move in a good way. . . . I believe The Milwaukee Idea has made a significant difference in Milwaukee, even though it still is in its infancy."
>
> —*Johna Rogovin*
> *community participant*

UWM. "I thought my experience [in the health care field] would be useful to the team," she said.

Steve Holt of the Milwaukee Jobs Initiative believed The Milwaukee Idea could help increase economic opportunity in Milwaukee's central city. Michael Morgan felt that he could offer the perspective of the private sector in service to the university.

Business leaders Sheldon Lubar and Roger Fitzsimonds, members of the Chancellor's Corporate Council, an advisory group of area CEOs who meet quarterly to provide guidance to the chancellor, saw The Milwaukee Idea as a vehicle for strengthening the academic status of the university. They wanted

UWM to "become a player" in the civic life of Milwaukee and offered their ties to the business community to help.

Wisconsin State Senators Rick Grobschmidt and Alberta Darling, both members of the Senate Education Committee, were active in Affinity Groups because they saw new potential for UWM to impact education across the state. And alumnus Ted La Tour, a financial planner, figured The Milwaukee Idea would finally give UWM the respect it deserved. Many others just wanted to see what the chancellor was doing and what all the excitement was about.

"The Milwaukee Idea seems like a new avenue for a community that's weary of long-term problems and not sure where to go," Jean Tyler said. "This is a rallying point."

THE HARD REALITIES OF PARTNERSHIP

The level of community awareness and excitement generated by The Milwaukee Idea was, perhaps, a measure of how much the community wanted to be more involved with campus—and how infrequently that happened. Timothy Sheehy, president of the Metropolitan Milwaukee Association of Commerce (MMAC), observed that while UWM's School of Business Administration was active, the university as a whole was an "under-utilized asset."

True Community-University

Engagement means:
- two-way partnerships
- a commitment to sharing and reciprocity
- mutual respect

Characterized by:
- problems defined together
- shared goals agendas, and definitions of success
- pooling of university and community resources
    —Kellogg Commission
    "The Engaged University"

Robyn Mayrl, a vice president for program development at the Helen Bader Foundation, believed the community was "hungry and anxious" for an engaged university. "The timing was right," she said, for the campus and community to come together.

While many individual faculty members, departments, and even whole schools had community initiatives of long standing, campus observers commented on the overall "cultural isolation of the university." One Action Team member who joined his group in an effort to become more familiar with the university said "institutionally there are no connections" to the city. That lack of connection also extended to within the university itself. Mayrl likes to tell about the meeting with UWM faculty that several foundations convened to discuss possible collaboration. Most of the conversation was among the faculty, who "were tripping over each other, meeting and learning about what their colleagues were doing on campus. They had no idea what others on campus were doing. It was pretty striking," she said.

Learning about collaboration involved—and continues to involve— more than figuring out who to invite to a planning meeting. "There's an awful lot of rhetoric about involving the community," Tyler noted. "But in a lot of instances, it doesn't happen. Inviting one or two people who happen to work in the community, to be the 'community rep,' just does not do it."

As James Austin of the Harvard Business School notes, collaboration across different sectors—like education and business or education and civic organizations—"involves entrepreneurial and managerial challenges of the highest order." He outlines the "Seven 'C's' of strategic collaboration," guidelines that UWM was not always successful in following. They include:

1) Connecting with people and with purpose

2) Clarity of purpose

3) Congruency of mission and values

4) Creating value

5) Communicating

6) Continual learning

7) Commitment to the partnership[1]

Efforts were made throughout the first 24 months of The Milwaukee Idea to "connect with clarity" and to "communicate better" by moving beyond token inclusion and involving as many community members as possible. Media reports, speaking engagements, fliers, radio broadcasts, neighborhood mailings, and personal invitations all combined to enlarge—somewhat—the pool of community participants beyond the "usual suspects."

All groups, from Affinity Groups to Evaluation Teams, had community members, although meetings scheduled on academic and not real-world time often meant scattered attendance. The Cultures and Communities Action Team, for example, was one of the most open, constantly striving to enlarge the conversation and involve the community. Kingsbury admitted, however, that at times she was the only community person at a meeting.

Other groups sought to get around meeting conflicts by holding online discussions and using email. But the electronic tools taken for granted by faculty and students often are unavailable to small nonprofits or inner-city residents. Affinity and Action Team leaders—as well as The Milwaukee Idea office—were forced to discover alternatives to keeping everyone involved—in itself a positive learning exercise for the university.

As Kingsbury said, "In theory email is a wonderful tool. In the field, you know that you may have to do phone calls as well as letters and notices." The university may have the ideas and expertise, but the community "knows what has to be done. And we make sure it gets done."

Community partners bring a sense of reality to the partnership, which can be valuable to the university. As one of the members of the Technology Center Action Team noted, the professors on his team were clearly well educated and intelligent, but they occasionally "missed the obvious practical stuff."

Determining how the community could contribute to The Milwaukee Idea was an ongoing challenge and invigorating opportunity. Tyler was the sole community member of her Affinity Group, but "they grew to like me," she said with a smile. "It was all right with them that I was there because I didn't seem to hurt them any. And sometimes I had things to say they thought were useful." Useful indeed. By the end of the process, Tyler was the acknowledged spokesperson for the group, the neutral peacekeeper for the sometimes stormy academic discussions.

Other community members fared less well. Kingsbury was informed by a faculty member that her community perspective did not hold equal weight with the academic one. "Of course you're not equal, we all know that," she was told. While this comment sparked debate within the group, it pointed up a fundamental difficulty in forging community-university partnerships.

A perception of inequality can be the death knell for a collaboration, as David Chrislip and Carl Larson write in their book, *Collaborative Leadership*. In their list of conditions for a collaboration to succeed, "strong stakeholder groups" is number two in a list of ten.[2] This was born out in the various Milwaukee Idea groups. Those teams that gave community members equal voice, encouraged more than token community involvement, or who had influential civic leaders able to balance university perspectives, resulted in partnerships that flourished. When groups had only one or two active community members, or university leadership that was unwilling or unable to involve them effectively, the outcomes of the group lacked important connections that would have made them stronger.

Another Action Team member remarked that he was given the unmistakable message that the community should not advocate anything that would interfere with the "real work" of the university. He sensed that, for many faculty, community partnerships are fine in theory, but only if the community's

"I realize that community demands often seem irrational or even bizarre—too many voices, too many variables, questionable commitment to long-term investigation. But we have to find a way to bridge this underlying cultural divide."
—*Action Team participant*

needs fit with a particular professor's professional pursuits. "To the university personnel, this is axiomatic. To me, it is thoroughly confounding," he said.

This divide between community and university perspectives is not unique to UWM, of course, or even to higher education. Collaboration is hard work, no matter the mix of groups or individuals involved. As Suzanne Morse, executive director of the Pew Partnership for Civic Change, writes, "Collaboration takes time away from prescribed responsibilities, it has an element of change that frightens people facing shrinking resources, and it frightens people personally because it challenges what they do and with whom they do it."[3]

Communication between university and community is vital because too often community members have unrealistic expectations about what the university brings to the partnership. Many community members came to The Milwaukee Idea expecting UWM faculty to provide everything from volunteer labor to large donations. According to Rose McManus, a former vice president for housing impact at Fannie Mae, universities need guiding principles and consistent communication to guard against raising expectations that can't be met.[4]

Most faculty, like most people, are comfortable working with their peers. They have devoted their careers to working independently so that their work can benefit their students and their community. Clark Kerr once defined a modern university as "an assemblage of faculty entrepreneurs held together by a common grievance over parking,"[5] a topic that has indeed brought together many at UWM. For many faculty, burdened with large classes, dwindling research support, and the competitive march to tenure, investing time and energy in a community alliance that has no guarantee of success is not a realistic option.

"Because we're a research university, we have to develop faculty that can work on a variety of levels—locally, nationally, and internationally," said UWM History Professor Margo Anderson. "You can't devote careers to The Milwaukee Idea at the expense of securing professional standards. The Milwaukee Idea has chewed up an awful lot of people's time. Only senior faculty can do that without falling on their own personal swords." As a former chancellor of UWM said, "Our job is not to save downtown. Our job is to provide an education to students and to run an academic institution."

At the same time, the taxpayers who support a public institution feel that they have a legitimate claim to help set the priorities of the university. The traditions of The Wisconsin Idea are based on a symbiotic relationship between academy and community: The needs of the community and the expertise of the faculty would create an institution worthy of its students. For many, it is not a question of either "save the downtown" or "provide an education," but "do both."

TAKING THE COMMUNITY SERIOUSLY

Zelda Gamson and others have argued that higher education will be reinvigorated when it becomes a more serious player in rebuilding the civic life of the United States. But to do that, it first needs to rebuild its relationship with its communities "in a way that takes them seriously." This will involve recognizing the value of community participation. "We must recognize that communities are not voids to be organized and filled by the more knowledgeable; they are well-developed, complex and sophisticated organisms that demand to be understood on their own terms—or they will not cooperate,"[6] Gamson writes.

> "You don't do public service to people. It's a partnership."
> —*Frank Horton*
> *Former chancellor of UWM speaking at The Milwaukee Idea 1999 conference*

In Kingsbury's words, it means treating community partners as equals, not suppliants—something UWM, like most universities, is still learning. Allen Zweben, Joan Wilk, and Hector Cruz-Feliciano of Healthy Choices worked hard to make the community members of their Action Team feel like equal participants. The interdisciplinary nature of their leadership (Wilk was from the School of Nursing, Zweben from the Helen Bader School of Social Welfare, and Cruz-Feliciano was a student) set a tone of cooperation that was mirrored by the group as a whole. Zweben, Wilk, and Cruz-Feliciano made community participation a priority and structured their process to keep everyone involved. There was no preconceived agenda, and the community helped develop the questions on which the team focused.

"I think that the community felt valued by us," Zweben said. "That was a very different experience for them. They usually have not felt that way in the university." The results were "amazing." New networks of community contacts have opened up a wealth of research possibilities and new opportunities for community health promotion.

"We've talked about a whole public health orientation I wasn't even thinking about," Zweben said, his voice excited. "This really gave us an opportunity to look into the future and say, 'this is what our community really needs.'"

LET'S DO MORE

For community members, The Milwaukee Idea opened new resources on a campus many had not even visited. Rogovin, who worked on the Healthy Choices team, reconnected with the university. "I believe The Milwaukee Idea has made a significant difference in Milwaukee, even though it is still in its infancy," she said. "I think there are many people like myself who have a renewed interest in the university and want to be part of this ambitious idea. This is something that will be enduring."

Henry Monaco, former president of the United Way of Greater Milwaukee, also found his work on the Consortium for Economic Opportunity Action Team to be "totally invigorating." As UWM embraced the community, he said, the community embraced UWM in a whole new way. "If we're really going to make change here, we need to do a lot more of this kind of collaboration."

Creating change can be difficult, however, especially when it involves partners unused to working together. Even when faculty and community found common ground in their Idea, their expectations for results often clashed. Steve Holt, of the Milwaukee Jobs Initiative, joined his Action Team because he believed Chancellor Zimpher would support innovative university approaches to economic development. It was a "chance to break some eggs," as he said. Others on the team, aware of real or potential university constraints, were more conservative in their approach, seeking to work within existing university structures.

While recreating the entire academic culture was not the goal of The Milwaukee Idea, in some cases the internal bureaucracy became a damper for community enthusiasm. "It was definitely a challenge to work with university politics," as Bonnie Sumner, an Action Team member and community consultant, delicately put it.

Some community participants felt that the chancellor's charge to the Action Teams to "take the wraps off and work in new and novel ways" was stymied by a university culture intent on preserving the status quo. Leaving the Action Teams alone to work independently during the summer may have provided the freedom the groups needed, but periodic motivation by the chancellor or Milwaukee Idea Office staff perhaps would have helped the groups think more aggressively. "Timid should not be part of the game plan," Holt said.

The academic penchant for analysis and reflection also bumped up against the community inclination to move forward. "More goal-oriented" is how architect Hanewell characterized the community perspective. Community members were frustrated by an unwillingness on the part of university staff to assume accountability for results. Reflecting on the divergent perspectives, one participant characterized it as the difference between focusing on process or on results. As he put it, "When the future of a city and its residents is at stake, I'll take the latter."

Two Perspectives on Community Partnership
By Jean Tyler, community leader and Milwaukee Idea participant

"Imagine." With that strong, one-word directive, UWM Chancellor Zimpher launched an unusual enterprise to create a community-university partnership culture that could "make things happen" on a scale not usually possible. Two years into this bold initiative, I am encouraged and excited by the several complex partnerships that have developed from this demanding challenge, and by the commitment of many Milwaukee folks, inside and outside the university, to use The Milwaukee Idea process to move both sectors in new directions.

> "More experience will, I believe, suggest that complex partnerships depend upon relationships that continue long enough to develop understanding and trust."
> —Jean Tyler

As a community participant and group facilitator, I've had a unique opportunity to work closely with two of these Milwaukee Idea efforts—one initiated by the university and one by the community. These two planning efforts had much in common: timing (approximately six months), participants (volunteers), format (small- and large-group meetings), and product (a written report containing recommendations). There were, however, some differences that may hold useful insights for future efforts.

The university-based initiative—the Frontiers of Knowledge Affinity Group—began with about 30 volunteers from the ranks of faculty, academic staff, and top administrators. This group defined the issues, provided background and information, and eventually wrote the final recommendations. The process spawned creative dialogue across many diverse campus disciplines, encouraging useful intra-university interaction. I witnessed collegial discussion and debate at its best with much stimulating give-and-take among dissimilar viewpoints. Almost everyone involved felt good about the process and the recommendations it generated.

There was, however, one missing element. Mine was the only voice from the community. This meant little chance to hear or learn from community experts in the subject areas discussed. In my opinion, the absence of diverse, possibly conflicting, community voices at the planning stage left the Ideas without an important reality foundation. Almost a year after this hopeful beginning, the creative and far-reaching Ideas generated through this process have not yet moved into action. It remains unclear whether the difficulties resulting from this initial community "partnership" omission can be overcome.

In contrast, the community-based initiative—the Nonprofit Management Education project, outlined in Chapter 6—began with the community when several well-known nonprofit leaders defined a problem and approached the university about assisting them in finding some solutions, a common sequence for traditional partnerships. By traditional, I mean those partnerships in which one party defines the need, another party provides one or more services, and the recipients are expected to benefit from the exchange.

This time, however, under the umbrella of The Milwaukee Idea, it was decided to invite many interested (or threatened) parties to join the initial discussions of needs, services, and benefits. Somewhat surprisingly in these busy times, almost 100 people from the community, UWM, and several other area colleges and universities accepted the invitation to participate. Given the somewhat unusual approach and the numbers of people who wished to be involved, The Milwaukee Idea hired an experienced community facilitator to oversee the planning.

The resulting participant diversity spawned an eclectic process marked by interest, energy, and a wealth of information. It also brought out misunderstandings, even mistrust. Former antagonisms, turf battles, ego, and politics all surfaced early in the process. Some participants worried that the pace was too rapid, while others complained that progress seemed too slow. "Too much diversity," huffed some; "Not inclusive enough," warned others. University participants sometimes felt unwelcome and unappreciated as community factions reacted negatively to each other and to the university. Yet a majority of participants stayed with the process, and at the end many, though not all, endorsed the final recommendations.

Within a month after publication of the recommendations from this sometimes collaborative, often confusing process, a new board, including agreed-upon university and community representatives, was formed to begin moving these Ideas into action. In my opinion, the process produced some listening, some learning, and some trust-building that had not existed before—all essential ingredients if a vision is to be translated into successful community-university action.

Has either approach succeeded? Not yet. To succeed, Ideas must be translated into actions that are useful in solving real-world problems. Is one approach better than the other? Not necessarily. The university-initiated process was easier, more straightforward but less inclusive. The community-initiated process involved many people and much information but was less visionary and often contentious. A group's ability to envision, while essential, is not enough. A group also must be able to share, change, and accept risks. Above all, a group must persevere long enough to see things tried and evaluated.

If this partnership business were easy, we would not need to work so hard, nor would we fail so frequently. The Milwaukee Idea invites us to try again and again until we succeed. Imagine!

THE JURY IS STILL OUT

When asked to assess their involvement in The Milwaukee Idea, every community participant interviewed felt that the exercise had been a positive one—in varying degrees. Some learned more about the internal workings of the university than they wanted to know, and some were keenly disappointed by the critical or defensive behavior of faculty to community perspectives. All believed, however, that The Milwaukee Idea was an effective beginning to a continuing relationship that would be valuable for city and campus alike.

Key to their support was trust in the integrity of the chancellor to remain true to the original vision and to create change. "Chancellor Zimpher's leadership has raised UWM's profile considerably and created cautious optimism in the community," Holt said.

The MMAC's Timothy Sheehy agrees. The key to raising the visibility of the university in the community was not only her tireless outreach, but also her ability to energize the university as a whole. "It goes beyond the chancellor," Sheehy said. "She also brought others to the table to actively participate. She opened the door to the university as a resource."

Robyn Mayrl goes further. She believes that it was the chancellor's willingness to take a risk and reach out to the community—"be vulnerable, and make us vulnerable with her," that has inspired many individuals and organizations to take risks, too. "I think what she's done has helped a lot of us say,

'Okay, if you're going to do it, we'll try too,'" Mayrl said. "We may all go down together, but at least we're going to give it a try!"

The effects of The Milwaukee Idea partnerships already have begun to spill over to other partnerships as well. The Milwaukee Partnership Academy for Teacher Quality is a collaboration of Milwaukee Public Schools leaders, representatives from the teachers' association, UWM, business, and the Milwaukee Area Technical College, focused on training for urban teachers. The Academy came together as new partnerships were being forged with the educational community. Early results of the partnership are promising. According to Sam Carmen, executive director of the Milwaukee Teachers' Education Association, working with the Milwaukee Public Schools (MPS) on the Partnership Academy has produced real results. Relationships between MPS and the union that were historically strained were given new life. Working together on the Partnership Academy "changed the way the union and MPS came to the bargaining table," Carmen said.

Jean Tyler worries, however, that the practice of partnering has not yet trickled down into the warp and woof of the university. "A lot of us believe at this point it's totally dependent on the chancellor. It would not survive without her, because it's so new." Other community leaders echo the fear that not all faculty are on board—and that they're missing out because they haven't become more involved.

But as the months pass, and as the First Ideas are launched, the university is slowly learning how to change, and to prove itself. While it's safe to say some people are saying, "Show me the deliverables," others recognize that UWM is doing things differently.

"UWM has come to the forefront with resources," Mayrl said. "There is a cadre of faculty members that are really committed and bring a lot of energy and excitement. The university is finally at the point where it can say, 'We don't have all the answers either, but we would like to work in partnership with you.'"

According to Tyler, The Milwaukee Idea has helped the university get better at collaborating. It has learned by doing. "People are learning how to involve each other," she said. Those individuals already involved in community partnerships have discovered "wonderful new avenues" for work through The Milwaukee Idea. "It's been very powerful," Tyler said. Others are learning who to contact in the community. And the university now has a pool of individuals with partnering skills with which to "sprinkle other planning processes."

Taking Small Steps

But Kingsbury has no illusions about the path ahead. It will be measured in small steps, individual victories, and painstaking relationship building. The "educational process from within" has been a valuable one for the university, she believes. "The Milwaukee Idea has brought a real sense of anticipation to the university. There's the possibility of good things to come," she said. "I really believe in the crawl of faith. I don't think you're going to get immediately large things happening. I think you have to build step-by-step. I'm a beader and a quilter, so I work in very small increments and after awhile you've built something. Maybe that's the way The Milwaukee Idea is going to be successful."

From the community's perspective, The Milwaukee Idea's greatest challenge lies in how well it becomes a measure of the way the university operates. Wendy Werkmeister, president of The Wisconsin Women's Business Initiative Corporation, has her office next door to the newly opened Consortium for Economic Opportunity offices, in the heart of Milwaukee. She summed up community expectations when she remarked recently, "The community is ready. . . . Is the university?"

Chapter 8 Summary

What UWM Should Learn About Collaborating

Previous chapters include summaries of lessons we've learned through The Milwaukee Idea. For this chapter on community perspectives, we've included lessons we've heard the community tell us we should learn about collaborating.

1) **Be an equal partner.** Too often the university comes to the table with an agenda or as leader. Community partnerships require that all participants have an equal voice in creating the partnership and measuring success.

2) **Be accessible.** The university has tremendous resources, but they're often difficult to connect to. Find ways to link more easily.

3) **Be accountable.** Research and scholarship is inherent to the university, but the community is interested in results. As a partner, the university is accountable for action as well as ideas.

4) **Be open.** The community has much to contribute to the partnership, and much to contribute to the university as well. Both sides benefit from partnership.

5) **Be tolerant.** Community partners deal with their own political and personal realities, which come to the partnership table as well.

Endnotes

[1] James E. Austin. (2000). *The Collaboration Challenge: How Nonprofits and Businesses Succeed Through Strategic Alliances.* San Francisco: Jossey-Bass, page 173.

[2] David Chrislip and Carl Larson. (1994). *Collaborative Leadership: How Citizens and Civic Leaders Can Make a Difference.* San Francisco: Jossey-Bass, page 52.

[3] From a 1996 Wingspread Briefing by Suzanne Morse, Executive Director of the Pew Partnership for Civic Change, sponsored by The Johnson Foundation, Racine, Wisconsin. Excerpted in *The Wingspread Journal, Vol 18, Issue 4,* edited by Mary Jane Brukardt and published by The Johnson Foundation.

[4] Gregory Wegner. (November, 2000). "Strategic Community Partnerships" in *Exemplars,* a companion to *Policy Perspectives,* published by the Knight Higher Education Collaborative.

[5] Ernest Boyer and Fred Hechinger. (1981). *Higher Learning in the Nation's Service: A Carnegie Foundation Essay.* Washington, DC: Carnegie Foundation for the Advancement of Teaching, page 57.

[6] Zelda Gamson. (January/February, 1997). "Higher Education and Rebuilding Civic Life," *Change* magazine, page 13.

MAKE IT REAL:
LAUNCHING THE MILWAUKEE IDEA

From *The Business Journal*, Milwaukee, Wisconsin
Week of June 5, 2000

Bringing The Milwaukee Idea to Reality
Editorial

To date, The Milwaukee Idea has been little more than that—an idea. The project's mission statements are riddled with vague but high-sounding management-babble, such as "create a guiding coalition," "empower people for broad-based action," and "communicate the change vision."

The project's early accomplishments have been cosmetic "quick wins." . . . But Zimpher's vision of a university and a community entwined is about to take a giant step forward with the creation of the Consortium for Economic Opportunity.

The consortium may mark a turning point for Zimpher's Milwaukee Idea. The Milwaukee Idea is gaining momentum. That demonstration of progress is needed to transform the project from an idea into reality.

On May 22, 2000, the Consortium for Economic Opportunity was officially opened in a restored building on Dr. Martin Luther King Jr. Drive, to "bring the university's resources right into the community where they are needed," as the *Milwaukee Journal Sentinel* wrote. The Consortium joined other tenants that include the Wisconsin Housing and Economic Development Authority and the Wisconsin Women's Business Initiative Corporation (WWBIC).

"I see good things from this," said WWBIC President Wendy Werkmeister. "I see the leveraging of excellent resources in the community and the university."

This wasn't the only Milwaukee Idea project to become reality. Within 24 months of the first Milwaukee Idea plenary session, Cultures and Communities (CC), Healthy Choices, the Global Passport Project, the Milwaukee Partnership Academy for Teacher Quality, the Milwaukee Industrial Innovation Center (the new name for the Technology Center), and Campus Design

Solutions also were launched, to great interest by both the university and Milwaukee. And the community-led Bader Institute for Nonprofit Management opened its doors at the University of Wisconsin-Milwaukee. From fellowships for new CC courses to experimental housing for the central city, the ideas of The Milwaukee Idea were coming alive.

But a press conference, newspaper article, and pictures on television do not necessarily add up to university engagement. And hiring a new director for an academic center marks not the end of the process, but the beginning— the beginning of a long road to transforming rhetoric into action. The kind of action the community will recognize and applaud.

The strength of The Milwaukee Idea was its diversity of ideas and people—the very things that formed its greatest challenge. What worked for one Idea did not necessarily apply to others; a successful strategy for mobilizing change for one Idea would spell failure for another.

For many of the Action Team leaders, the Negotiation process was one they survived, but with cuts and bruises. Dollar requests were invariably sliced, discussions on who would lead the new initiatives were sometimes contentious. The Partnerships for the Environmental Health Idea languished because of disagreements over who would direct it and which school would host it. It was eventually split into two separate Ideas. The Fresh Water Initiative spent months reworking its action plan because it was too ambitious and had not addressed the issue of how to merge leaders at the off-site WATER Institute and those on campus, reflecting a tension that had been festering for years. Agreement over where to house the Global Passport Project was won only after two existing units were reorganized and combined.

But when the dust settled, after the chancellor had held her last closed-door meeting with warring factions and the budgets were signed, what remained were Ideas, some dollars, and some passionate people convinced they could make them work.

And so the launches began. Over the space of six months, the Ideas began to set up shop, hire staff, and begin to implement their plans. Each Idea faced different challenges, yet by looking closely at the first months of "settling in," there are lessons learned that point toward ways in which real change can be implemented in an organization as large and hierarchical as a public university.

The Ideas fell into three categories: 1) those that began an initiative "from scratch," 2) those that were built on an existing academic unit, and 3) those that created a new unit by merging existing ones. Each category has its own challenges, but across these three models are five shared characteristics. All of the successful First Ideas:

1) Put support in place

2) Selected the right leadership

3) Forged strong partnerships

4) Created new structures

5) Learned by doing

Put Support in Place

Never underestimate the importance of dollars to change. It is, says Provost John Wanat, the single most critical element. The Ideas that were able to move forward in concrete ways started with the advantage of sizable external grants, well-funded existing support, or ready access to new sources—beyond the dollars pledged in their UWM budgets. While the promise of UWM money up front was vital to producing results and creating community trust, additional external dollars gave the Ideas a running start.

Just as important was a good sense of how to use those dollars well. Cultures and Communities strategically used seed money to encourage faculty involvement in curriculum development and to jump-start community partnerships. Small amounts awarded through short-term fellowships to faculty and community committed to the project paid off in results and a growing base of support.

Campus Design Solutions kept its budget lean but was able to draw on existing partnerships to leverage community dollars for individual projects. Using relationships already established by the School of Architecture and Urban Planning (which had been active in the community for many years), Campus Design could connect new projects with vendors, supporters, and community consultants instead of investing its own dollars. This helped not only to conserve funds, but also to involve a wider net of participants in Milwaukee Idea projects.

Select the Right Leaders

As dedicated to their Idea as many of the Action Team leaders were, not everyone stayed on as project leader. What was more important than a history with the Idea was a passion for it. All the leaders brought their unique vision to implementation and a style of leadership suited to its needs—which varied. Bob Greenstreet of Campus Design Solutions favored an open, network-based style. The Consortium for Economic Opportunity divided duties between its two directors. Greg Jay of Cultures and Communities preferred a team-oriented organization. One size does not fit all, but all leaders were characterized by a willingness to be flexible, inclusive, and creative.

Forge Strong Partnerships

At the heart of The Milwaukee Idea is the notion of partnerships across campus and throughout the community. If there was a critical ingredient for the survival of the First Ideas, it was the ability of each Idea to hone sustaining connections with diverse groups. Author Sally Helgesen calls this kind of network a "web of inclusion," and borrowing from quantum physics says that "identity is inseparable from relationship."[1] So is successful change. The Milwaukee Idea partnerships took many forms, from the network of community advisors who continued with Cultures and Communities after its launch, to an international group of scholars who supported the Milwaukee Industrial Innovation Center, to the collaborations of students and faculty on Campus Design Solutions' projects.

Create a New Structure

Each of the First Ideas needed to create an infrastructure that was supportive of individual goals and working style. For some like Healthy Choices, which grew out of an existing university center, the structure was clearly defined and helped to give shape to the new organization. The Nonprofit Management Education project spent months studying other models to determine how best to create an organization that would be able to support the nonprofit community.

Other initiatives, like Campus Design Solutions, were more loosely organized with an emphasis on flexible response to new situations. A team of students and faculty was pulled together to address specific needs, then disbanded when the project concluded. Each successful Idea, however, was able to capitalize on existing infrastructures, or move quickly to get operations up and running.

Learn by Doing

For five months, 200 people labored over Affinity proposals. For another five, specialized Action Teams analyzed the Ideas and set forth workable plans. For another six months, administrators and external reviewers assessed the Ideas and developed infrastructure to support them. Despite the planning, visioning, and nitty-gritty details, when the signs went up over the doors of the First Ideas, the real world called the shots.

Leaders learned to be creative, dissolve, and rework on the fly, continuing The Milwaukee Idea's founding principle borrowed from Michael Fullan to get "Ready, Fire, then Aim!" As Bob Greenstreet, dean of the School of Architecture and Urban Planning and head of Campus Design Solutions said, "It's the human interaction that helps determine your rules." Which, of course, are constantly changing.

What follows is a closer look at how each start-up model illustrated these five characteristics.

START AN IDEA FROM SCRATCH

Cultures and Communities

UWM's Curtin Hall is a nine-story concrete tower, home to the Departments of English, Foreign Languages and Linguistics, Philosophy, and the Center for Twenty-first Century Studies. Its maze of hallways lead to a warren of faculty offices, where two small second-floor rooms were designated the home for Cultures and Communities. Behind the bookshelves and desks and boxes of printed brochures, Director Greg Jay, Assistant Director Sandra Jones, Office Manager Michael Lowry, and two Teachers-in-Residence from the Milwaukee Public Schools began to transform learning at UWM.

The lean staff and cramped quarters belie CC's fiscal resources. Thanks to a partnership with the School of Education and a major U.S. Department of Education grant, CC had five years of funding in place before it had administrative approval to proceed as a Milwaukee Idea. With a financial safety net in place, CC hit the ground running, completing UWM negotiations in December 1999, opening its small office in January 2000, hosting a community conference in August, and offering its first course in September. The secret?

"We worked our butts off," Jay said. "All 50 of us." The 50 are the network of community and campus people who had formed the basis of the Action Team and who, thanks to Jay's aggressively inclusive management style, continued to remain actively involved in getting CC operational and steering its direction.

> **Cultures and Communities**
>
> An all-university curriculum that speaks to a distinctly urban setting, interacting with the metropolitan community.
>
> Students who participate in this one-of-a-kind curriculum are exposed to all aspects of the community, from within the classroom and without. CC blends community-based experience and service learning with traditional academics. It brings together students and educators of diverse backgrounds, ages, and races to learn from each other.
>
> During its first year, CC developed and offered two courses, funded faculty fellowships to develop others, and offered mini-grants to community-faculty collaborative projects.

CC leadership was creative and mission-focused. Jay was one of only a few individuals who were involved in The Milwaukee Idea from its first plenary session through final launch. He began as a skeptic and ended up running an initiative to create a campus-wide alternative General Education

Requirement (GER) program. (The GER is the list of required courses all students must complete—usually during their first two years—to obtain their bachelor's degree.) What drove his involvement was a dedication to what he saw as his ultimate goal: serving students. He had a clear sense of mission, so the implementation fell into place.

His implementation, however, was fueled by a keen understanding of what he termed "the coin of the realm." Jay knew what worked with faculty and campus staff.

"To get buy-in, you've got to do buyout," he said, referring to the CC faculty fellowships that sponsored curriculum development and to the mini-grants awarded to community/faculty partnership projects. Faculty were awarded small grants to help develop courses that aligned with the goals of the new Cultures and Communities curriculum. Jay recognized that faculty and community participation would be enhanced if their contributions were rewarded. "You have to give money away, even to outside groups," he said. "You can't be competitive; it's the kiss of death to new ideas." When people support the new initiative, "you fund what they want to do."

The buyouts worked. Thirteen faculty fellowships were awarded the first year to encourage development of courses with a cross-cultural focus and innovative pedagogy. Those courses would be woven into a roster of CC courses until enough were developed to form the core of a proposed alternative GER. Fellowship recipients were from departments across the campus, from health science to film, anthropology to occupational therapy.

The first class, "Introduction to Multicultural America," was launched to test student and faculty response. Master teachers from Milwaukee Public Schools joined Jay and Jones in providing 30 students with a wide-ranging, multicultural experience—everything from tours of the Black Holocaust Museum to presentations by Chicano film makers. "We bridged theory and practice... we made it real," said master teacher Darryl Terrell of the teaching experience.

In addition, nine mini-grants were given to faculty-community projects that included public presentations of contemporary African films and an oral history project in one of the city's oldest neighborhoods. Response to the second round of funding was even more enthusiastic.

Funding small projects, starting a curriculum with a single course, and encouraging existing pockets of interest is, in Jay's words, a "grassroots approach to reform." Believing that evolution is more powerful than revolution, Jay's team consciously modeled CC after The Milwaukee Idea Affinity Groups—small groups of diverse individuals, working creatively on focused projects. Together they build a foundation—and momentum—for change.

"The wrong thing to do would have been to get a small group of people to write up a curriculum on a napkin and try to drive it through the governance structure," Jay said. "We resolved to build a program through a series of initiatives and experiments so that we could see what worked, what faculty wanted, and what students responded to." It's a long-term process that it's hoped will bring long-term change.

The Helen Bader Institute for Nonprofit Management

While CC was started from scratch, it nonetheless was framed within an existing structure: the academic culture. The Helen Bader Institute for Nonprofit Management, on the other hand, was truly "homeless." A community-initiated Idea (see Chapter 6 for a description of how this Idea was started), it had the enviable task of literally creating itself from the ground up. Supported by the philanthropic community, its collaboration of funders, universities, and nonprofits came to consensus on the Idea only after many months of wary debate.

It was decided that UWM would be the new Institute's temporary home, opening an office within The Milwaukee Idea, with ties to the School of Business Administration. But first, the university had to prove itself a trustworthy partner. Robyn Mayrl, of the Helen Bader Foundation and a key community liaison to the project, recalls that initially the university "wasn't even on the radar screen." The planning process, as arduous as it was, became the opportunity for the nonprofits to see UWM as a credible partner with important resources—among them, creative faculty, strong curriculum, and national connections to research. Like CC, it was the partnerships forged throughout the planning process—across a truly broad range of nonprofit, educational, and philanthropic organizations—that formed the core of the new Idea's support.

> **The Helen Bader Institute for Nonprofit Management**
>
> The Institute aims to strengthen the community's nonprofit sector with programs that promote effective management and leadership.
> Its goals are:
> - to develop degree, non-degree, and continuing education courses
> - provide technical assistance to nonprofits in the areas of human resources, financial management, fund development, and planning
> - strengthen diversity—locally and nationally—in the nonprofit sector
> - generate new knowledge about nonprofit management

"We've been at the table continuously and I think that we've all contributed to the conversation," said Rita Cheng, who, as associate dean of the School of Business Administration, had played an active role in representing UWM. "Through that time, we've become a team."

Just as CC gained launch momentum through early grants, the Institute for Nonprofit Management was buoyed by almost $2 million in funding from the Helen Bader Foundation and other area foundations to set up shop, staff it, and begin introducing educational programs in support of nonprofit leadership. The foundations had been leaders in promoting and developing the Idea, and their financial support signaled vital community support.

"We want to make sure that the Institute has the resources that it needs, especially during its start-up period" Mayrl said. "We don't want it to be dependent on soft money, focused only on grant-writing. We want to give it a chance to really fly."

Preparing to soar also involves focusing on leadership. One of the first things the newly-named Helen Bader Institute for Nonprofit Management did was to underwrite a community planning initiative to focus on organizational issues, goals, and priorities. Strategic planning was built into its leadership model.

Milwaukee Industrial Innovation Center

Leadership also involves more intangible measures. The ability to supply creative energy for an initiative was a common factor across all the Ideas. William Gregory, dean of the College of Engineering and Applied Science, is a gregarious and infectious storyteller and idea generator—the perfect head for the Milwaukee Industrial Innovation Center, another of The Milwaukee Ideas that started "from scratch."

The Center did not exist before The Milwaukee Idea process. It was an Idea that came out of the Frontiers of Knowledge Affinity Group, which called for a "technology transfer center" at UWM. The idea was shepherded by William Rayburn, dean of the Graduate School, until Gregory was hired with the express purpose of also heading up this Milwaukee Idea. A physicist, lawyer, philosopher, and business consultant "with a bunch of patents," Gregory came to The Milwaukee Idea with an eye for the potential of business connections—and business opportunities.

Milwaukee Industrial Innovation Center

Drawing on the University of Wisconsin-Milwaukee's substantial research capability, the Center fosters technology innovation and helps generate new business and jobs in the city and across the state. The center:

- Provides technical training and intellectual property support services to help commercialize innovations in bioengineering, software development, and information technology
- Has a focus on intelligent maintenance systems, supported by an international collaboration of business and higher education institutions

And so, even as the Center was assembling staff, he reached out to make two evolving initiatives part of his efforts. A new research venture at UWM for Intelligent Maintenance Systems (IMS) was among the first of the Center's contributions. TechStar, a separate community initiative focused on providing research expertise from area universities to the region's diverse clusters of business and industry, offered future opportunities for partnerships with the Center. Both projects had UWM ties and fit nicely within the goals of technology transfer set for this Idea.

This creative approach to growth also offered financial advantages: IMS came with a stable of Fortune 500 underwriters and federal funders promising almost $1 million, and TechStar was attracting significant local and state dollars. Both projects also offered connections into the business community this Idea had targeted. Like CC and the Center for Nonprofit Management, the Milwaukee Industrial Innovation Center was able to quickly produce results and connect with critical supporters.

SECTION SUMMARY

How do you launch a transforming Idea from scratch?

1) **Select leaders** who know the environment and know how to partner.

2) **Focus on providing adequate and long-term dollars** for the project so efforts aren't diverted by fund-raising.

3) **Use the carrot rather than the stick.** Find what interests key supporters, then give them the resources, time, support, and dollars they need to help advance the goals of the initiative.

4) **Evolve.** Don't be afraid to take small steps, test results, regroup, and build.

5) **Dynamic leadership is important** for new projects to help gain visibility and keep momentum.

6) **Reach out creatively.** Look for existing projects that are a good fit and bring needed dollars, expertise, or opportunities.

Quick Wins Revived

One of the original Affinity Groups was called "Quick Wins," tasked with soliciting ideas from campus for small projects that could be implemented quickly and inexpensively (see Chapter 5). It began with a series of small initiatives, but then languished for lack of staff support until Negotiations began. That's when René Gratz, the Knowledge Fest Action Team leader, decided to rekindle Quick Wins while she waited for the go-ahead on her Idea. She updated the name—Quick WINS (Ways to Implement New Solutions) and, armed with a file box of suggestions, she plunged in.

A Quick WINS committee with members from across campus was selected to provide help in directing the suggestions that continued to come from across the schools and colleges. They included everything from "the doors bang shut in the Fine Arts Lecture Hall" to "let's put up tables and umbrellas in the Plaza this summer."

Soon Gratz had the process down cold. A link on the campus web site allowed anyone to submit a suggestion. Within 24 hours, Gratz sends an acknowledgement advising when the committee meets. Suggestions are measured against four criteria:

1) Quick—can be accomplished within the academic year

2) Affordable—must fit into the relevant unit's budget

3) Beneficial—will improve the campus

4) Positive—will have a good outcome

Gratz advises the submitters about the committee's decision, then forwards qualifying suggestions to relevant managers with a request for a reply within ten days.

Posters and bookmarks across campus advertise the program and more than 100 suggestions are received each year. Thanks to Quick WINS, UWM has improved bike parking on campus, offered Spanish language instruction to medical professionals, listed web sites in the campus directory, and placed convex mirrors at driveway intersections in parking ramps to improve the view of oncoming traffic.

Thanks to Gratz, Quick WINS is back and the campus is the winner.

Transform an Existing Program
Into Something New

From the windows of the cluttered corner office on the tenth floor of UWM's Enderis Hall you can glimpse the steel and brick façade of the School of Architecture and Urban Planning a block away, and the second-floor window that belongs to the dean. These offices are the respective homes of two Milwaukee Ideas: Healthy Choices and Campus Design Solutions. Both grew out of existing programs and faced the similar challenge of how to graft new and bigger Ideas onto already flourishing organizations. Both kept the same leadership, but how they handled the transition was as different as night and day.

Healthy Choices

When the Healthy Choices Action Team proposed an initiative to share research, education, and support with the Milwaukee community around issues of substance abuse, UWM's nationally recognized Center for Addiction and Behavioral Health Research was the natural home for the Idea. Its director, Allen Zweben, had co-chaired the Action Team with Professor Joan Wilk and student Hector Cruz-Feliciano. Zweben's center already was providing research to the community and had strong community partnerships. Healthy Choices would be a natural extension of the Center's work. The trick, of course, was how to graft a new Idea without smothering the old one—or perverting the new.

> **Healthy Choices**
>
> Taking advantage of the collective expertise of the community and the university to address health concerns related to substance use and abuse, this Initiative focuses on sharing strategies for good health.
>
> Healthy Choices oversees research in concert with the community, shares cutting edge information with healthcare providers, is an information clearinghouse for substance abuse resources, screening and referral, and provides educational programs for students on such subjects as binge drinking, stress management, and strategies for making healthy choices.

"I didn't want to destroy the strengths we already had in the Center, " Zweben said. "I've kept intact my consortium, because their goals were always large and, at least so far, they've supported our broader mandate." Keeping this support has involved a clear understanding of both the mission of the Center and the goals of the new Idea—and arranging a productive marriage of the two.

What that has meant for Healthy Choices is a broadening of possibilities as the Center began to expand its reach into areas it might never have considered before. First on the list was a campus-wide survey of student drinking, a project the Center had been unable to tackle in the past. Zweben now had the luxury to refocus on new issues and expand operations. He had plans for a new training institute, a national conference, and new community partnerships. The Center was able to do that with the addition of staff funded through The Milwaukee Idea. And with that staff came a whole new organization.

Divisions, goals, constituencies, boards, and advisory committees—Zweben had the plans for Healthy Choices carefully diagramed, with staff working on research, community health promotion, technology transfer, and grant-writing. The goal was clear: Provide a guiding structure to the new enterprise so there was no confusion about the new Idea or its relationship to the Center.

This structure was important because, during the Negotiation phase, there were questions about which college would house the Center (with its significant Milwaukee Idea funding). The new organizational structure now protects Healthy Choices and provides assurance to the team of deans that oversees it that it can respond across disciplines. In a sense, Zweben's organizational chart was a "firewall," something he admitted he didn't have when, as Action Team leader, he was asked to create Healthy Choices in the face of conflicting requests from deans.

Fortunately, the budget struggle that characterized the early days of the Deans Council was resolved, resulting in the creation of a pool of funding to staff Healthy Choices with an interdisciplinary team that enriched the expertise of the Center. Zweben also actively involved members of his former Action Team to include community perspectives in setting the direction for the Center.

Campus Design Solutions

Campus Design Solutions focuses on improving the physical environment of campuses in the University of Wisconsin System and their neighborhoods. It brings together groups from the university and community to explore issues of mutual concern.

Housed in UWM's School of Architecture and Urban Planning, projects include a neighborhood plan with university community members, assessment of the use of public space on the UWM campus, design and renovation recommendations for Milwaukee Public Schools, and creation of a system to monitor energy use at a visitor's center at the Schlitz Audubon Center.

Campus Design Solutions
Bob Greenstreet, head of Campus Design Solutions, agrees with Zweben that organization is the key to successfully grafting a new Idea onto an existing program.

"If you've got the structure right, everything else follows," he said. Not a surprising statement for an architect, yet Greenstreet's vision of structure is diametrically opposed to Zweben's. Campus Design created an organizational plan that was an amorphous, highly flexible, permeable network of just-in-time teams to handle new projects as needed.

Like Zweben, Greenstreet was also an Action Team leader, heading up Campus Design Solutions. As dean of the School of Architecture and Urban Planning, the idea of providing design and planning expertise in service to the campus, neighborhood, and statewide system of Wisconsin's public universities was a natural fit. The School was already a campus leader in community partnerships and was eager to ramp up its outreach. The decision to have the dean continue to head the initiative after its launch made equal sense. It was one of the First Ideas ready to launch.

The Milwaukee Idea House

As ideas go, it's pretty solid. A house in the heart of the city. Modestly priced, built of reconstituted building materials, energy and environmentally friendly. Bright and airy, it fits right into the neighborhood of turn-of-the-century homes.

It's The Milwaukee Idea Home, an idea developed by UWM's School of Architecture and Urban Planning, funded by local business and community development agencies, and championed by Campus Design Solutions.

"It's appropriate for us to focus the university's resources on communities that have significant needs, " said Stan Wrzeski, the UWM faculty member who heads the project. "We want to re-envision how whole city blocks can be organized as compelling alternatives to sprawling suburban development."

It's a vision that has appealed to a range of partners, including Milwaukee's Neighborhood Improvement Development Corp., Wisconsin Energy Corporation, and Wells Fargo Bank. More than a vision, it's a tangible example of the power of building community-university partnerships.

But unlike Zweben, Greenstreet faced no conflicting interests for staffing, funding, or space. As a dean, he had the freedom to graft Campus Design Solutions onto an already existing habit of community outreach at the School. His solution, mirroring Zweben's, was to "refine, not reinvent." What Greenstreet didn't anticipate was the demand.

"We hit the ground with so much demand from the campus and community, we had to go back and get more money in order to create some structure," Greenstreet acknowledged. The structure, however, was minimal: a part-time assistant director and paid student help. It was, in the dean's words, "a little bit of management," but it fit the needs of the new initiative perfectly.

When the community calls, the campus has a facility need, or faculty have a community-based project, a "Rapid Response" team of faculty and students is assembled to handle projects as needed. It might involve two faculty working with a business district on a community charrette or a class of 75 students developing designs for an entire neighborhood redevelopment. They come together to meet a need, then disband when the project's complete.

The dean's task was to be a catalyst and encourage interdisciplinary team building. He also tackled the funding. For Campus Design Solutions, Greenstreet purposely kept the budget small so that its contributions would be focused at the planning and research stages. Its work is with community groups who usually cannot afford to hire consultants and so UWM does not compete with existing community businesses. What Campus Design Solutions can do, however, is connect the community to other funders, through the broad network of the School of Architecture and Urban Planning.

Unlike The Milwaukee Ideas that started from scratch, funding dollars are not the driver for success when working with existing programs. Healthy Choices already had a well-developed grant-seeking engine at the existing Center. Campus Design Solutions kept costs low by focusing on catalyst projects. Both Ideas found their impetus in the new opportunities of the Idea rather than in new funding. As Greenstreet noted, Campus Design Solutions "takes us into the heart of things"—engagement with the community.

"The mere act of engaging with our neighbors is beneficial," he said, but the tangible reality of Campus Design Solutions adds a concrete dimension. "If you structurally plug directly into the community, link the campus to the city, that's when partnerships happen and you have growth in that change. And it just builds over time."

SECTION SUMMARY

How do you transform an existing campus program?

1) **Anchor your change in a structure** that works for both the new Idea and the existing program. Make it explicit.

2) **Make clear the relationship** between the new Idea and existing reporting structures.

3) **Link the new Idea structurally with the community.**

4) **Use the new Idea as an opportunity** to expand the vision, seize new directions, and reinvigorate the mission of the existing program.

5) **Use existing partnerships and dollars** in service to the new Idea.

Round Two: Looking for More Big Ideas

When Chancellor Zimpher first announced The Milwaukee Idea, most people on campus and in Milwaukee understood it in terms of the "big ideas" being discussed: new academic programs, research initiatives, community partnerships. And the "First Ideas" as they were called were wonderful illustrations of the potential for engagement.

But from the beginning, The Milwaukee Idea was more than ten (and then 11) First Ideas. It was to be an overarching vision for what the university could be and could achieve through its teaching, research, and service. And so even while the Affinity and Action Teams were working on the details of the First Ideas, plans were being laid to continue the process and to make ongoing the creative process of finding new connections across campus and community.

As the Evaluation Team made its final recommendations to the chancellor on the First Ideas, The Milwaukee Idea office announced "Round Two." This time there was no Committee of 100—the word already had gotten out and such a formal group was unnecessary. Instead, a request for proposals went out asking for "Next Ideas." (See Appendix G for detailed support materials.)

The campus community was asked to submit concept papers for Ideas that would be judged on five criteria:

1) Community collaboration and partnerships

2) Advancement of diversity

3) Interdisciplinary work

4) Imagination

5) Capacity to generate external support

The process for Round Two mirrored the successful Milwaukee Idea process, with a few modifications. The Milwaukee Idea office continued to consult with proposers to assure quality submissions. Detailed packets that included a template and guidelines were available from the office and online.

A Reading Group, composed of representatives from campus governance groups and community leaders, evaluated the concept papers. This kept the process open and representative. Those Ideas that met with approval were assigned Action Teams, as the First Ideas had done. Leadership and membership was selected by The Milwaukee Idea office, in consultation with the sponsors of each Idea. An Evaluation Team then assessed the final action plan, with recommendations to the chancellor for implementation as appropriate.

Seventeen concept papers were submitted. Of those, the Reading Group recommended that three move forward to Action Teams: proposals for a Center for Women's Health Research, an information technology computer training project that targets at-risk youth, and an Age and Community initiative. These most clearly were comprehensive and had strong community backing and financial viability. Of those not accepted, several held promise for further development, and small planning grants were offered to the Team leaders to develop them further.

The Center for Age and Community proposal represents how the spirit of The Milwaukee Idea had already begun to produce results—and how the community had begun to take the initiative to involve UWM in new projects. A group of faculty and staff, including Professors Karen Riggs, Carol Haertlein, and Sharon Keigher, had been part of a multidisciplinary research group on campus that focused on issues of aging. They were approached by members of the age services community in Milwaukee to develop a targeted university program on aging. Even before the call for Round Two went out, Riggs and others on campus had been meeting with community members and funders to develop the project. It was a natural next step to formalize their collaboration and submit a proposal to make it a Milwaukee Idea.

Interestingly, the group's work paralleled the Affinity Group process: Almost 50 people from across the city—of all ages, backgrounds, and expertise—met to discuss community needs, divided into small working groups, and created a detailed plan. Meetings with faculty and with other colleges and universities also yielded interdisciplinary support for the proposal. The message from the community was: "Let's see UWM turn its research into practice and show the community what it can do."

As the proposal for the Center for Age and Community illustrated, strong, diverse community partnerships were beginning to form across the campus in response to key issues. Round Two represents the continuing spirit of partnership that is the soul of The Milwaukee Idea.

CREATE A NEW IDEA BY MERGING EXISTING PROGRAMS

The challenges facing all the First Ideas were big ones: Create something from nothing. Transform what already exists. But perhaps the most difficult challenge was faced by those Ideas charged with putting one and one together — and getting a product that was better than the sum of its parts.

Both the Global Passport Project and the Consortium for Economic Opportunity (CEO) called for a merger of existing university centers, with all the political, logistical, and philosophical problems such a union implies. Marc Levine, associate professor of history and director of the Center for Economic Development, had been involved with CEO from the beginning of The Milwaukee Idea—heading up both the Affinity and Action Teams. Patrice Petro, a film history scholar and coordinator of the Graduate Program in English, had only heard about The Milwaukee Idea and was getting ready to take a sabbatical when she was asked to head up the Global Passport Project.

Despite their varied backgrounds, Petro and Levine attacked the merger of their respective centers with remarkably similar strategies. Both kept their vision central. Both used location to advantage. And both focused on communication: early, often, and constantly.

Global Passport Project

The last time Petro counted, there were at least seven centers or institutes that coordinated international learning and programs at UWM. Several of them were housed in the College of Letters and Science, whose dean at the time, Marshall Goodman, headed up the Global Passport Action Team. His vision for a renewed focus on international learning, study abroad, and research programs soon pointed up the obvious: Consolidation of some of the centers would offer better coordination and strengthen impact. Global Passport could best be implemented as an initiative housed in a larger and stronger Center for International Studies—which just happened to be in Letters and Science.

Global Passport Project

The Global Passport Project brings an interdisciplinary, collaborative, and cooperative approach to international education at the University of Wisconsin-Milwaukee. It provides students with expanded opportunities for study abroad, helps to increase the number of international students and faculty on campus, and offers the community an array of programs on international issues.

Global Passport also offers a new degree program in global studies designed to give students an academic foundation and practical training to understand, predict, and respond to global change.

It was not a view that was shared by the rest of his Action Team, nor by many of the directors of the other existing centers. The debate was heated and delayed the launch of Global Passport as a plan to merge the Center for International Studies (CIS) and the Office of International Studies and Programs (OISP) into the Center for International Education under Petro's leadership was hammered out.

"I immediately found myself in the middle of a kind of firestorm," Petro admitted, as some staff from OISP left and she struggled to find ways to combine two groups that served different constituencies.

"I wanted to do something interesting with this Idea," said Petro, who saw great potential in linking both study abroad and international student programs. She anchored her efforts in what she believed was the core mission of her new center, strong research and curriculum development.

Then she worked on building a new team. She began by ignoring the battle and working with the individuals who could get the work done. "We pulled people together to meet monthly to get to know one another, to figure out where we can collaborate and how to work together."

By building networks of information across disciplines at the staff level, Petro created a foundation for shared growth as people discovered things that others were doing, ways in which they could partner, and even the possibility of making the new organization work.

She also concentrated on what she called her leadership style: being transparent. She made her goals for the center explicit. She involved people. She met with people individually to answer questions, allay fears, and share information. All with the ultimate goal of "creating a different kind of community" among the faculty and across disciplines and schools.

"After all, we can't export our riches until we are organized ourselves. Unless faculty know each other and work with each other and have a common program in mind, it's all smoke and mirrors," Petro said.

As Petro worked with her new team, she also paid attention to the often overlooked detail of workspace. As structure was to Campus Design Solutions, space was to Global Passport and the Consortium for Economic Opportunity. The new, merged Center got a face-lift so that the offices that the staff moved into were newer and better than they'd had before. As Dean Goodman noted, "We took pains to see that people got larger offices." On a campus strapped for space, it was a tangible message that change could be positive.

Consortium for Economic Opportunity

Space also was a key ingredient in the launch of the Consortium for Economic Opportunity, but in a different way. CEO brought together Levine's center and the Small Business Development Center from Continuing Education, headed by Lucy Holifield. She had been an Action Team co-chair with Levine and the two centers were logical partners, linking her small-business outreach with his research and technical assistance. And Levine and Holifield worked well with each other.

The Consortium for Economic Opportunity

The Consortium builds on partnerships with nonprofit organizations and small businesses to extend the benefits of economic growth to all of metropolitan Milwaukee, particularly the city's low- and moderate-income neighborhoods. CEO focuses on increasing family-supporting jobs and employment—generating business through a variety of efforts, including:

- A Small Business Development Center offering counseling assistance to entrepreneurs and small-business owners;
- A Center for Community Economic Development providing technical assistance to nonprofit groups;
- Action-oriented research on economic opportunity and applied research on local economic development policy; and
- Enriched educational experiences for UWM students and faculty by integrating real-world urban issues into the curriculum.

But merging an on-campus, faculty-focused center with an off-campus, outreach-focused center (Continuing Education is headquartered in downtown Milwaukee) was not without its challenges. Reporting structures delayed the launch, a common problem with The Milwaukee Idea, as existing structures were asked to bend in new, interdisciplinary ways. At times, Levine felt that they would become bogged down in the details of leases, space demands, and budget concerns. The campus culture was new for Holifield, and the communication demands of coordinating the needs of two centers at times overwhelming.

Levine and Holifield agreed that a third, separate location was ideal, one that would put CEO closer to its core community constituency and form a "neutral ground" for its growth. A renovated building in the heart of the city linked CEO with potential clients and also was home to other community organizations with which CEO sought to partner. The building's restored brick walls, exposed pipes, and large windows provided a welcoming environment and a warm new identity for CEO.

The transition was eased by the strong working relationship of the two leaders. They shared goals, understood each other's style, and were able to provide continuity to a growing staff. They also both recognized and responded to opportunities the Idea presented. Like Campus Design Solutions and Healthy Choices, The Milwaukee Idea offered new potential for existing programs.

"We've gotten off to a good start because we were fortunate to have really functioning base units on which to build," Levine said. Holifield was able to expand her staff to increase community outreach, and Levine's staff hit the ground running with a new certificate program and requests for research in support of the neighborhood. CEO also solidified the partnerships it had built up with community advisors, providing a continuity of connection.

A Good Fit: What Happens When an Existing University Center Meets The Milwaukee Idea

By Lucy Holifield, Assistant Director, Consortium for Economic Opportunity

I have directed the Small Business Development Center (SBDC) at Continuing Education for three years. We provide information and support to entrepreneurs and small businesses throughout Southeastern Wisconsin through UWM's outreach campus, located in the center of Milwaukee's downtown mall in a restored office building.

We serve about 150 people a year, providing free one-on-one business counseling and business management education, and connecting people to classes or resources that build business skills. But the need always has been greater than what we could provide from a single small office.

When I received the letter from the chancellor inviting me to participate in the first Milwaukee Idea plenary meeting, I must admit I went primarily because I wanted to be more connected to the main campus. Even though it's important for SBDC to be downtown, close to small business, it does isolate us from what goes on at the main campus. I wanted to meet people who might offer some new ideas or partnerships, and in that The Milwaukee Idea has more than delivered.

I became involved with the Economic Opportunity Affinity Group and through it was asked to work with Marc Levine on the Consortium for Economic Opportunity Action Team. Our partnership was a natural, since he heads the Center for Economic Development at UWM, which focuses on the research component. He was able to connect our Idea through his dean to the College of Letters and Science at UWM. In addition to lots of support from my dean, Susan Kelly, I also was able to connect to the Minority Entrepreneurship Program at the School of Business Administration through another team member. The counseling that the SBDC offers was a nice fit with the School's ten-week business course on operating a start-up. Our partnership is a great example of the benefits of teaming up to deliver services.

The campus and community contacts through The Milwaukee Idea have also heightened awareness of SBDC and what we do, something that's been invaluable in reaching out to new clients as well as new supporters. We have started a Consortium Dialogue—something that would not have been possible without the community-wide publicity for The Milwaukee Idea. We're pulling together leaders of lending institutions, development groups, community-based organizations, and corporations to explore new partnerships, discover what the needs are for new business, and what the resources are so we don't duplicate efforts. Our goal is to create a seamless delivery of services so that our clients can have access to everything they need through one contact point. By working together, we can accomplish more. The Dialogue is a first step in that direction.

I've been asked if The Milwaukee Idea's Consortium will "take over" the SBDC. If anything, it's helped to make it stronger. Because the Center is an important component of the Consortium's efforts, we've been able to expand our staffing to offer more counseling to more people. We're broadening our services to target people who, in the past, were left behind: minority and inner-city entrepreneurs. We're also looking to fill new opportunities, such as helping existing businesses to grow or manage growth. There's no one doing that right now.

Our new home at the Ameritech King Commerce Center is in the heart of the inner city, so that, finally, we can engage the university with the community we serve. The mission of CEO is to mobilize all the resources of UWM to partner with Milwaukee for economic growth, specifically by targeting those communities that haven't shared in the prosperity of the past decade. We're now in the right place to do it, and that's a good thing for the SBDC and for UWM.

I didn't realize when I went to the first Milwaukee Idea meeting how it would open so many new possibilities. Our Center has more visibility, a new home, more staff to better serve our clients, new connections to campus and to business, and a mission that is growing every day. That's going to make a big difference for the future of Milwaukee.

SECTION SUMMARY

How do you merge two centers into a new Idea?

1) **Create a strong leadership team.** Key word here is "team." A single or shared leadership approach works if members of both centers are involved in making decisions.

2) **Be clear about mission.** From the beginning, everyone needs to know the mission of the new center and how the new organization will get there.

3) **Build on strengths.** Create new goals, but use the best of what each center brings to the new identity.

4) **Building relationships is vital.** This truth was demonstrated repeatedly throughout the entire Milwaukee Idea process. Find ways to connect people at the staff level to keep communication open and encourage team building. Provide opportunities for creative work and new working partnerships.

5) **Pay attention to place.** It's a concrete way to create a new, shared identity. Reward successful change with new or better offices.

Reflections

Nancy Zimpher and Steve Percy talk about educational partnerships and the launch of The Milwaukee Ideas.

Nancy Zimpher
There isn't a week that goes by that I don't find myself standing before a service group or professional organization telling them about what we're doing at UWM.

Milwaukee Partnership Academy for Teacher Quality

The Milwaukee Partnership Academy is a community-wide effort to revitalize urban schools. Partners include UWM, Milwaukee Public Schools, Milwaukee Teachers' Education Association, Milwaukee Area Technical College, and educational organizations throughout southeastern Wisconsin, joining together to:

• Prepare more students for college, particularly those from culturally and linguistically diverse families. Middle and high school students are supported by enrichment courses to help ensure college success.

• Create and expand a strong, diverse, and energetic teacher workforce through a collaborative, interdisciplinary teacher education program.

• Integrate technology into teacher education programs to enhance student learning in the urban environment.

I tell them about our 11 Ideas. I tell them we're not just talking. We're not just making plans. We've started to translate our rhetoric into action.

I tell them about our Partnership Academy—a truly unique collaboration with Milwaukee Public Schools, the Milwaukee Teachers' Education Association, the School Board, our area technical college, the Association of Commerce, and civic organizations. Together we sought and won more than $20 million in federal grants to prepare teachers more effectively.

As I describe this partnership, I remind my audience that what we are doing is not the way higher education usually operates—and I'm not just referring to this kind of extensive community-university partnership.

I tell them universities do not typically ask to be held accountable for student learning in the public schools. And that's exactly what we're doing at UWM. As a member of a partnership working with the school teachers and school system to improve learning, we are stepping out and say-ing to the community that, as a partner, we also are accountable for what happens. We are saying our reputation is only as good as our partnership results.

Steve Percy
The idea of accountability is important to The Milwaukee Idea, because ulti-mately our success as an institution will ride on whether we are able to do what we say we will do. From the beginning, our measurement has been results, not reports. That has meant that some ideas—like Fresh Water and our health initiatives—are still working through important planning. Others, like Campus Design Solu-tions and Cultures and Communities, were ready to go early and begin moving ahead.

We have given each Idea the freedom to create its own structure and organi-zation, while supporting them by bringing the leaders together regularly to learn from each other. We continue to remind the leaders that they need to tell us clearly what they intend to accomplish and then we need to have results, not only to prove that we are worthy community partners, but also to help us measure what we have done, both inside the university and in our communities.

While we are forthright about holding ourselves accountable, ultimately it is the community who will be the judge of whether we have succeeded. We've been public from the start of this initiative, and that openness has helped to keep us focused, on target, and responsive to community needs.

Nancy Zimpher
Our public spirit also has been risky, because we are, in some ways, changing the equation of what is expected from a modern urban university. In essence, we are saying that scholarship, learning, and research must remain part of our mission, but they are not enough. Today's world needs a university that also can deliver applied research, as well as basic discovery. As a cornerstone institution of our soci-ety, we are accountable to contribute to the common good in real and concrete ways, in ways that go beyond learning and basic research.

When UWM opened its doors in the middle of the last century, it was chal-lenged by University of Wisconsin President Harrington to "experiment, generate and try out original ideas and approaches in instruction, research and public serv-ice." We are taking that challenge literally and, through The Milwaukee Idea, are doing the hard work of reinventing.

These Ideas are really breaking new ground for UWM. In them, our faculty, staff, and students will be able to see tangible examples of what it means to weave our triadic mission into engagement. These Ideas are the strongest argument I know against "the tyranny of the 'or'"—that our work is either teaching or service, research or engagement. Faced with the Consortium for Economic Opportunity on Martin Luther King Drive and the new Helen Bader Institute for Nonprofit Management on campus, with the Milwaukee Industrial Innovation Center partnering with business and Healthy Choices and Cultures and Communities working with students, it will be impossible not to understand the value of our social mission to make "the boundaries of the university the boundaries of our world."

That wise social commentator, Mae West, once said that an ounce of performance is worth pounds of promises. I stick by that.

<hr>

CHAPTER 9 SUMMARY

What we learned about launching The Milwaukee Ideas

Whether ideas started from scratch, were built on an existing academic unit, or created by merging existing units, all shared five common traits.

1) **Support the Idea.** Provide adequate start-up funds or access to immediate funding so the idea can focus on implementation, not fund-raising.

2) **Get the right leadership.** Good leaders are vested in the idea, have a vision for what can be accomplished, and work collaboratively with campus and community.

3) **Focus on partnerships.** Collaborating doesn't end when the visioning and planning stop. It's a continual process that involves hard work to keep the networks expanding.

4) **Create new structures.** To work in new ways, you need new approaches to organization that grow out of the spirit of the Idea.

5) **Learn by doing.** Keep the "ready, fire, aim!" motto in the forefront.

<hr>

Endnote

[1] Sally Helgesen. (1995). *The Web of Inclusion: A New Architecture for Building Great Organizations.* New York: Currency/Doubleday, page 16.

INTO NEW TERRITORY

Speech given to the Faculty Plenary
September 21, 2000

A New Perspective on a New Territory
By John Wanat, Provost and Vice Chancellor, UWM

"Universities are dedicated to seeking truth wherever it is. In our own disciplines, we are always overturning the received wisdom. New theories replace the old. Novel interpretations challenge tradition. New data force reconsideration of past practice. That dynamism in our intellectual lives, however, often rests on a desire for stability in the day-to-day conduct of our university lives. That traditional stability will not necessarily be there.

To cope with the changes that have been occurring and will continue to occur, we will need more than our basic five senses of sight, hearing, taste, smell, and touch. We will need a sense of humor, a sense of forgiveness, and a sense of selective amnesia."

There is an apocryphal story about Wayne Gretzky, arguably the best hockey player who ever played the game. When asked the secret to his success, he is reputed to have said, "I skate to where the puck is going to be, not where it's been." While the story makes for good hockey strategy, it also expresses the challenge the University of Wisconsin-Milwaukee faced as The Milwaukee Idea launched its first initiatives. With community and campus expectations high, the pressure for major increases in program funding mounting, and momentum for change growing, the university administration found itself skating on thin ice. The traditional ways of operating a large, public university could not meet the demands of people and systems eager to try new ideas. UWM needed to be looking ahead to where it wanted to be, not backward to the "way it's always been."

From the beginning, The Milwaukee Idea was not only a way to implement some innovative experiments in community outreach, but, more importantly, it was also the means to weave the idea of engagement into the very fiber of the university. It was the process of lining the organization up around a Big Idea—the Idea that the community and university were partners in building a better world and preparing women and men to create it.

Just as the First Ideas needed to translate vision into action, so the university itself needed to find concrete ways to change.

Nancy Zimpher on Change in the Academy

With The Milwaukee Idea, we launched a huge transforming process that was bold and by every dimension daring. It was public; it was structured. It was real, with money behind it. It wasn't subtle and it wasn't incremental. Few institutions in the country that I have read about have tried to line the whole organization up around the idea of engagement.

We really are facing head-on the idea of institutional change, something that has been written about extensively and which we've studied. I have been influenced by Michael Fullan's books on change and his notion—not unique to him—about creating a learning organization, one that operates on the edge of chaos. That certainly describes The Milwaukee Idea!

Essentially we have been living within a spirit of uncertainty, which we have tried to use in a positive way. At the same time, we have sought a balance that provides people with a comfort level adequate to help them get their work done. Easy to talk about, of course, this finding a balance for change. No books I know of, however, tell you exactly where this fine line is—or how to stay on it.

We have tried to find that balance. We didn't always succeed, but what we discovered is that change is what you can get away with. We knew what we needed and what we wanted to do. Now, what could we actually do? What would people help us accomplish?

The reason we could get away with change, the reason we could live on that edge of chaos is because people wanted us to be better. They knew UWM was capable of great things. They knew our dream for a premier research university was what they wanted as well. And so faculty, staff, students, community stepped outside their comfort zones. They tried things differently. They put up with uncertainty. Because they believed we could be better. That's how we changed UWM. We trusted the institution to change. And it did.

Of course we're not there yet. We're really still in the middle act of a three-act play. But already, the outlines of the finale have been foreshadowed. As the curtain rises on the next act, we launch an innovative form of strategic planning and resource building.

DOING IT DIFFERENTLY

To support The Milwaukee Idea and to transform the institution, UWM needed three things:

1) A focused message

2) Targeted resources

3) Connections

By the time the First Ideas were readying for launch, Nancy Zimpher and Steve Percy had taken The Milwaukee Idea across the community and campus. Literally thousands of people knew about the 11 Ideas that would connect the university to the community.

But if these Ideas were to survive long-term, they would need extensive funding—beyond UWM using dollars from increased enrollment and before significant external grants could be accrued. They would need additional state support. Just as important, the notion of partnership needed to extend deeper into the university, and broader into new relationships across the city and state. This would require a strategic plan as broad as The Milwaukee Idea process itself.

And so Chancellor Zimpher returned to the principles of The Milwaukee Idea: the "Connectors" of diversity, partnerships, interdisciplinarity, communication. With these values in mind, she repeated the process, this time, with an eye to the institution.

A Focused Message

The launch of the First Ideas was timed to coincide with the biennial request for funding to the state legislature. In formulating the budget request, it was essential to find ways to connect the new potential of the university with a message that would resonate with public funders. So a new Strategy Team was assembled, with representatives from across the campus to help support an aggressive state budget request. As on previous teams, there was a mix of leadership and staff so the work got done. Some members were chosen for the perspective they could provide—whether on the workings of the university or the legislative process. Others had the ability to help the group think through issues. Others had important connections to civic and business leaders. And some were just there to learn.

The Budget Strategy Group (as members called themselves) met twice monthly, and one of the first things they did was refocus the message of The Milwaukee Idea for a broader audience. The 11 First Ideas were grouped into three categories: education, environment, economy—the 3Es. Together, these three areas of UWM focus would enhance the quality of life (QL) for the people of Wisconsin—from more jobs to better educated students to healthier cities. In shorthand, $E^3 = QL$.

This formula would form the basis for UWM's budget pitch and frame its discussions within the university and beyond its walls.

"These notions resonate with what ails society, with what people worry about, with what meets our scholarly curiosity," said John Wanat, UWM's new provost. "By looking at those three foci, we got the attention of those who control dollars, an attention that had eluded UWM for decades."

Targeted Resources

Before the university could make a request for state support, it needed to determine its resource needs: how much, when, and why. It was the discussions within the university that next took center stage. Just as The Milwaukee Idea could not be imposed from above, so too a comprehensive plan for seeking and implementing major budget changes needed to originate from across campus. In April 1999, the chancellor convened a retreat of 50 individuals—much like the Affinity Group process—to identify major areas of funding need. They arrived at a list, of which The Milwaukee Idea was but one of five that also included enhanced research, enrollment, and learning; the Milwaukee Commitment (a plan for increasing campus diversity); achieving competitive salaries; and improving technological infrastructure.

Armed with these priorities, the CBAC was enlisted (UWM is famous for its administrative acronyms). The Chancellor's Budget Advisory Committee—individuals drawn from across governance groups and departments to advise the chancellor—was asked to take on the function of an Action Team to translate the priorities into budget proposals from which the university would make its requests to the state legislature for funding. Working over the next year, the CBAC took the report from the original planning retreat—"Investing in UWM's Future"—and used it as a blueprint for an aggressive budget agenda, ratified by

From "Investing in UWM's Future"

"This planning document represents a unique, optimistic and aggressive approach to institutional planning... We have identified our vision and aspirations for UWM. This document provides a single merged blueprint charting UWM's aspirations over the next five years, and, most critically, makes sure that we have the pocketbook to achieve them. It goes beyond describing what we will do—it also provides strategies for building our resource base and investing these resources in those activities prioritized in this planning process. It is a plan based on willingness to take charge of our future, and willingness to assume some risk in the process."

every major campus governance group. The committee then worked with the APBC (Academic Planning and Budget Committee) for further refinement. The bottom line: about $75 million would be needed to fund UWM's dreams, drawn from increased state support, extramural funds and gifts, a major gift campaign, and reallocations. The biennial request to the state— also called, for simplicity's sake, "The Milwaukee Idea"—was based on that long-range outlook.

Working with the Campus

As the new investment plan was being ratified, UWM's provost and vice chancellor, Ken Watters, retired. His replacement, John Wanat, a former vice provost at the University of Illinois-Chicago (UIC), arrived in the summer of 2000 with a mandate to focus on the "inside"—reinforcing communication with faculty, nurturing relationships on campus, finding ways to integrate The Milwaukee Idea structurally.

Wanat was no stranger to the idea of engagement, having worked with UIC's "Great Cities" project, that institution's program to reach out to its urban neighbors. As an outsider, Wanat could appreciate The Milwaukee Idea's strengths (it was campus-wide) and its challenges (giving the campus a voice).

"One thing that I think UWM did right was to get faculty buy-in early on," Wanat said. "We have more to do, of course; I see my goal as working on the inside with faculty, to build the 'crosswalks' that will connect us and make our teaching, research, and service easier and more fulfilling." And so he walked the campus, talked with everyone, and launched key initiatives, including task forces on research and information technology.

Connections

To get the faculty and staff more involved in the implementation of The Milwaukee Idea—and its budget plan—Wanat burrowed down to where the work gets done, to the departments across campus. And to do that, he enlisted the deans, as the intersecting points, to be the managing team. At a deans' retreat that echoed the formative one held when the chancellor first arrived, the deans identified areas of excellence on which to encourage growth, such as the Honors Program, urban education, information resources, and The Milwaukee Idea. These "skyscraper" themes, as Wanat called them, offered rallying points to the faculty and they complemented the crosswalk connections—interdisciplinary relationships and networks that The Milwaukee Idea encouraged.

Then, as an exemplary political science professor would, Wanat took the budget plans from the CBAC and created a giant grid: what funding would arrive when, laid over the financial needs of the campus, such as new faculty, infrastructure expenses, Milwaukee Idea, research upgrade, etc. To complete the grid, he asked the deans to solicit proposals from every department for how they would add faculty and staff to fulfill the goals of the budget plan. He was, in effect, getting the campus to think more broadly about how to put it all together.

"Our budget request to the state was the broad brushstrokes of what we wanted to accomplish in the next two years," Wanat explained. "We needed to refine the picture, to put in the detail to make the masterpiece."

The call for proposals came with conditions. Each proposal must 1) meet at least one of the "Investing in UWM's Future" goals and 2) fit within the framework of the 3Es of The Milwaukee Idea.

The response signaled a far-from-disconnected faculty. Two hundred and forty-five proposals—totaling $68 million—were received. Marshall Goodman, then dean of Letters and Science, received more than 60 proposals from his department chairs alone.

"What I tried to do was send strong signals to the departments that the train's leaving the station and it's good to be on the train, because if you're not, the resources aren't going to follow," Goodman said. "This is where we're going and the faculty are excited by it because they recognize that growth is going to occur in this direction. One of my faculty came to me the other day and said, 'You know, one thing about UWM right now: It's fun.' We now have a lot of people who are willing to collaborate."

Expand the Circle

Collaborate—and spread the news. As more people, especially those at the departmental level, became involved, more voices were heard in support of The Milwaukee Idea and the university's investment plan. As Provost Wanat said, this expanded the circle of individuals who could "help us walk into the future." The commitment, which started with the deans, expanded.

"I would say there hasn't been a faculty meeting that's gone by where in some way I don't talk about the integration of research and teaching and community engagement in one way or the other," said Sally Lundeen, dean of Nursing. "They've heard it from me so often, I now have other people lined up to say those things—key faculty who are well-funded, respected researchers who get it, who have been willing to be champions."

More important, she's put her money where her mouth is. Realizing that community-based research can often be a luxury young faculty can ill afford, the School of Nursing offered a competitive buyout for one faculty member each semester to develop a fundable project proposal. One of the criteria for acceptance was that the project relate to the goals of The Milwaukee Idea.

"It's all well and good to talk about your dreams," Lundeen said. "But if you put a little money behind you, people get very intrigued about how to redefine what they do with their lives." It was a lesson, by the way, that Greg Jay in Cultures and Communities also had learned with the success his faculty fellowships had encouraging faculty to create new curricula.

Impact of New Faculty

Redefining how to do the work of the university soon began to bump up against the traditions of the academy as newly hired faculty tested the boundaries. When Letters and Science wanted to hire a new math instructor to focus on teacher education as part of a partnership with the School of Education, there were no guidelines for tenuring someone who wasn't going to be bringing in grants and doing research. But the department was flexible and Dean Goodman developed different tenure criteria, spelled out in the appointment letter outlining expectations.

"We work with departments on developing more flexible criteria for tenure," Goodman said. "People can wear different hats and live within the same department. Faculty realize that a person is going to play a special role in developing links that, in the long run, will lead to more math majors and more budget for the department. We've added several key staff people from Milwaukee Idea money and they're making a world of difference."

Subjects like tenure and promotion, which the chancellor had vowed not to "tackle head-on," were beginning to be discussed across campus in different ways and in different forums. Independently, individuals and groups were looking at what community engagement means to the professional lives of faculty and staff. It was an essential discussion—by no means resolved—on a campus where acceptance of engagement varied widely across departments.

Create Consistent Criteria

Meanwhile, with 245 faculty proposals for what would only be an anticipated $20 million or less in new funding in the first biennium, Provost Wanat needed to identify which ones to implement first. With assistance from the deans and the APBC, Wanat asked faculty "Action Teams" to devise criteria to determine which proposals would make the first round. They would meet:

- UWM's internal goal to be a premier, urban, student-centered, engaged, research university

- UWM's external goals, the promises to the community

- The 3Es of The Milwaukee Idea

- The growing need for distance learning
- The Milwaukee Idea's Connectors: interdisciplinary, partnerships, diversity, potential for funding
- Quality and capacity goals

The result of the work by the faculty teams was 92 proposals slated for implementation, dependent on state funding. The proposals reflected a truly collaborative vision of major institutional priorities. Staffing for the proposals would be handled by the departments, and dollars would stay on campus.

A Closer Look

Changes for The Milwaukee Idea Office

By the start of the budget initiative, The Milwaukee Idea office was a much different place. Original staff had moved on and new Assistant Director Fran Luebke and Communication Director Deborah Fagan found themselves in changing roles. Gone was the scrappy meeting planning and convening (although the office was still one of the best last-minute event planners on campus). Instead, the office was increasingly a support organization, helping the First Ideas with logistics, making community connections, and responding to questions and partnering opportunities.

It was called on to help create the institutional structures needed to support the new Ideas, everything from creating approval forms for joint dean signatures to new spreadsheets that could accommodate funding from two different colleges. If the office had the luxury of working outside university procedures in its formative days, it needed to live by the rules now—or at least help create some that would work better.

In large part, the office served as the conduit across campus. "Linking the Ideas to the campus is a challenge," Luebke said. Fagan agreed that providing internal communication about The Milwaukee Idea was an ongoing challenge, limited by the size of the campus, indirect access to the chancellor's office, and the independence of the various Milwaukee Idea initiatives. Monthly meetings of the team leaders helped to ease the process and provide a forum for leaders to share what was working and offer help for problems encountered.

The office also became another voice for the university in the community, connecting people and making collaborations easier. "The role of the office has changed, now that the initial excitement of The Milwaukee Idea process has subsided," Fagan said. "Promoting The Milwaukee Idea has become a university-wide function. Our task—beyond supporting the various initiatives—is to find ways to involve the community more completely and to facilitate discussions, on campus and off, about what The Milwaukee Idea is and can be."

Now its goals are to:

- Identify new opportunities for community-university collaboration to bring under The Milwaukee Idea umbrella
- Communicate results and achievements to campus and community
- Work with governance groups to explore opportunities for engagement
- Support campus capital campaigns and state legislative requests
- Assess the results of The Milwaukee Idea

As the 11 First Ideas become more independent, The Milwaukee Idea office is finding that The Milwaukee Idea is not just "Big Ideas," but includes a range of activities that encourage engagement at all levels. The Milwaukee Idea, for example, has partnered with several schools and colleges to facilitate a city-wide forum on health-care solutions. It hosted a session for public defenders of the City of Milwaukee to reflect on how better to serve individuals with mental health needs. In some cases, it links community groups to university expertise, facilitates several meetings, then steps back as the new collaboration takes off. Together with the chancellor's office, The Milwaukee Idea office is now the connecting point on campus that can spark innovation through small grants, group facilitation, and networking.

"We've grown tremendously from our conceptual roots as an initiative for engagement," Fagan said. "I think The Milwaukee Idea office can become an 'intellectual base' for understanding engagement at UWM—for the campus and the community."

Make the Connections

While Provost Wanat managed the inside communication, Chancellor Zimpher focused on the external agenda: the political process to lobby the state for increased dollars. To do this, she needed to connect UWM in the minds of the legislature and people of Wisconsin with their goals for a better future. The formula of E^3=QL did that. What was missing were explicit connections that would amplify the message. Zimpher set out to "connect the dots." She found them in the University of Wisconsin System.

The UW System has two research universities, 11 comprehensive universities, 13 two-year campuses, and a statewide extension. UWM already had several partnership arrangements with nearby two-year colleges to make student transfers easier, and a new program making it possible for working students to get a four-year UWM degree in their hometown also was being launched. This kind of collaborative arrangement was a natural for UWM—and a natural way to extend UWM's services across the state. And so "College Connections" was launched, a program to offer System campuses a partnership with UWM so that students could receive a four-year UWM degree at their local campus, through faculty exchanges and distance learning. It was a great opportunity to become, in the words of the *Wausau Daily Herald,* "the university to whom hometown Wisconsin turns."

And so the chancellor, provost, and several deans took to the road, meeting with leaders at 14 campuses to discuss joint programs and to explain how The Milwaukee Idea offered opportunities for their students and communities as well. Over the course of a busy summer, from La Crosse in the west to Marinette in the north and the towns along Lake Michigan to the east, Zimpher made a point of insisting that meetings on campus include community leaders and UWM alumni. From them, the UWM team heard what the needs of each community were: from more international opportunities to better technology training. The result was partnerships for joint degrees at five campuses, with four more in line. More importantly, UWM had a mandate for statewide educational support to add to its state budget request.

At the same time, UWM was exploring ways to connect more effectively with business leaders in Wisconsin. Concerned that many of the state's best and brightest were being lured south and west, business had long complained about a "brain drain." UWM plunged in, using the opportunity to address the needs of a new economy as a partnering bonanza.

Corporate Council

The chancellor convened her Corporate Council, a group of leading CEOs who meet periodically to provide counsel to her and to UWM. After meeting regularly for years, the Council became a "strategic resource to the university," providing advice, support, and lending their names to key initiatives—including support for the investment plan.

> "We are seeking ways to bring intellectual capital from our educational institutions out to businesses to help the new economy grow in Wisconsin."
> —*Mark Mone*
> *Associate Dean*
> *UWM School of Business Administration*

From their group, several leaders agreed to fund a proposal that would help UWM address the challenges of increasing jobs and attracting new business. The result was TechStar, a proposal that united UWM with four major Milwaukee universities and the Milwaukee Metropolitan Association of Commerce in creating a technology center that would serve the needs of the state's business and industry. (TechStar also was linked to the Milwaukee Industrial Innovation Center.)

But that was only the beginning. A statewide Economic Summit in the fall of 2000, organized by the University of Wisconsin System, identified the need for more regional coordination in support of increasing high-technology related jobs and businesses. Thanks to partnerships already formed around TechStar and ongoing Milwaukee Idea collaborations, UWM was ready to take the lead. Civic, business, nonprofit, labor, and educational leaders were convened from a seven-county region. The Joint Venture for Regional Development was formed, with UWM a strong partner. UWM was making explicit the important role that education had to play in supporting and expanding the state's economy.

These kinds of connections expanded the reach of the university and its ability to ask the citizens of the entire state to invest in UWM's vision. UWM was a long way from the days when community leadership could afford to ignore it. It had become a major player.

State Investment

The web of connections created by the chancellor, provost, Milwaukee Idea staff, and leaders finally came together in the fall of 2001. UWM's proposal to the state legislature made its way through committees and hearings and finally to the governor's desk. Governor Scott McCallum signed into law the 2001–2003 budget with millions of dollars in additional funding for UWM. It was an unprecedented show of support from the legislature and it also was recognition by the people of Wisconsin that UWM's new role as a partner in the economic, educational, and environmental future of the state was a reality. Now, UWM—and The Milwaukee Idea—would need to deliver on that promise.

A Closer Look

A View from the Outside
By Alan Guskin, consultant to higher education, former chancellor of the University of Wisconsin-Parkside, and former president of Antioch University

As the First Ideas are launched, and as the next phase of The Milwaukee Idea begins, two key questions regarding The Milwaukee Idea should be raised: What are its successes and what challenges lie ahead?

WHAT ARE THE SUCCESSES OF THE MILWAUKEE IDEA?

A New Profile
First and foremost, the continuous espousal of The Milwaukee Idea as the new theme at UWM has had an enormous impact in the community and state. From an image-enhancing perspective—a very important issue in a state-supported university—The Milwaukee Idea remains a powerful and successful effort and may well have importance considerably beyond the internal programs developed to implement it.

Momentum for Change
Within the institution, the external message, the reorganization of the institution's administrative structure, and the call for programs to implement The Milwaukee Idea and the support of them have together created a momentum to think anew about UWM's relationship to its surrounding communities. Even if some of the early efforts fall short of the grand conception of The Milwaukee Idea, the context for creating future academic and institutional programs may well have been altered by the consistent and persistent message of the chancellor and the internal changes already made, as well as the financial, political, and symbolic rewards that have accrued to UWM as a result of this new institutional vision.

WHAT ARE THE CHALLENGES FACING THE MILWAUKEE IDEA?

Promises
In many ways the implicit problems are the shadow side of the successes. First is the danger of unfulfilled promises. The Milwaukee community, like almost

all urban communities, has heard many times how their urban university is going to serve their interests. While The Milwaukee Idea—and Chancellor Zimpher—sound different, the very implications of the partnership model require a considerable amount of time to implement. This may create some political difficulties and credibility problems in the long run if UWM does not show progress toward meaningful partnerships with the Milwaukee community in a reasonable amount of time.

Institutionalizing The Milwaukee Idea

While many people throughout UWM, like their community counterparts, are intrigued with The Milwaukee Idea, even some of its strongest advocates are struggling to figure out how they can deal with it on an institution-wide basis. A number of major issues are at the heart of these struggles:

1) There's a difference between partnership and service. A partnership between two entities indicates that there is a sense of equality between the partners and that the boundaries between the two entities are relatively fluid with easy movement back and forth. While there may be different skills and functions between the partners, even complementary skills/functions, both are equally valued.

Service to others, especially in the context of a university, indicates that those providing the service have more value than those receiving it. The relationship is not one of equality but of inherent inequality, with the implications for all parties. In a service relationship the boundaries are not permeable, there is little back and forth movement, those providing the service come out to perform, and those receiving the service either accept or reject it; they have little else to offer the provider.

In effect, the model of community relationship common to universities is one of service and not partnership. Unfortunately, while people have felt the need for the service, they often have not been happy with the institutions providing it.

2) Faculty criteria for success. The primary criterion for success at a university—tenure and promotion—remains research productivity or what some are beginning to call the scholarship of discovery. There remains considerably less emphasis on teaching and service. Yet, if The Milwaukee Idea is a primary part (or the essence) of UWM's mission, then teaching and engaging in community partnerships (and the scholarship of teaching and community experience) should be at least equal with research in these critical decisions.

3) *Academic policies and administrative services.* The major changes inherent in a conception of The Milwaukee Idea require significant changes in the institutional policies dealing with who can be a faculty member, the nature of faculty workload, and what constitutes academic credit, among others. This raises many questions:

- Can a community member without all the "right" academic credentials be considered a faculty member? Can such a "community faculty" member grant credit?

- How does community engagement count toward faculty workload?

- How does the institution credit student experiential learning in the community?

Restructuring

The very power of The Milwaukee Idea as a partnership with the Milwaukee community is that it is a significant reconception of UWM requiring a considerable restructuring of the institution. Yet, creating such change is not a simple venture, since many of the most supportive faculty and administrative leaders are unfamiliar with the nature of such institutional change efforts and uncomfortable with them. On the other hand, these leaders are comfortable with less significant change efforts that emphasize incremental changes, thereby staying within the present institutional values and academic policies and administrative processes.

Therein lie some of the most difficult issues in the implementation of The Milwaukee Idea. For, while some of these incremental changes are good additions to the university's academic offerings and some are enhancements of UWM's service to the Milwaukee community, together they will not, I believe, lead to the reconception of UWM as a partnership with the community. Because these incremental changes do not deal with the underlying issues of how the institution operates—e.g., service versus partnership, faculty criteria, existing academic and administrative policies—they cannot lead to the desired transformational changes. In effect, the accumulation of incremental changes can lead to a better institution in its old forms, but not to a new institutional conception. Such efforts may be good additions to the university but do not make UWM distinctive in the state or national higher education arena and are not likely, over time, to mobilize community and political leaders to seek special support for UWM.

Faculty Support

While the new institutional identity fostered by The Milwaukee Idea is consistent with the public's conception of or desires for UWM, it is at considerable variance with many faculty members' conception of the university as an aspiring research university. Given the past, it is likely that without some significant changes in their institutional perspective, many faculty members will have difficulty letting go of their competition with Madison and will view any movement away from a traditional research university model as a rejection of their aspirations.

In effect, fully realizing the implications of The Milwaukee Idea requires significant changes in important administrative systems (e.g., the way in which faculty workload and student credit hours are counted) and in some of the basic institutional values (e.g., the criteria for faculty promotion, the separation of the university and community boundaries, the legitimacy of experiential student learning). Implementing such significant changes requires change strategies very different from those involved in incremental changes.

What Next?

It is, of course, too early to assess the success of The Milwaukee Idea, but this case story raises important questions about the nature of community-university partnerships and how change is institutionalized. I believe the single most important issue in the implementation of The Milwaukee Idea is a powerful and sustained focus on the development of a long-term community-university partnership that involves the primary academic interests and skills of the university and the interests and expertise of the community. To be successful, I believe, this focused effort will have to challenge existing institutional values and academic and administrative systems by creating and inventing new structural models in which these new visions, educational values, and systems are embedded. There should be a number of such models that reflect the potential variations that can exist in these new visions, educational values, and operational systems.

For The Milwaukee Idea to be successfully implemented, it will be necessary, I believe, for UWM to avoid tackling other good institution-wide program ideas unrelated to the basic tenets of The Milwaukee Idea. Too many good ideas can dissipate the symbolic power of institutional leaders as well as their energy, and can confuse many institutional members about the primary strategic direction of the university. The lack of clear, sustained, and unrelenting institutional focus significantly decreases the capability of key faculty and administrative opinion leaders to hold, advocate, and implement the university's agenda.

As in all significant change efforts, consistent, persistent, and sustained institutional focus is the key to success. I eagerly await the coming months as the progress of change unfolds at the University of Wisconsin-Milwaukee.

CHAPTER 10 SUMMARY

What we learned about taking The Milwaukee Idea into new territory

1) **Don't create limits.** The Milwaukee Idea was not just 11 First Ideas. It became a state budget proposal, small and large community collaborations, and a culture of change, because UWM remained flexible about what it could be.

2) **Stay true to values.** As The Milwaukee Idea was expanded on campus and externally throughout the state, original values of inclusiveness, communication, and interdisciplinary partnerships continued to guide efforts.

3) **Find the message.** Connect to new audiences by listening carefully to what they need and linking to real resources. The Milwaukee Idea could address statewide economic concerns because it could offer tangible resources in return.

4) **Don't forget the internal audience.** Even as UWM took The Milwaukee Idea to a broader statewide audience, connections to faculty, staff, and students continued.

5) **Encourage creativity.** Deans, faculty, and staff responded with creative solutions because they were given the freedom to think in new ways about how their interests could support The Milwaukee Idea.

11

TEN EARLY LESSONS
FOR CHANGE

From the Chancellor's Plenary Address
To the UWM Faculty Senate
September 21, 2000

Celebrating a New Kind of University

That famous philosopher Vince Lombardi once said: "Winning isn't everything. The will to win is everything." We have the way. Do we have the will?

Let's begin by being very clear about our goal. We will be nothing less than a premier . . . urban . . . research . . . university.

To reverse the order, we are, first and foremost, a university, with all the glorious promise that appellation entails. We are not a social service organization; we are not a business. We will fulfill our triadic mission to be a place for learning, service and discovery, with the responsibility to "give voice to truth" and to fulfill the potential of those we teach.

Our strength as an institution is our research and scholarship, the foundation on which we build our expertise, our teaching and service. Without it, we cannot excel. With it, we have ignited the lives of countless students and changed the face of knowledge—and our world.

We are also an urban institution, positioned at this unique time in history at the forefront of a revolution in human development. . . .

All of this offers us the opportunity to become a premier institution, ahead of the pack in our vision, revolutionary in our creativity, and leaders in our willingness to try new ideas. . . .

We celebrate a new kind of university. The University of Wisconsin-Milwaukee.

Three years after the first Milwaukee Idea plenary session, the University of Wisconsin-Milwaukee was indeed on its way to becoming a "new kind of university," one that, as the Kellogg Commission predicted, would be "as much a first-rate student university as it is a first-rate research university, one that provides access to success to a much more diverse student population as easily as it reaches out to 'engage' the larger community."

"Perhaps most significantly, this new university will be the engine of life-long learning because it will have reinvented its organizational structures and reexamined its cultural norms in pursuit of a learning society."[1]

But the journey is far from over. The success of The Milwaukee Idea is by no means assured. While the First Ideas are launched, the strength of the new interdisciplinary structures and community partnerships is still being tested. Organizational infrastructures are becoming more flexible, but change is incremental. Enthusiasm for The Milwaukee Idea is growing, but resistance can be found in pockets throughout the campus. Many community leaders know more about The Milwaukee Idea than do some faculty who are watching—from the sidelines—holding out for some concrete results before they cast their vote for or against. Others want to see the dollars first. "It's just too early to tell," is heard on campus and off.

LESSONS FOR CHANGE

But it is not too early to begin reflection and learning. While the final chapters on the results of this brave experiment have yet to be written, the early lessons learned from the work done by almost 400 individuals from campus and community will shape what happens next. Many of these lessons have already been outlined in the preceding pages: involve campus leadership from the beginning, be inclusive at all costs, find new ways to encourage community and student involvement, foster a "Yes" attitude, be accountable to the community for results, stay flexible to beat the inevitable roadblocks.

But if, as Michael Fullan says, success is found in "the discovery of patterns that emerge through actions we take,"[2] the success of The Milwaukee Idea can surely be found in ten well-earned lessons of change.

Here, then, are The Milwaukee Idea ten early lessons for change, with personal reflections by Nancy Zimpher and Steve Percy.

The Milwaukee Idea
Ten Early Lessons for Change

1) You've got to have a Big Idea
2) You need a process
3) Partnering is crucial
4) Be nimble
5) Experiment and evolve
6) Morph
7) Brand it
8) Create a network of support
9) Move to action
10) Be accountable

Lesson One:
You've Got to Have a Big Idea

Like most states, Wisconsin has a state bird (the robin), a state animal (the badger), and a state beverage (milk, of course). It even has an unofficial state hat—the cheesehead. But unlike the other 49, Wisconsin claims a state philosophy: The Wisconsin Idea. It was by anchoring The Milwaukee Idea in this strong tradition that UWM could imagine change. Some UWM faculty felt that The Wisconsin Idea was "the way you do things." It was integral to UWM's founding mission and was the natural source for the evolution of The Milwaukee Idea.

It also offered another advantage as UWM looked for the impetus that would rally faculty and students for change. It was big enough.

Reflections

Nancy and Steve comment on each of the lessons learned

Nancy Zimpher

There are moments in the life of an institution when it all seems to come together: a happy convergence of leadership, opportunity, and resources. The Milwaukee Idea happened at the right time (UWM was ready for bold action), the right place (an urban research university), and the right tradition (The Wisconsin Idea).

The Milwaukee Idea is not some radical concept imposed by a new chancellor eager to make her mark. It grows out of our understanding of our social mission as a public institution. So when I came to UWM, I wanted to find a Big Idea that was true to the institution.

Setting the goal of being a premier urban research university is a lofty one, but it doesn't pass the "shiver test"—no spine-tingling reaction that makes you want to join in. The Milwaukee Idea passes that test. It meets Collins and Porras' definition of a Big Hairy Audacious Goal: It reaches out and grabs you.

> "We will accept no small plans."
> —Nancy Zimpher to Committee of 100 at first Milwaukee Idea plenary

The Milwaukee Idea is large enough to encompass the entire academy, from freshman business major to emeritus professor of history. Many faculty, it is true, struggled (or rebelled) at the notion of how engagement in the urban community could apply to their scholarship or teaching, but what began as "change at the margins" is elastic enough to offer opportunities across the academic spectrum—to those willing to imagine.

It's important to note, as Collins and Porras caution, that big ideas do not replace the organization's core mission.[3] Student learning, scholarship and discovery, and public outreach are at UWM's core. They are the reasons the university exists. The Milwaukee Idea, with its urban priority and its commitment to com-

munity collaboration, is the creative spirit that invigorates that mission. Professor René Gratz describes it as a "way of doing business and an idea, rather than an event or thing."

It's all that. It's ideas, it's our budget plan, it's our process of organizational reinvention. And, as Steve likes to say, The Milwaukee Idea is an attitude. That's what a Big Idea can do.

Lesson Two: You Need a Process

The measure of a bold vision lies in its capacity to encourage everyone involved to imagine something better and inspire each individual to be a part of that change. It is a dream that is dreamed together. One of the greatest results of the first two years of The Milwaukee Idea is that students, faculty, and staff at UWM had the opportunity to think in new ways.

> "You can't get to radical, energizing change without a transformational process."
>
> —Greg Jay
> Action Team leader

"We were given a chance to be creative," said Professor Laurie Glass. "That is a rare opportunity, not frequently offered—in any organization."

"When was the last time a chancellor came to you to discuss a decision *before* it was made?" asked Union President Stan Yasaitis as he described how The Milwaukee Idea process had changed the way he interacted with the UWM administration. "What's interesting about The Milwaukee Idea is that it said everybody can contribute and everybody needs to, for the well-being of the university."

Steve Percy
The Milwaukee Idea process—from Affinity visioning to Action Team planning to evaluation and negotiation—succeeded because it was based on inclusivity. Diverse voices from on and off campus were encouraged at each stage. This built shared ownership of the process that continues to expand as leaders draw more and more people into the circle of participation. The very practice of inclusion strengthened the process itself, so that it was mutually reinforcing.

Nancy Zimpher
The other key to getting the process right was making sure that significant groups of people were playing ball. I created my Cabinet, for example, made up of leaders of every major organization on campus: faculty, labor, deans, students, administration. I keep them in the loop so they are able to share information across campus. Just as importantly, they inform my decision-making from the various perspectives they bring to the table.

Steve Percy
The Milwaukee Idea process has proved to be an effective and new way of work-
ing—one that has spilled over into how administration works with staff and fac-
ulty, how decisions are made, and how colleagues are treated. The Milwaukee
Idea has given people permission to start thinking about doing things differently,
and how they do their work has changed because of that.

Just as importantly, The Milwaukee Idea has rewarded faculty and staff for
innovation—rewarded them with new positions, funding, and time to expand
their ideas. This process has kept the momentum for change moving forward.

Lesson Three: Partnering Is Crucial

Central to The Milwaukee Idea was the notion of partnering. This value
applied internally to the process itself and to the focus on interdisciplinary
collaborations, and externally, in the university's commitment to renewed
engagement with the community.

Like most universities, UWM needed to learn how to work as a community. As Professor Greg Jay notes, large metropolitan universities are notoriously fragmented places, and UWM was no exception. Through The Milwaukee Idea, faculty met peers from across campus for the first time at Affinity Group meetings. Interdisciplinary relationships became possible through
shared work on Action Teams. In some ways, as René Gratz suggests, the
process of partnering is The Milwaukee Idea's most important product. Secretary of the University Ellen Murphy echoes that idea. The Milwaukee Idea,
she says, demonstrated repeatedly the importance of relationships. Perhaps
the single most defining element of success for each of the Ideas was how successfully new partnerships were formed and strengthened.

If nothing else, The Milwaukee Idea fostered a new spirit of community
that is beginning to change the way the university interacts. Assistant Vice
Chancellor Ruth Williams commented on how the budget planning process
became more open and attributed the change in part to The Milwaukee Idea
model. A student leader observed that The Milwaukee Idea had helped the
institution relate better to students. "There is a clearer sense of mission, a
sense of self, and a sense that it's going in the right direction, through coalition building, working with the community, and realizing it needs to be relevant."

If UWM needed to learn how to partner among its faculty, staff, and students, it also had much to learn about partnering with the community. The
"reciprocal, two-way relationships" [4] that the Kellogg Commission says char-
acterize true engagement are not easily forged. "We're good at giving, but not

so good at taking," said Dean William Rayburn, describing the academic propensity for independent action.

UWM's experience in community partnerships was as old as the university itself, but it was not a hallmark of every school and college. As Jean Tyler observed, The Milwaukee Idea experience was really just a first step in helping to identify new opportunities for partnerships and to raise awareness of which community members needed to be included in future efforts.

Nancy Zimpher

Partnering is not just one of the several key attributes of The Milwaukee Idea. It is pivotal. As one of the first web site bulletins announced, The Milwaukee Idea is all about partnerships. And that is the secret to the success—or failure—of the change process.

We're still learning to get it right. Partnering is not the university seeking a community collaborator to help complete a project. It is a reciprocal relationship where university and community together decide what's important and how it is to be accomplished. Dean Sally Lundeen told me she must constantly monitor herself to make sure she isn't taking a position that fails to acknowledge the role of her community partners. We must all be deliberate in our relationships.

We also are trying to find ways as an institution to be more supportive of faculty and students who want engagement, and who see it as a way to truly animate their scholarship and research. As I had the opportunity to rethink my administrative team, a priority was to make partnership integral to our structure. So we created the position of vice chancellor for partnerships and innovation with the mandate that it be filled by someone from the community—someone who brings a network of connections with her. This has helped to bring the community into and onto the campus in both a real and symbolic way.

In the end, one of the best measures of the success of The Milwaukee Idea is how well UWM collaborates, in truly authentic ways.

Lesson Four: Be Nimble

You can't move the battleship of higher education without a lot of hands to help push. It takes leadership and vision at the top—and middle and bottom. Nancy Zimpher's first year was spent stretching talents, identifying needs, and finding the right people for a team that could manage change.

Building a "nimble team" doesn't involve hiring the best and highest-priced talent available. According to many business innovators, the best teams evolve, allowing the organization the freedom to try out changes before making major commitments, to see what works and what doesn't before structures are put in place.

The key word is structural flexibility—how well the team can bend to new ideas and new challenges. This process relies on individual innovation and responsibility, which, as the team coalesces, builds strong group allegiance, with nimble response.[5]

Nimble. Flexible. Responsive. These are words that must increasingly be used to describe institutions of learning. As James Duderstadt writes, the best way to predict the future is to invent it, and the future for higher education may well be "divisionless." By this he means less specialized, a "web of structures" that integrate disciplines and colleges both horizontally and vertically.[6] This kind of structure—or lack of it—is something that every institution will need to create on its own.

UWM, according to some long-time faculty, had a history of flexibility, based in part on a loose organizational structure. Faculty and staff were given the leeway to try new things, if their other work demands were also met.[7] It was not difficult, then, for the chancellor to build a matrix organization that overlays the traditional academic organization chart: Deans collaborate across disciplines, directors of Ideas report to multiple deans, chancellor's deputies focus on specific projects, and campus leaders serve both campus and community.

This matrix overlay was an ideal solution to an academic environment in which traditional structures change slowly. The matrix retains the academic framework, but allows for more flexible inter-relationships.

One way to build a strong matrix is to use generalists. Change experts tell us that people who can think broadly and have many interests and skills help them better combine disparate ideas, techniques, processes, and cultures—a skill essential to the change process.[8]

The secret is to create an environment that encourages relationships. As Greg Jay said, if you're going to change the culture of an institution, you must create structures to bring people together in meaningful ways, to cross boundaries and be rewarded for doing so.

A matrix organization that relied heavily on networks of individuals connected to functions and to the chancellor provided a flexible—and responsive model. As business consultant Sally Helgeson has written, these kinds of web organizations, by emphasizing process as well as structure, by encouraging new connections, help to transform the organization as well. They are teams that can "go the distance."[9]

Nancy Zimpher
I recall a conversation I had with the University of Wisconsin Regents during the early days of my tenure. I had just outlined the scope and process of The Milwaukee

Idea and the group was nodding politely. Then Regent Olivieri asked "What about your bench?"

He knew, of course, that you can't go it alone. I believe that change in the academy must be initiated and constantly supported from the top.

My job as chancellor is to provide the encouragement and environment for everyone at the university to advance our mission more effectively. Without my constant and vigilant support, The Milwaukee Idea would not have succeeded.

But I also believe that leadership, while essential, is not sufficient. A strong bench is vital, and a key source of that strong bench is diversity. I can only be as effective as the range of ideas and perspectives I can access. Broadening my Cabinet to all groups was immensely valuable for me as I reaped the benefits of new ideas. Widening the ethnic and cultural diversity of my staff opened doors to new communities and new voices. Creating a matrix organization gave staff freedom and flexibility. It's designed to create a little disequilibrium in the academy. We can't go on with the silos and the turf battles. We have to be more nimble.

While UWM has often operated in the shadow of UW-Madison's remarkable leadership, being number two has given us the luxury of being able to take more risks. We can experiment, try new organizational approaches, and respond more quickly.

Someone once described this kind of structurally flexible organization as "Jell-O nailed to the wall." [10] *As shaky as that sounds, it works.*

Lesson Five: Experiment and Evolve

Provost John Wanat likes to tell the old joke about the definition of a university. It is, he says, the only institution in which a vote of 34 to one is seen as a tie. That's why, from the beginning, alignment with The Milwaukee Idea was more important than 100% consensus.

Moving forward—at what sometimes seemed a breakneck speed—drew people into the initiative more powerfully than waiting for everyone to agree. Alignment also encouraged experimentation.

No one had time to impose a rigid structure, so participants could find individual ways to incorporate the new direction of the university into the way they worked. When crises hit, staff scrambled to find the best creative decision—often working outside the established "way we've always done things around here." This gave The Milwaukee Idea an essential elasticity that has been a core attribute. It also relieved people of the mandate to be perfect. There was room to make things up, and also room to fix things when they didn't work the first time.

For example, when the selection of leaders and resource allocation for launching the First Ideas met opposition, Percy and Zimpher decided to put

> "A living systems thinker might listen for 'where the system wants to go.' By amplifying or intensifying people's overall awareness of that direction, new behaviors will naturally emerge, and propel the overall pattern of the system into a new form."
> —Peter Senge
> *The Dance of Change*

everything on hold until the deans and governance groups could help invent a new process. The Trustee Council, an innovative administrative model, was the result.

UWM's experiments often led to positive discoveries. When implemented as a response to a real need, the solution worked. If it had been imposed from above or implemented as a grand reorganizational scheme, it might have failed. UWM's process is a good example of the notion that intractable problems cannot be solved by challenging them head on. Instead, as change guru Peter Senge describes it, effective organizational change is organic. It deals with "living systems." It starts small and starts within. As in nature, organizational change happens best when new growth is nurtured, not when old battles are fought. [11]

The Milwaukee Idea focused the university's efforts on new possibilities, not on old problems. It also grew out of an already established notion, The Wisconsin Idea. By encouraging the university to refocus its energies on engagement—a practice and tradition that was well rooted—The Milwaukee Idea could flourish. And flourish it did, with 11 First Ideas—and growing. Many observers, both inside and outside the university warned that growing 11 Ideas would tap valuable resources. That is a danger, but there is also the potential, inherent in living systems theory, that new activity produces change—and that more activity produces more change.

But all change, especially evolutionary change, must be protected. UWM has been very deliberate in constructing supports to nurture the new growth of The Milwaukee Idea: a strong financial base for the visioning and planning stages; a major funding effort for implementation; and resources, access, and flexibility for The Milwaukee Idea office.

Protection also involves pacing. Eric Abrahamson, in the *Harvard Business Review,* talks about the importance of interspersing major change with periods of smaller, organic change. He calls it "dynamic stability" and it involves both "tinkering" and "kludging." Tinkering is obvious: It's the fine-tuning activities that take what already exists and makes them work for the new organization. Several of the First Ideas are perfect examples of this process: ramping up existing projects in Architecture for Campus Design Solutions. Combining study abroad and international students at the Center for International Studies. Broad scale, comprehensive change wasn't necessary to make these Ideas successful.

"Kludging" is tinkering on a larger scale: adapting assets and skills for new purposes. When UWM created the TechStar collaboration it was a great "kludge" change. It created a separate initiative that nonetheless drew on many of the existing First Ideas and didn't require ground-up development. [12]

Steve Percy

One of the deans once told me I should stop calling The Milwaukee Idea an "experiment." She said all the scientists on campus would lose faith because scientists know that most experiments fail. And, of course, The Milwaukee Idea has hit opposition and unexpected problems. There were turbulent times when The Milwaukee Idea's headlong rush led it straight into a brick wall. And then we just had to stop and correct things.

This freedom to experiment is professionally rewarding and provides an example to campus for how to introduce change in other areas. If The Milwaukee Idea has a watchword, it is "experiment."

Nancy Zimpher

In some ways, Lesson Five: Experiment and Evolve, and Lesson One: Have a Big Idea, seem diametrically opposed. How can you nurture incremental change and at the same time tackle big challenges?

The answer lies in seeing the whole. The cathedral is built one stone at a time. Each brick must be placed correctly, according to the grand vision of what can be. The Milwaukee Idea is certainly huge. It's daring and inspiring. But it must be created. And that's where the organic approach to seeking evolutionary change seems right. We are experimental to the bone. We have to be!

Of course we don't know exactly what our final product will be. In fact, there will be no final product, just a continuing process of creating a premier institution. But the outline is The Milwaukee Idea. Within those guidelines we grow.

Steve Percy

As The Milwaukee Idea has evolved and as more people on campus and in the community become involved, it's fair to say that it is becoming "institutionalized." It's taking root. The attitude, philosophy, and practice of The Milwaukee Idea are more and more expressed through traditional mechanisms—you'll see The Milwaukee Idea mentioned in job descriptions for hiring new staff, in applications for sabbatical, in proposals for resource allocations.

As opportunities to hire new faculty and deans arise, their alignment with the goals of The Milwaukee Idea is becoming more a part of the consideration process.

In a way, that's important because The Milwaukee Idea is becoming an integral part of UWM, not just a reflection of our leadership or our chancellor.

Community people often ask me what will happen if the chancellor leaves. I do not believe that The Milwaukee Idea is dependent on just a few isolated individuals any more.

Nancy Zimpher

Institutionalizing The Milwaukee Idea is a very important issue, because there's no pride in saying it will fall apart if the chancellor or executive director leaves. UWM has taken a big step in defining its goal to be a premier urban research university—as an institution we are certain of this.

Just as important, this community concern that UWM continue to remain engaged has suddenly changed the entire conversation. Now it is no longer about who is the leader, but how much the community and the campus want to continue on this path. The community truly has new power in affecting the potential of this institution. The campus and community together will determine the future of this initiative. It's bigger than an individual or a single idea.

Lesson Six: Morph

There is change. And then there is morphing. The change process is what the organization experiences—its processes and structures. Morphing is what happens to the brand and the message. Much like the high-tech Hollywood process that allows figures to seamlessly change form, The Milwaukee Idea also has shifted roles and become different things to different people.

The Affinity Groups talked about Big Ideas. The Action Teams fine-tuned them into the First Ideas. The First Ideas have been launched as new centers and institutes. And "Round Two" of The Milwaukee Idea solicited another set of ideas.

For the university, The Milwaukee Idea is a way to reinvigorate its mission. For Milwaukee, it is a way to connect to new research and ideas. For the UW System, The Milwaukee Idea is urban partnerships. For Wisconsin, it is an investment in the future.

As new initiatives are launched, The Milwaukee Idea will redefine itself again. Morphing allows the BHAG to become even more comprehensive and, more importantly, to become more meaningful to the people it touches.

Steve Percy

When I'm in the community or walking across campus, I often hear people talking about The Milwaukee Idea. If I didn't know what they were talking about, sometimes I'd think they were talking about completely different things. At City Hall I hear it described in terms of economic development. Faculty in Letters and Science speak in terms of new approaches to student learning. In the business community, I hear about job training and the new economy. For others, it's the reason why they want to be a part of our capital campaign. Grad students talk in terms of community-based research. Nonprofits think leadership training when I say "Milwaukee Idea."

And that's fine. The Milwaukee Idea, like all BAHGs, can be described in "100 different ways, yet easily be understood by everyone." [13] *That's because there is a common core: The Milwaukee Idea is the campus and community working together. That's the only thing people need to understand—and they get it.*

Lesson Seven: Brand It

"Imagine a community filled with economic vitality, rich in cultural and educational opportunity, healthy and safe. And, at its heart, a vibrant partner, the university." The vision of The Milwaukee Idea began with the words of the chancellor's first faculty plenary address and continued throughout the entire three-year process. The Milwaukee Idea is now used across campus, on banners and posters, in newspaper articles and among civic leaders.

The secret to a successful vision, say Collins and Porras, is a vivid description—pictures, as well as words, of what the future can hold. And so Zimpher, joined by Percy and many of the Affinity and Action Team members, "made visible the public work" [14] of the university: describing storefront economic development, students traveling in India, kids playing on restored brownfields.

> Communication is more than the words used. It's how, where, and by whom. And it is in the intangibles of communication that the strongest messages are conveyed. For UWM, that intangible message was "integrity." By talking about—and, more importantly, modeling—values of inclusivity, diversity, and partnership, the chancellor signaled that The Milwaukee Idea would keep its promises.

Branding means creating an image backed by communication that is thematic, on-message, and consistent. For The Milwaukee Idea, all materials had a bold, vibrant look—a brand identity—that built equity for UWM. The bright gold and black colors, the support materials, all reinforced the messages of change, growth, and excitement.

Most importantly, everyone worked from the same page. Zimpher, Percy, and UWM leadership quoted each other and soon heard their comments reflected back by community leaders. These community "echoes" were important ways to hear how UWM's vision was being received by the community and also provided Milwaukee Idea leadership with added dimensions, as civic participants put their own spin on the vision. It also reinforced UWM's accountability to the community. When Milwaukee began to take notice of The Milwaukee Idea, through the public vetting and innumerable presentations, UWM had to produce results.

Nancy Zimpher
I've repeated The Milwaukee Idea message so often, I've lost count. I'm sure Steve feels the same way. Being on-message has been key to our progress.

    Together with team and campus leaders, we accepted every Rotary, Kiwanis, and Junior League invitation tendered. I've held up gears to illustrate UWM's new research for Milwaukee's industry. I've sat with business leaders and used charts and graphs to talk about everything that UWM was already doing for Milwaukee and the new jobs it could help to foster.

    When I arrived at UWM, we had no clear identity. No one knew our colors were black and gold, the logo was undistinguished, and you could count the people who could sing our fight song on one hand. We needed to create the UWM brand from the ground up. Today we have banners in black and gold touting both UWM and The Milwaukee Idea across campus. We have "Black and Gold Days" and we're working on getting that fight song updated. The Milwaukee Idea is on signs around the city and at the airport. We are now a presence in this community.

Lesson Eight: Create a Network of Support

Part of the rationale for taking The Milwaukee Idea message to the community was to create an external network of support that mirrored the internal one. As important as it was to "build a bench" with flexible, strong leadership, it also was essential to nurture champions on the outside who would provide feedback, analysis, support, and financial backing. As a public institution, UWM is servant to the wishes of the people of Wisconsin—and to state funding. When the university proposed a large increase in state funding in support of The Milwaukee Idea, a rich web of influential supporters was vital to getting the message to the capitol that this proposal was worth funding.

    While UWM did have a board of directors in name—the UW System Board of Regents—it oversees the entire System of 26 universities and colleges. Regents needed a reason to pay attention to UWM so the chancellor used an annual on-site Regents meeting to inform the Board about UWM's new directions and to build enthusiasm through recreational and social activities that highlighted UWM capacity. From cruises on UWM's Lake Michigan research vessel to breakfast at the new ballpark, the Regents were introduced to a new UWM.

    The chancellor and campus leadership also began to build support networks in the community. Some happened when people engaged in The Milwaukee Idea process—several legislators participated in Affinity Groups and became advocates for UWM. Other participants were leaders of educational and social service organizations who could encourage new collaborations at their agencies and in their classrooms. Other supporters came from the chancellor's countless speaking engagements, inspired by the idea of new directions for the university. And still others were wooed through business breakfasts, alumni receptions, and foundation dinners.

Nancy Zimpher
A university can't go it alone. Public or private, external support is crucial. That's why building a brand is so important. Why consistent and frequent communication is vital.

The good news for UWM—and the bad news—is that we don't have a board of directors—no ring of fire to project us. What that means, however, is that we also have some latitude to create the kind of support network we need.

So we began with the institutions on campus that had external ties: the UWM Foundation, the Alumni Association, the Board of Visitors. We invested in staff and focused on activities that reinforced The Milwaukee Idea. Our friends needed to know—and love—The Milwaukee Idea as much as we did.

Early on we created the Corporate Council, a group of leading CEOs from area business and industry. We held quarterly breakfast meetings with a strict one-hour time limit with the stated purpose of soliciting their advice, not their donations. We needed their input, to find out what the needs of that community were and how UWM was perceived. They were flattered to be asked and became a vital resource and counsel. When the time came to ask the governor to back The Milwaukee Idea, every one of them signed a statement in support of UWM—signatures that had meaning for state leaders. When we needed them to advocate for UWM—sometimes with only a few hours' notice—they responded. This kind of support from external stakeholders is essential if change is to occur.

Lesson Nine: Move to Action
Vince Lombardi would agree: It's results that count. From the first plenary meeting it was clear that the results of The Milwaukee Idea would not be minutes from meetings and a dusty report. The outcomes would be concrete and real. The goal always has been to take those theoretical pictures of what The Milwaukee Idea vision is and turn them into actual photographs of community-based results.

The process has generated a mentality and momentum for action. This was accomplished by clearly defining the desired outcomes for Affinity and Action Teams (transformative ideas) and setting an aggressive timeline for results (work the summer; launch your Idea).

For some, the process itself has been a significant outcome. But the process is not enough. "What we want in the end is real change," Greg Jay said. "We want product. We want a better education for our students. We want more collaboration among our faculty. We want the community to recognize UWM for the leader that it is. We want tangible achievements for these partnerships so that people can look back and say 'This would not have happened if it hadn't been for The Milwaukee Idea.'"

Nancy Zimpher
One of my favorite quotes is "Ideas without action are meaningless." Action is important as a demonstration of our intent to deliver. But it also has another function. Action is the means through which change is integrated into an institution. In The Dance of Change, *Peter Senge's book about sustaining momentum in learning organizations, he talks about the three processes necessary for generating profound change.*

The first is at the personal level, when individuals become involved in an idea because it matters to them. The Committee of 100 became involved because participants believed—for many different reasons—that they wanted to be part of making the university better. The strength of The Milwaukee Idea was its power to speak to individuals at a personal level about a renewed mission they could support. Marcia Parsons, for example, talked about faculty who, despite well-earned fears about "just another call to change," became involved because they believed that "this could actually be for real."

The second process necessary for profound change is at the team level, when people join because "my colleagues take it seriously." By the Action stage of The Milwaukee Idea, more people across campus and in the community were involved because they had been in contact with others who spoke passionately about its potential.

And the final stage in the process is at the institutional level, when people invest in change "because it works." By this time even the nay-sayers cannot deny that the new order may hold potential to make life better. They see new ways of working, new ways to organize or partner. They can work from a tangible model. [15] Getting to this final stage is only possible when the process produces results.

For The Milwaukee Idea, results are only now being achieved. But across the campus and throughout the community and state, there is a growing chorus: "This could be for real."

Lesson Ten: Be Accountable
Shortly after the launch of the First Ideas, the state budget process began. Chancellor Zimpher and her administration approached the Regents with a

bold plan for significant funding increases for UWM, and in support of The Milwaukee Idea. The pitch to the Regents and to the state legislature was that an investment in UWM was an investment in Wisconsin. This was because UWM's goals were not just to increase faculty and student numbers but also to make a concrete, measurable difference in the quality of life of the people of Wisconsin. The Milwaukee Idea, with its educational, economic, and environmental initiatives, was the visible proof that the investment would pay off in results.

In essence, UWM said to its supporters and to the people of Wisconsin that it was willing to be held accountable for its end of the social partnership. And it followed up this remarkable offer with some real numbers.

The current high school graduation rate for the Milwaukee Public Schools (MPS) hovers around 43%—unacceptable by any measure and especially in a city that is looking for economic growth.[16] UWM, home to the School of Education that prepares more than half the teachers in Milwaukee's schools, pledged to partner with MPS to radically improve graduation rates by doubling the number of prepared urban teachers and double the graduates trained in information technology. And it would quintuple the number of students enrolled in pre-college programs.

UWM matched its willingness to be held accountable in economic and environmental issues as well, pledging to impact the regional economy through technology transfer and assistance to minority business, and through new initiatives in urban and environmental health.

In short, UWM said that part of partnering is also being willing to be held accountable for results and for change. To this end, as First Ideas are launched, measurement of results is a priority for each initiative.

And Wisconsin has responded. When the state awarded millions in additional funding to UWM in 2001, it was acknowledging the university's commitment to tangible results. The state's investment came with a single string attached: Make a difference.

But the budget success also signaled a growing belief that UWM was capable of achieving those results. "Our budget success is a huge indicator of confidence, as was UW System's initial investment in The Milwaukee Idea at the beginning," said Dean Bob Greenstreet, head of Campus Design Solutions. If UWM was willing to step up to the plate as a community partner, the people of Wisconsin said, then we are willing to play ball.

Nancy Zimpher
I can't emphasize enough how important I think accountability is to university-community engagement. The academy is only too eager to measure our success in

institutional terms: graduation rate, research dollars received, time to degree, pro-ductivity.

At UWM, we took what I consider to be a radical step when we said we also would be held accountable for public school graduation rates, levels of lead in our children's blood, the growth of our regional economy. We can do no less. If we are to be taken seriously as partners, if we are to earn the trust of this community, we must shoulder our responsibility to make a real difference.

John Gardner, founder of Independent Sector, talked about civic engagement in terms of "networks of responsibility." Through our collaborations and through The Milwaukee Idea, we are part of that civic network, accountable to our com-munity for results.

Is it risky? You bet! We don't have any magic bullets. The solutions we offer can only be in partnership with others. There is the very real possibility—if not certainty—that at times we will stumble. But we will get back up and try again. It is our accountability for action that gives meaning to UWM and to The Mil-waukee Idea.

Looking back over what was a three-year process, the University of Wiscon-sin-Milwaukee made great strides. Asked to imagine what its future would be, the faculty, staff, students, alumni, and community said nothing less than a premier, engaged, urban research university would do. And then they rolled up their sleeves and began to make that vision real.

Through brainstorming and debates, planning and campaigning, The Milwaukee Idea has become the way in which UWM defines itself and its future. It has launched ambitious First Ideas and expanded its faculty to meet growing enrollment. It has strengthened its research focus and forged hun-dreds of new partnerships. Most importantly, it has captured the imagination of both campus and community to believe that more is possible.

And there is still much to do. The Milwaukee Idea needs to become more clearly a part of the university fabric, for faculty, academic and classified staff, and students. The university continues to struggle with how these new ways of working can be integrated into its governance traditions and how they can help to transform tenure and faculty recognition. Issues of diversity and stu-dent participation are ongoing. These are big concerns and they will continue to shadow the efforts at UWM.

At the same time, the community also has much to do. It is just now learning how to work with the university: what it can expect, what it needs to contribute, and how ongoing collaborations can be sustained. Relationships and leadership are still evolving. The community itself also needs to continue to assess its needs and goals so that it can use the resources of the university more strategically.

But as these pages have described, UWM already has gone far in the continual quest of defining for a new century what it is about. It has found practical—and sometimes messy—ways to begin conversations about what matters, to dream about what can be, and, perhaps most importantly, to take action to make a difference. UWM is leading the way in what is a national conversation about the role of higher education, the contributions that urban universities can make, and the ways in which faculty, staff, and students can become more involved in the lives of their communities.

Helen Keller once said that we must never consent to creep when we feel the impulse to soar. For UWM—and for countless other institutions of learning across the country—now is the time to soar.

Endnotes

[1] The Kellogg Commission on the Future of State and Land-Grant Universities. (2000). *Renewing the Covenant: Learning, Discovery, and Engagement in a New Age and Different World.* National Association of State Universities and Land-Grant Colleges, page 10.

[2] Michael Fullan. (1993). *Change Forces.* New York: The Falmer Press, page 20.

[3] James Collins and Jerry Porras. (September/October, 1996). "Building Your Company's Vision" in the *Harvard Business Review,* page 74.

[4] The Kellogg Commission on the Future of State and Land-Grant Universities. (1999). *Returning to our Roots: The Engagement Institution.* National Association of State Universities and Land-Grant Colleges, page 30.

[5] Sally Helgesen. (1995). *The Web of Inclusion: A New Architecture for Building Great Organizations.* New York: Currency/Doubleday, page 37.

[6] James Duderstadt. (February 4, 2000). "A Choice of Transformations for the 21st-Century University" in *The Chronicle of Higher Education,* Arts & Opinion Section.

[7] Jon Wergin and Jane Grassadonia. (May, 2001). "The Milwaukee Idea: A Study of Transformative Change," a paper prepared for the Office of University Partnerships, U.S. Department of Housing and Urban Development, page 19.

[8] Eric Abrahamson. (July/August, 2000). "Change Without Pain" in the *Harvard Business Review,* page 79.

[9] Helgesen, *The Web of Inclusion,* page 33.

[10] Ibid., page 24.

Callout page 179: Peter Senge et al. (1999). *The Dance of Change: The Challenges of Sustaining Momentum in Learning Organizations.* New York, NY: Currency/Doubleday, page 144.

[11] From a radio conversation with Peter Senge and Christopher Lydon on *The Connection* on WBUR, Boston, May 10, 2000.

[12] Eric Abrahamson. "Change Without Pain."

[13] Collins and Porras. "Building Your Company's Vision," page 73.

[14] Harry Boyte and Elizabeth Hollander. (1999). *Wingspread Declaration on Renewing the Civic Mission of the American Research University,* page 6.

[15] Peter Senge. *The Dance of Change,* page 46–51.

[16] Sam Schulhofer-Wohl. (November 13, 2001). "Report shows big chasm in graduation," *Milwaukee Journal Sentinel.*

EPILOGUE

As we end this chapter of The Milwaukee Idea, we offer two final thoughts. First, we recognize that The Milwaukee Idea is a work in progress—the story is not complete. We are reporting from what we hope is still an early point in our history. We know The Milwaukee Idea is dynamic and we recognize our perspectives will change. We anticipate a second volume, and only time will tell how much the insight and learning reflected here will prove useful. Surely, we will have more reflections and learning to share. We also hope to have our ambitions and achievements examined by those outside the University of Wisconsin-Milwaukee.

To this end, we are pleased that The Milwaukee Idea has been selected as a case study of a university engaged in forging stronger relationships with its community. The Office of University Partnerships in the U.S. Department of Housing and Urban Development (HUD) has commissioned a case-study volume that will track varied models of engaged universities. UWM's Milwaukee Idea will be one such case. Professor Jon Wergin in the School of Education at Virginia Commonwealth University has visited UWM and prepared an assessment of The Milwaukee Idea. His work will serve as a chapter in the HUD volume and will offer another perspective on our efforts.

THE MILWAUKEE IDEA

*Remarks Prepared for University of Wisconsin-Milwaukee
Faculty Senate Plenary Session, September 17, 1998*

By Nancy L. Zimpher, Chancellor

If one were to count the days since my arrival at UWM, they would surely be logged in miles and meetings, not in days! What does a chancellor do? Here's a glimpse: four editorial board meetings; two alumni gatherings; one ethnic festival; a circus parade; a cruise on UWM's Great Lakes' research vessel *Neeskay*; two times at bat with the Brewers; a back-to-school picnic; testing the world's largest architectural grill; three trips to Madison; freshman move-in day; a walking tour of the campus. I have made numerous trips downtown to meet business CEOs, community and civic leaders, and the mayor himself.

I've also attended neighborhood and community celebrations and dedications; and as many standing committee and college-school-division and department meetings as one could fit into your basic eight-hour day. Homes have been opened to me, maps drawn, and endless trips made across the bridge to the south side of Milwaukee, even when it wasn't my original destination! What an introduction to an exciting world-class city, and what a personal outpouring of welcome from the UWM community.

As I have met people, I've asked, "What are your hopes and dreams for UWM?" Expectations are incredibly high! Literally everyone hopes for the best for UWM. What can the university do for the city? What can the city do for the university? And most important, what can we do for each other and together?

While these are the questions I intend to address today, there are certainly other important issues we face. I have talked about them on WUWM; I have written about them in the *Report*; you have read about them in campus and community newspapers:

- Our commitment to enhancing the quality of student life. Already we are planning the "New Student Convocation" and other efforts to enhance the ritual and culture of the campus.

- The profound opportunity presented us by the UW System's Plan 2008, and the emerging plan for UWM in succeeding drafts of the Milwaukee Commitment. I am proud to have come to a state that had the courage to articulate its continuing commitment to diversity.

- Our efforts to streamline the university's infrastructure and become more user friendly and service oriented.

- Our need to continue with important planning initiatives that began well before I came here: strategic planning and the faculty perspective thereof; the program array review; long-term facilities plans; advertising campaigns; and information technology support systems. These efforts must be continued because they represent clear steps in reaching this institution's full capacity.

But today, I will invoke the past only to address the future.

Beginning with my earliest visit to Milwaukee back in March, I heard reference to the notion of The Wisconsin Idea. Everyone spoke of it with such obvious familiarity. It became abundantly clear to me that The Wisconsin Idea was really something special. I heard it in casual conversation, I heard it at Regents meetings; and President Lyall referenced it most recently at the celebration of the University of Wisconsin-Madison's sesquicentennial, as did Chancellor David Ward and Governor Tommy Thompson.

I've kept asking myself, where do we fit in The Wisconsin Idea? So we searched the web, and the sesquicentennial edition of Wisconsin's *Blue Book,* the source for all things legislative and statutory. And, there it was: "The boundaries of the University are the boundaries of the State"—the notion that the university's faculty serve all the citizens of the state, not only those on campus.

Many of the university's efforts through The Wisconsin Idea became part of the national fabric—the drafting of national legislation for social security, civil service, workers compensation, agricultural research that eradicated disease and improved crop production, and development of concepts that led to wildlife ecology, game management, reforesting—and frankly, better sauerkraut!

Judging from the UW sesquicentennial celebration, launched in Madison just a week ago today, we will continue to bring attention to modern-day examples of The Wisconsin Idea, through technology transfer and specialized expertise, applied and direct research for real-world applications, and outreach and training. We at UWM will do that, as Katharine Lyall observed, not as a carbon copy of UW-Madison, but in our own distinctive way, as a significant member of this great university system.

We must cast a vision of ourselves and our future that distinguishes us not only in Wisconsin, but nationally across that group of peer urban institutions who face, as we do, the incredible heralding of the 21st century, and the promise of an urban renaissance.

By the year 2000, the world population is expected to rise to the 6 billion figure, 50% of whom will be living in cities in the next century, a 100%

increase in a period of only 20 years. Already, 40% of our state's citizens reside in the greater Milwaukee area.

As Wisconsin's only public urban campus, UWM already has a powerful presence. In the Milwaukee of the 21st century, UWM can surely thrive and, I believe, become a centerpiece of metropolitan life. For us, The Wisconsin Idea gives us a firm foundation, but it does not take us where we need to go.

Thus, the working title for our destiny: The Milwaukee Idea. This title recognizes that cities are the hallmark of civilization; frontiers of imagination and innovation (President Lyndon Johnson).

Mayor Norquist has observed, "America is an urban society. In cities we find the first signs of social and cultural upheaval. The problems of poverty, illiteracy, joblessness, and social conflict are concentrated in our cities.

"Despite these stresses, cities are also our country's best hope for change. They are fertile with talent, ideas, and opportunities—and Milwaukee is blessed with more of these resources than most cities."

As observed on the cover of the Norquist text, "cities should not be looked upon as a problem that needs to be fixed, but as a source of limitless potential that can be unleashed through policies based on a clearer understanding of how cities generate lasting value—to their citizens and to the nation as a whole."

A FRAMEWORK FOR THE MILWAUKEE IDEA

It is clear to me that the University of Wisconsin-Milwaukee is one of Milwaukee's greatest assets, if not its greatest. But how do we assert our case? How do we express the essence of The Milwaukee Idea? It's not just us serving the city. It's not just the city serving us. It is the notion of together building a city and a university that are the heart of Metropolitan Milwaukee. This is the essence of The Milwaukee Idea!

But how do we make The Milwaukee Idea evident and commonplace in the minds of our constituencies and, frankly, in our own mind's eye?

We begin, as all good ideas do, with ourselves.

Our goal is nothing less than to change forever the quality of our life together—yours and mine, theirs and ours—by endeavoring to join the urban renaissance of Milwaukee; and the transformation of ourselves as Milwaukee's, and someday the nation's, premier urban university.

Undoubtedly such a concept will play itself out in a network of, for lack of a better word, "urban environments"—the life space in which you and I live. It's my life and your life, our children's lives, our neighbors' lives that define the quality of our life together. Nowhere more than in the cities does the quality of my life depend so heavily on the quality of your life. Our lives are reciprocal, symbiotic. If they educate my child but ignore your child, the city lives in ignorance. If I go to work but you go hungry and without purpose in your life, then the city has no purpose or life.

In order to reach that goal, we need hope, hard work, vision, and a little imagination.

Imagine . . . An Urban Environment of Economic Opportunity

Nowhere more than in the city do we need better job readiness. This is as true for the college graduate as it is for an 18-year-old who dreams of holding a high-skilled, high-paying job. Students have to be better prepared to meet the educational and technological challenges of the 21st century. Business and intellectual enterprises have to provide better ways for young people to realize the dreams of full and productive employment. We need enterprise zones and business incubators, and accessible, state-of-the-art learning facilities that make the new work an integral part of the authentic learning experiences of learners, whether they be kids in high school or adults in college.

To do this, we will have to create educational and employment networks that rival any school-business partnership ever dreamed of in the 1980s and 1990s. We talk about the new world, but none of us has truly attained it in the ways we think about preparation for school and work.

Many of us on this campus are already strongly engaged in the metropolitan marketplace:

- In peer training in technology on campus and with our business partners
- Through a new Masters program in Human Resources and Labor Relations
- Through our Institute for Global Studies

But we have to do more, like the creation of inter-institutional research and service networks. We have to dream a vision of our economic future as an integral part of the Greater Milwaukee and Wisconsin community.

Imagine . . . An Urban Environment
Rich in Cultural and Educational Opportunity

In the 20th century, we built art museums and schools, botanical gardens, zoological wonders, and cultural exhibits, and we called these the fountains of knowledge. In the 21st century, we will see the real potential of total knowledge expansion, the growth of the web, the dependence on information technologies whose future can only be dimly imagined today. These technologies will catapult over traditional notions of teaching and learning, and of our cultural and artistic understanding. Some kids will still read to learn, others will listen to learn, some will feel to learn, or experience to learn. Others will create to learn.

How will we greet the learning and cultural attributes of the 21st century, when art is created electronically and knowledge is stored in gigabytes? This is the educational environment of the future. We must not only come to understand it, we must frame it.

Again, many on this campus are making a profound difference in the artistic, intellectual, and educational landscape of metropolitan Milwaukee:

- Science Vans and the Science Bags

- Professional development for teachers across multiple disciplines

- Our pervasive presence in the arts and our multiple partnerships with the Milwaukee Public Schools

But together with the city, in partnership with Milwaukee Area Technical College, the Medical College of Wisconsin, Milwaukee School of Engineering, Cardinal Stritch College, Marquette University, Alverno, and the rest, we must become *the* urban educational hub of Wisconsin, networking and brokering educational and cultural experiences for young and lifelong learners, equivalent to any airway hub America has to offer. And perhaps most importantly, we must become the portal campus for the University of Wisconsin System, opening doors for metropolitan Milwaukee that do in fact truly extend the boundaries of the city to the boundaries of the state.

Imagine . . . An Urban Environment of Health and Wellness

The past five years have seen a massive transformation of our medical delivery system. We are on the verge of redefining personal independence and interdependence through state and federal welfare reform.

Again, this campus is directly engaged in that transformation:

- Through evaluative research on W2 [Wisconsin Works] welfare reforms

- Our community nursing centers

- Our Center for Addiction and Behavioral Health Research

- Our System-supported urban environmental health initiative

Imagine . . . An Urban Environment that Transcends Our National Boundaries

We have the unrivaled advantage of Milwaukee's location as an international port. The commercial, industrial, manufacturing, and business interests of the Greater Milwaukee community are unequivocally international. Corporations that were once just local now trade daily in the international marketplace. UWM possesses the capacity to contribute through language proficiency, cultural awareness, and international exchange programs to the metropolitan community. Milwaukee and UWM together have the capability to become the essence of our international port, creating unique public/private partnerships, an international business park, and a window for the metropolitan area to the international expertise available throughout the UW System.

Again, this is happening, step by step, today:

- Through our Institute of World Affairs

- Our role in an international initiative to lead the UW System in globalization

- Overseas liberal studies and library science programs

Imagine . . . The Environment of Our Urban Environment

Sound redundant? Well, it's really not. While we have borrowed from our colleagues in architecture and urban planning a cityscape term like "environments," we are acutely aware that the urban landscape needs our continued vigilance and creativity. What will or should the spaces of the 21st century look like? How will we define the 21st century neighborhood? Better yet, what is your personal vision of the neighborhood in which you would most like to live in the new millennium? We have the talent to design, to inform, to create, to stimulate the most creative and sensitive aspects of our environmental growth, from the waterways of the Great Lakes to the back alley passageways that so define urban life.

Already, much of this city's "environment" has been at UWM's design:

- Student architects working one-on-one with city planners

- More than I have time to say about our Great Lakes WATER Institute

- Partnerships between schools/colleges and community agencies in the city, focusing on our urban settlement

How will we achieve this vision of our future?

First and foremost, to be a player in the urban landscape of the future, we have to have ideas. We have a notion that the 21st Century Idea Factory might somehow become a pseudonym for the modern-day university. That's what UWM is—an Idea Factory. I know you say, why does everything have to be in retrofit? OK, have it your way: an Idea Zone, an Idea Sphere, an Idea Icon. Or an "intellectual merchandise mart." But any way you cut it, that's us. We are the developers of new knowledge, we are the developers of modern-day application. We're the ones investigating the quality of the water we drink, the reproduction of lake perch, the invasion of the zebra mussels. We're concerned about these issues not just for our city, but for the nation as a whole.

So, while I see the renaissance of these urban environments as only the skeletal beginnings of framing The Milwaukee Idea, they can become its cornerstones. We must do the hard work of figuring out the reality of our dreams, the actions that transcend our rhetoric.

THE MILWAUKEE IDEA PROCESS

So how to make The Milwaukee Idea a reality?

In my 30 working days on campus, I have visited numerous groups whose hopes and dreams are critical to the future of this campus:

- The University Committee and other standing committees of our shared governance structure

- The Academic Staff Committee

- Student leaders

- Union representatives

- Deans and directors

- Our Alumni and Foundation Boards, and soon our Board of Visitors, and numerous individuals and groups in the community, including business executives, civic leaders, community association and neighborhood groups, elected officials, and of course, our Milwaukee Regents

Many, if not all, of these groups are represented in this audience.

Today I call you to action, and propose that we roll up our collective sleeves and go to work on defining the essence of "The Milwaukee Idea."

To do so, I have asked the groups above to do several things:

First and foremost, I have asked them to share with me their early thoughts and expectations in defining the distinctively urban nature of this great university.

Then I asked them to give me a process that would so distinguish our work that all who participated and were informed could someday embrace The Milwaukee Idea as their own. Then I asked them to volunteer themselves and others for this very deliberate work.

I am proud to say today that they have done so.

They have agreed to become party to a plenary group that will be convened immediately and oversee the work of this campus and its community during the next 100 days. That's about 100 people, working over the next 100 days, all the while feeding information to their constituent members and carrying their input back into the discussion process. This is not a strategic planning process, per se. Rather, it is a captivating opportunity to redefine our mission and vision, the core values, and most important, the critical action steps that will define UWM for the decade and century to come. It is a rare opportunity to create our own distinctive 21st century identity. I know the sacrifices I am calling for. I deeply appreciate the commitment I've already encountered.

These groups have agreed to meet consistently over time, to promote creative thinking, and most of all to participate in the framing of actions that would unfold during the months and years to come as The Milwaukee Idea.

They, in turn, will keep close to their constituents to share information frequently, to be open to new ideas, and to help us all serve as friendly critics for each others' thinking. They have asked for assurance that this phase of the process would have not only a beginning, but also a clear ending. We have promised each other to commit ourselves to action.

Eventually we will need to enhance the curriculum at both the undergraduate and graduate levels and engage our students, faculty, and community resources to craft a curriculum-in-motion; that is, loan staff and resources from the campus and the community to this effort to get it off the ground.

We will have to continue to examine the quality and relatedness of our graduate and undergraduate and outreach programs to this urban vision, and the quality of our faculty to sustain our research and instructional commitments. We will have to look closely at the interdependence of our arts and sciences programs to the professional schools and colleges on campus.

We can also expect that the schools and colleges, divisions, and departments would ultimately be asked to reallocate resources in the direction of The Milwaukee Idea.

Crafting The Milwaukee Idea will require the time and talent of key community players. We must seek the agreement of important constituent groups in the community to make The Milwaukee Idea a reality. This commitment has been enthusiastically forthcoming. Finally, we must work hand in glove with our Board of Regents and System administration. I have briefed President Katharine Lyall on our intent to define The Milwaukee Idea, and we have her full support.

Katharine and I are not the only people who think the time has come to redefine ourselves.

As Ernest Boyer remarks: "As we move towards a new century, profound changes stir the nation and the world.... It is a moment for boldness in higher education."

"Our nation's institutions of higher education are crucial to the fight to save our cities. The long-term futures of both the city and the university in this country are so intertwined that one cannot—or perhaps will not—survive without the other," says former Secretary of Housing and Urban Development Henry Cisneros.

Hear HUD Officer Marcia Feld: "I don't want to say it is an idea whose time has come. Rather, it is a concept whose need has finally been understood. By starting to talk about how universities can care for their communities, they are beginning to understand *why* they have to care."

So, what will we achieve with our 100 people for 100 days?

My hope is that we will create a statement of The Milwaukee Idea that defines this university and its role in all of our lives in a way that will become generally accepted and widely recognized for simultaneously capturing the essence of the great university that is UWM, and the great city that is Milwaukee.

Moreover, my vision is that this statement of The Milwaukee Idea will be as animating for our university as The Wisconsin Idea has been for the University of Wisconsin, and that it will clearly point the way for action and initiative in both the immediate and longer-term future.

THE MILWAUKEE IDEA PROCESS

Visioning: The Affinity Group Process

August	September	October	November	December	January	February	March
	Chancellor presents Milwaukee Idea at community events and meetings →						
		Mke Idea office opened					
		Web site and hand-out created					
		Affinity Groups formed: open to campus and community					
			Monthly articles on Mke Idea in campus publication				
			Strategy Group formed to advise Chancellor Community and Campus vetting sessions				
• Deans Retreat • Meeting with Chancellor's Cabinet and Staff • Outline of Mke Idea and areas of focus determined	• Chancellor announces Mke Idea at faculty plenary • Letters invite Committee of 100 to 1st plenary	• 1st Plenary • 7 Affinity Groups created • Co-convenors self select • Chancellor sends letter to campus announcing Affinity Groups and inviting participation	• 2nd Plenary • Affinity Groups share preliminary ideas with peers • Convenors Meetings outline goals, Connectors and template for final report • Affinity Groups continue meeting; new members join	• 3rd Plenary • Affinity Groups begin finalizing ideas; present to peers • Chancellor meets with University Committee to discuss how to vet ideas with governance • 1st drafts of Big Ideas submitted by Dec. 30	• 4th Plenary • UW System's President Lyall pledges support to Mke Idea • Reading Group meets to evaluate drafts; work with Affinity Groups to fine-tune Big Ideas	• 5th Plenary • Participants assess lessons learned • Final ideas presented at faculty plenary • Mke Idea report written	• University-Community Engagement Conference • Chancellor's Inauguration; Ideas announced to community • Corporate Council created • Action Team leaders selected by Strategy Group

THE MILWAUKEE IDEA PROCESS

Planning: The Action Team Process

April	May	June–August	September
	Chancellor presents Milwaukee Idea at community events and meetings		
		Action Teams meet independently through summer Mke Idea office coordinates team meetings	
		Chancellor holds regular, informal meetings with faculty	
• Action Team leaders meet, receive charge, review team member lists • First UWM Budget Planning Retreat held to set funding priorities	• Chancellor announces Action Teams, Advisory Councils • Action Teams meet for Kick-off, receive charge • President Lyall of UW System announces $1.5 million in funding for Mke Idea • Video describing goals of Mke Idea created	• Action Teams meet independently throughout summer • Strategy Team creates Evaluation process; Evaluation members solicited • Chancellor presents Mke Idea to Board of Regents • Corporate Council meets to provide counsel to Chancellor	• Sept. 15 final report due; reports received by all groups by Oct 15. • Evaluation team formed • School of Education receives major grants for teacher training

THE MILWAUKEE IDEA PROCESS

Implementation: The Evaluation Process

September–January	November–February	March and Ongoing
Chancellor presents Milwaukee Idea at community events and meetings		
Mke Idea office coordinates team meetings; drafts summary reports		
Strategy Group meets with Chancellor as needed		
Chancellor holds regular, informal meetings with faculty, students		
• Evaluation team reviews action reports, meets with Action Team leaders • Final recommendations made to Chancellor for implementation of First Ideas • Reports to Faculty Senate for input on administrative infrastructure • Chancellor sends all-campus email updating faculty and staff on progress	• "Thanksgiving" party in November recognizes Action Team members for hard work and contributions to Mke Idea • Percy meets with Administration and Deans to negotiate implementation plans • Deans Councils formed for each Idea to oversee administration • Trustee Council formed to oversee implementation and facilitate new infrastructures • Planning begins for major funding request to State for 2002 biennium • Ongoing faculty meetings regarding budget process; *Investing in UWM's Future* help to integrate Mke Idea into UWM governance process	• **First Ideas launched:** - **Cultures and Communities** introduced at community dance showcase. - **Campus Design Solutions** unveils plans for The Milwaukee Idea House, a prototype low-cost, energy-efficient home. - **Partnerships in Education** announced at Milwaukee Partnership Academy for Teacher Quality board meeting, chaired by Chancellor. - **Global Passport Project** launched at International Trade Day sponsored by Milwaukee World Trade Association. - **Consortium for Economic Opportunity** launched with Secretary of Commerce during National Small Business Week. - **Healthy Choices** launches a campus-wide survey of student drinking habits. - **Milwaukee Industrial Innovation Center** supports UWM's new Center for Intelligent Maintenance Systems. - **Helen Bader Institute for Nonprofit Management** announces new director. - **Urban Health Partnerships** forms to address community and family health issues. - **Partnerships for Environmental Health** supports research on urban environmental illnesses and how to implement preventive health practices in diverse populations. - **Knowledge Fest** promotes UWM's community partnerships at summer lakefront festivals. - **Quick WINS** continues to support innovative change on campus through faculty, staff, and student suggestions.

AFFINITY GROUP SUPPORT MATERIALS

Memorandum
To: Milwaukee Idea Affinity Group Members
Re: Affinity Groups

> *Our goal is nothing less than to change forever the quality of our life together—yours and mine, theirs and ours—by endeavoring to join the urban renaissance of Milwaukee; and the transformation of ourselves as Milwaukee's, and someday the nation's, premier urban university.*

I first heard Chancellor Zimpher describe a variation of this vision at the deans' retreat in late August. What can be more rewarding, compelling, engaging, and challenging than to be part of an initiative that has the genuine opportunity to change a community, a state, a region and, perhaps, whole chunks of the world? I was hooked!

Much has happened, on many fronts, since that retreat. As a member of The Milwaukee Idea working group, you are an integral part of this initiative, this "adventure," as Chancellor Zimpher called it.

This letter and packet contain the following:

- A brief overview of the concept of "Affinity Groups," introduced at the first Milwaukee Idea plenary session, along with "Frequently Asked Questions"

- An Affinity Group member's role description

- An Affinity Group co-convenor's role description

- A template for Affinity Group meetings

- A suggested timeline for Affinity Group work, and products from their efforts

Together, we have the opportunity to set in motion initiatives that will have positive impact for decades to come and touch millions of people around the world. The work over the next three months will be, by turns, gritty, contentious, ambiguous, frustrating, and time-consuming. And the ripples of our combined efforts can lead to benefits we can only imperfectly envision right now.

What a wonderful opportunity we have to make a difference!

AFFINITY GROUPS OVERVIEW

The Milwaukee Idea flows from a vision for the role of UWM as a member of the Milwaukee community, the state, and the world. This vision, articulated by Chancellor Zimpher and informed by interactions with hundreds of people during her early contacts with UWM, is made up of "imaginings."

During the first plenary session, participants were asked to imagine the future of UWM from their own perspectives. This is the beginning of the process of developing shared vision. The diversity of The Milwaukee Idea group assured that the collective vision elements would also be diverse. The imaginings include an urban environment:

- With economic opportunity

- Rich in cultural and educational opportunity

- Healthy and well

- That transcends national boundaries

- With a vibrant physical environment

- With UWM at the frontiers of knowledge and research

An additional Affinity Group was added, called "Quick Wins."

FREQUENTLY ASKED QUESTIONS ABOUT AFFINITY GROUPS

What Is an Affinity Group?

The definition of "affinity" in Webster's *New Universal Dictionary* is: "a condition of close relationship; conformity; resemblance; connection." Members of The Milwaukee Idea Committee of 100 were asked to select one of the preceding vision elements for which they felt a close relationship or connection, and meet with that "Affinity Group" to expand on the vision. They are also expected to creatively involve others in the Milwaukee community in the work of their group.

What Do Affinity Groups Do?

> "First and foremost, to be a player in the urban landscape of the future, we have to have ideas. [W]hile I see the renaissance of these urban environments as only the skeletal beginnings of framing The Milwaukee Idea, they can become the cornerstones. We must do the hard work of figuring out the reality of our dreams, the actions that transcend our rhetoric."
> —Chancellor Nancy Zimpher

Research Administrators

What our families think we do

What PIs think we do

What deans/directors think we do

What we think we do

What our bosses think we do

What we actually do

Chancellor Zimpher identifies two critical tasks for Affinity Group members: to "have ideas" (preferably "Big Ideas") and "the actions that transcend our rhetoric." When the Affinity Groups have finished the planning phase of their work in the new year, they will have identified big ideas and recommended specific action steps for their implementation.

Who Makes Up the Affinity Groups?

A cross-section of the UWM community, along with representatives from various Milwaukee groups. The Milwaukee Idea Committee of 100 was never intended to be statistically representative of the community. Its makeup reflects the necessity of involving a wide range of positions, personalities, and backgrounds. It is expected that the Affinity Groups will, in turn, draw in others to fill out the spectrum of groups represented.

Why "100 People, 100 Days"?

One hundred people (give or take 20%) is the practical limit for meaningful and positive group interaction. One hundred days is an acknowledgment that a new chancellor, or any new leader, has little more than three months to have a significant impact. Newness creates a unique window of opportunity for a short period of time. The Milwaukee Idea is starting fast, in the belief that the window of opportunity for change is still open and that dramatic advances are certain to continue after the "100 days."

What Are Quick Wins?

Consistent with the belief that the first 100 days of a new leader's tenure opens a unique window of opportunity, a list of ideas for quick victories is being collected. To qualify as a "quick win," the following conditions will be met:

- The win is inexpensive (it fits in a department's budget now, rather than next year).

- Time from identification to completion is relatively short.

- The win is viewed as positive, not controversial, by those involved in it or affected by it.

- The win has an appreciable (although not necessarily measurable) positive outcome.

AFFINITY GROUP MEMBER ROLE DESCRIPTION

MAJOR GOALS

Participants in an Affinity Group will contribute to the work of the group in such a manner that the group creates recommended action steps consistent with the vision of The Milwaukee Idea.

Members will:

1) Work with the Convenors to keep meetings on time and on topic so that the best use is made of people's limited time.

2) Seek to involve others in the work of the group, even if they are not members, so that the work is informed by a variety of viewpoints.

3) Strive for fact-based decision-making, when possible, to reduce the impact of bias and personal impression on group decision-making.

4) Participate and contribute in a manner that builds mutual trust and respect and brings out the best work of the group.

5) Participate in a manner that is at the same time respectful of the past and also focused on the future of The Milwaukee Idea.

Affinity Group Convenors Role Description

Major Goal

The Convenors will be responsible for leading an Affinity Group in such a manner that the group creates recommended action steps consistent with the vision of The Milwaukee Idea.

Leadership

Convenors will:

1) Lead the Affinity Group to create action recommendations for consideration by The Milwaukee Idea team so our vision is achieved.

2) Conduct meetings in a manner that promotes dialogue among participants so that different viewpoints are respectfully considered and recommendations represent the best thinking of the group.

3) Be responsible for creating a workgroup environment that promotes mutual trust and respect and is respectful of the time group members commit, so that all participants believe their contributions are valued and valuable.

4) Work with other members of the group to seek out and include diverse groups in discussions so that the whole group benefits from the rich variety of the Milwaukee community.

5) Challenge their group to make decisions and recommendations that are fact-based so that the impact of perception, bias, and "turf" is reduced.

Communication

Convenors will assure that:

1) Communication happens with other Affinity Groups, The Milwaukee Idea office, and other constituencies so that all groups can benefit from, use, and avoid overlap with the work of others.

2) Communication happens at agreed-upon times, using agreed-upon methods so that good order is maintained and the aggressive timeline for this project can be met.

3) Materials posted to the web by other groups are available to their own team members. In addition, they will see to it that requests for review

and feedback by other groups are done on time so that information bot-
tlenecks are reduced or eliminated.

COORDINATION

Convenors will coordinate:

1) The resources necessary to achieve the purpose of the Affinity Group.

2) The activities of the "note-taker" and an "office-liaison." These positions
   can be filled by any member of the committee or by the Convenors
   themselves.

AFFINITY GROUP MEETING TEMPLATE

PURPOSE

This is a suggested template for organizing Affinity Group meetings. It is only a suggestion. Convenors can organize their group's meetings in the way that best meets the needs of their groups.

OUTLINE

Open, Greet, Welcome (5 minutes)
- Introductions of new people, if any
- Assign a note-taker unless someone has already taken that responsibility

Review Purpose of Meeting and Agenda (5 minutes)
- Review to-do list from previous meetings, if any
- Confirm time frame for meeting

Discussion Topic #1 (set a time limit for discussion)
- At the end of the discussion, agree on:
  - Next steps
  - Who will do what
  - Timeline

Discussion Topic #2, #3, etc

Close with Review and Set Next Meeting (10 minutes)
- Review list of action items from the meeting, who will do what, by when
- Establish next meeting date and tentative agenda items
- Close

SUGGESTIONS

1) Distribute the agenda in advance.
2) Distribute a written agenda at the meeting.
3) Establish an end time for the meeting and abide by it.
4) Use The Milwaukee Idea staffing office for support: getting meeting notes sent to group members, posting notes or documents to the web, etc.
5) Send copies of meeting notes to participants as soon after the meeting as possible.

AFFINITY GROUP TIMELINE

PURPOSE

This document outlines the progression of tasks envisioned for the work of Affinity Groups. These tasks are suggested, not required. The members of the group will be the final arbiters of tasks, products, and timeline consistent with their ability to do their best work. The deadlines, listed in the "By" column, are recommendations only. Our goal is that all groups finish their work at approximately the same time and with the same level of detail.

Task	Outcomes	Delivered to:	By:
Team mandate: 1) Why the team exists. 2) Final outcomes or results that define completion.	Documents describing: 1) Definition of the vision element the group worked on (e.g., what is "an urban environment of economic opportunity"). 2) Why the team exists. 3) How the team will know it is done.	The Milwaukee Idea staffing office, so documents can be posted to the web for review and comments by others.	Before the November plenary.
Vision five years from now: A definition of the future state of UWM in the area the group has chosen to work, e.g., in the area of "economic opportunity" what will be different or better five years from now, as a result of The Milwaukee Idea.	Documents describing: 1) A clear description of what is different or better five years from now as a result of UWM's work in the chosen area. 2) A clear description of the current state as it relates to the vision element. The purpose is to identify the "gap" between the current and future state and the future vision.	The Milwaukee Idea staffing office, so documents can be posted to the web for review and comments by others.	Before the November plenary (at least in draft form).
November plenary meeting.	A report by the Convenors and/or team: 1) A summary of the completed outcomes. 2) Information needed from other groups. 3) Topics for discussion, either at the plenary or in some other forum (web, meeting, etc.).	Plenary group.	November.

Task	Outcomes	Delivered to:	By:
Describe barriers and enablers that are likely to be encountered in moving from the current state to the future state.	Documents describing: 1) Perceived barriers. 2) Perceived enablers. 3) Brief descriptions of how the group recommends overcoming those barriers and leveraging those enablers (note: this will be used in developing the initiatives and action plans later).	The Milwaukee Idea staffing office, so documents can be posted to the web for review and comments by others.	Finished before the December plenary, along with final versions of the preceding work.
Develop key strategies that will have the greatest impact on reaching the vision (1–2 key strategies will be sufficient).	Documents describing: 1) Descriptions of the key strategies (1–2) to move to the vision. 2) A description of how enablers are used. 3) A description of how barriers are overcome. 4) A clear description of the expected outcomes (this is a high-level description—detail will come later).	The Milwaukee Idea staffing office, so documents can be posted to the web for review and comments by others.	Draft version by the December plenary.
December plenary meeting.	A report by the Convenors and/or team: 1) A summary of the completed outcomes. 2) Information needed from other groups. 3) Topics for discussion, either at the plenary or in some other forum (web or meeting). 4) As part of the meeting we will look for overlaps, congruence, and dependence among strategies.	Plenary Group.	December.
Key Initiatives ("first things") to take action on, based on the strategies identified above.	Documents describing: 1) Recommended key initiatives. 2) What the expected results are of acting on those initiatives.	The Milwaukee Idea staffing office, so documents can be posted to the web for review and comments by others.	Before the January plenary.

Task	Outcomes	Delivered to:	By:
Action steps to get commitment for the strategies and initiatives the group is recommending (what has to happen to begin taking action—who needs to commit to this? Where will the money come from? etc.).	Documents describing: 1) Proposed action steps to gain commitment for the group's strategies and initiatives, including: • Who needs to commit to this? • What resources are needed? • Who will be responsible for what activities? • Recommended timeline.	The Milwaukee Idea staffing office, so documents can be posted to the web for review and comments by others.	Before the January plenary.

CONNECTORS

(Cross-cutting themes relevant to all Affinity Groups)

DIVERSITY AND MULTICULTURALISM

Truly one of the strengths of our institution, diversity is also a challenge. How can we better reflect our community? How can we encourage the riches of the cultures on campus through each Big Idea?

PARTNERSHIPS AND COLLABORATION

The Milwaukee Idea process is a textbook example of collaboration. How can we model it in the action steps we recommend? What new partners can we bring into the process? How can we better reach out to the community?

INTERDISCIPLINARITY

As we develop our proposals, what opportunities can we find that will link across disciplines? How can we encourage thinking outside the boxes of our departments, disciplines, and colleges?

CAMPUS LIFE AND CULTURE

The UWM we are envisioning five years from now will have a vibrant culture, rich in traditions and identity. How will we strengthen and enhance that culture? What will give it meaning and excitement?

COMMUNICATION AND SUPPORT

As we develop Big Ideas, what are we doing to improve the image of UWM and to increase UWM's standing in the community? How can we better communicate the partnership/relationship between UWM and the community to a broad audience, including elected officials, potential donors, community leaders, neighbors, and business people?

GUIDELINES FOR CREATING BIG IDEAS

In moving forward to create "Big Ideas" for The Milwaukee Idea, Affinity Groups are encouraged to consider the following guidelines.

1) Emphasize the *Connectors* that have been created as part of The Milwaukee Idea:

  - Diversity and Multiculturalism

  - Partnerships and Collaborations

  - Interdisciplinarity

  - Campus Life and Culture

  - Communication and Support

2) Anticipate the necessity for collaboration among multiple UWM units (it should not be possible for a single unit to perform an Idea)

3) Require substantial community input, participation, and involvement

4) Create lasting and widely recognized change at UWM

5) Substantially encourage wide participation among all people and organizations on campus, including:

  - Faculty

  - Academic staff

  - Classified staff

  - Students

  - Administrators

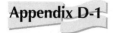

ACTION TEAM CHARGE

As part of the Action Plan, each Action Team is requested to:

- Devise a conceptual vision statement that outlines the fundamental rationale and anticipated outcomes of initiatives within the Big Idea.

- Craft a set of workable strategies and initiatives that will be launched and executed as part of the Big Idea within a five-year time frame. [Note: it may be necessary to pare down and/or reorganize some of the many ideas contained in Big Idea reports into a workable set; many of the reports are extremely ambitious in terms of the number of different actions that could be launched effectively as part of the Idea.]

- Explore options and make recommendations for the organizational structure within UWM that will be utilized to administer the execution of identified strategies. [Note: we encourage people to think outside the box here and explore nontraditional strategies for management and administration that embrace interdisciplinary contributions, diversity, and community connections.]

- Identify community partners who will join with UWM in pursuing strategic initiatives associated with the Big Idea and describe how the university-community partnership will be configured so as to ensure meaningful and sustainable collaboration.

- Describe how the Idea promotes interdisciplinary approaches and work, diversity, and collaboration across schools, colleges, departments, centers, and institutes.

- Estimate the resource needs associated with launching strategic initiatives including personnel (by type and function), space, equipment, travel, and other related expenses. Since some phasing-in of initiatives is likely, teams will be asked to prepare a budget plan for a five-year time horizon (see "Criteria for Awarding Funding" document).

- Identify potential funding sources that might be tapped to support identified initiatives, including federal and state grant programs, national and local foundations, private corporations or business associations, and other sponsors.

- Describe the anticipated outcomes and achievements that will result from implementing the Idea and how the initiative can be evaluated using appropriate indicators.

THE MILWAUKEE IDEA ACTION PLAN OUTLINE

In response to requests from Action Teams for a template to guide preparation of Action Plans, The Milwaukee Idea has prepared the following baseline plan.

1) Executive Summary

On one or two pages, outline your vision, goals, structure, collaborations, and funding plans. This can be in narrative or outline form. Readers should be able to capture the essence—and excitement—of your Idea from this summary. This is a "sell" piece, not just a summary!

2) Action Plan Narrative

Your narrative explains the full extent of your Idea and the plan for implementation. It should feature not only a description of your plans, but the rationale for your proposals and how your decisions were made. It should be based on the "Action Team Charge" and should include:

- **Vision statement.**

- **Work plan.** Outline the strategies or activities that will implement the Idea. For each strategy, include objectives, timelines and staffing responsibilities.

- **Organizational structure.** Describe how the Idea will be implemented and administered within UWM's overall structure, including the kinds of decisions that will need to be made to take it to action.

- **Partnerships and collaborations.** List the internal and external partners that will be involved (including the level of their participation in action planning) and strategies for their inclusion. Describe which partnerships already exist, how they will be used or expanded, and how new partnerships will be formed—both within UWM and the community. Describe how the partnerships represent interdisciplinary approaches and are inclusive of multiple schools and colleges.

- **Support for diversity.** Outline specific ways in which inclusion and diversity will be integrated into the successful launch of the Idea.

- **Launch.** Describe how your Idea can be launched at UWM, in the community—and beyond! Present ideas for special events, media involvement and key participants as well as suggestions for ongoing marketing activities and how they will be supported.

- **Evaluation.** Outline your indicators for success and a timetable for evaluating them, recognizing that each initiative will report annually on progress toward achieving stated outcomes.

3) Budget Narrative

Complete the Budget for the First Ideas, using the template form provided. Separate narratives, using the attachments provided, will explain significant expenditures and resources. Using "best estimates" complete the following:

- **Staffing chart.**

- **Supplies and expenses.** Describe and provide budget figures for any consultants, off-campus space rental, and space renovations. We anticipate that all projects will require travel and office expenses (including postage, reproduction, telephone, office supplies, software, and hardware). Describe any expenditures for these that exceed $5,000 per year.

- **Capital costs.**

- **Current sources.** Describe sources and amounts.

- **New sources.** Describe your assumptions and how the figures for new sources were calculated.

- **Space needs.** Describe space needs of the First Idea, including square footage, specialized facilities, renovation needs, preferred location, and number of offices, labs, and classrooms.

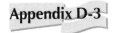

CRITERIA FOR AWARDING FUNDING TO FIRST IDEAS

Early in The Milwaukee Idea process, all Affinity Groups were asked to incorporate five themes into the creation of their First Ideas. These cross-cutting characteristics were called Connectors and are integral to the success of The Milwaukee Idea.

We have taken these Connectors and used them to inform and structure the criteria for our funding guidelines, which we have consolidated into four points:

    1) Links   *3) Building Blocks*

    2) Partners   *4) Wow!*

Each Idea must demonstrate fulfillment of all four criteria in its funding proposal.

Milwaukee Idea Connectors

Diversity and Multiculturalism
Not only must a commitment to diversity and multiculturalism be a hallmark of the Idea, it must also be reflected in its implementation, both in the diversity of approaches and the people it involves.

Partnerships and Collaboration
The engaged university is anchored in a culture of sharing and reciprocity. Partnerships are multidimensional, across the university and with our communities.

Interdisciplinary Work
All Ideas must bring together diverse groups of individuals, across disciplines, departments, and schools, sharing expertise and new thinking.

Campus Life and Culture
The Idea must contribute in significant ways to making our campus life more vibrant, our traditions richer, and our students' learning more powerful.

Communication and Support
No Idea will succeed without the support of our campus and community. To do so, we will need to effectively communicate our vision and reach out in new ways to new partners.

---

1) LINKS

No Idea is an "island." To be implemented, it must, by its nature, structure, and funding, require links within UWM that cross disciplines, divisions, departments, schools, and colleges.

Questions to Answer:

- Does the focus of the project demand new links?

- Do the people involved represent diverse groups?

- Does participation in on-going implementation link across disciplines?

- What are the explicit funding links?

Connector: Interdisciplinary Work

2) PARTNERS

The links within UWM must be mirrored by the partnerships with our community, UW System, and the state. Engagement is a "productive involvement with the community," according to the Kellogg Commission.

Questions to Answer:

- Who are the community partners who will collaborate in planning and in implementation?

- Who are the potential partners who will be added to the process as implementation advances?

- What is the documented level of community interest in the Idea?

- How does the Idea relate to other UWM community/university engagement initiatives either planned or underway?

- How does the Idea relate to other UWM initiatives of knowledge generation and learning?

Connectors: Partnerships and Collaboration, Diversity and Multiculturalism

3) BUILDING BLOCKS

The chief charge to the Action Teams is to "make the First Ideas real." Building Blocks is the proposed infrastructure that will support and make possible the implementation of the Idea. It involves developing four components: 1) funding sources, 2) a workable administrative structure, 3) a realistic budget within a two- to three-year timeframe, and 4) a comprehensive communication plan outlining how perceptions of UWM will be enhanced with our various publics, including the media, elected officials, funders, local community, and national and international audiences.

The funding proposal will specifically identify multiple streams of funding sources and it will outline a realistic timetable of when the dollars will be raised and spent. Sources and timelines must employ a working model of a "1/3, 1/3, 1/3 funding split" from the menu of funding sources below (departures from the model must state rationale):

- *Federal: grants and/or contracts*
- *New State: biennial budget, agency contracts, fees for service, loans*
- *University: UW System, reallocation, chancellor, fees, program revenue, tuition revenue, endowment income*
- *Local: city and/or county contracts, grants, fees for service*
- *Private: grants, gifts, fees for service*

Questions to Answer:

- Does the administrative structure involve both UWM and the community?

- What administrative support will be required to satisfy the funding plan?

- How does the funding plan and budget create a foundation for future activities?

- What key audiences need to hear about the Idea? What communication strategies will reach those audiences most effectively?

Connector: Communication and Support

4) Wow!

In addition to the steak, you need the sizzle. In short, where's the "Wow!" in the Idea? Specifically, the Wow! should address our campus life and culture, the Milwaukee Commitment, student learning opportunities, our enhanced role within System, and opportunities for a stronger presence locally, regionally, nationally, and/or internationally.

Questions to Answer:

- How is the Milwaukee Commitment integral to planning and implementation of the Idea?

- What are some of the anticipated synergies that will result from this Idea?

- How are student learning opportunities expanded or made more relevant? What role does service-learning play? What are the opportunities for international learning?

- How does this Idea help UWM become the lead institution within System? How might it enhance the flow of funding dollars?

- How does this expand UWM's connections to our communities? How can this increase the diversity of our entering students?

- How can the activities of the Idea find a regional, national, or international profile?

- What makes this Idea great? What will "sell" it on campus, to a community partner, to a funder?

- What will change as a result of this Idea?

Connectors: Diversity and Multiculturalism, Campus Life and Culture

EVALUATION TEAM CHARGE

THE EVALUATION TEAM

The Evaluation Team will have 13 members and will include:

- Three civic leaders from metropolitan Milwaukee

- Two faculty representatives nominated by the University Committee

- One representative nominated from each of the Academic Staff Committee, Student Association, and Classified Staff

- One representative from the Academic Deans Council

- Four representatives from The Milwaukee Idea Strategy Group

The team will be facilitated by the Executive Director of The Milwaukee Idea, The Chancellor, Provost, Secretary of the University, and Director of Business Services will be ex-officio members. The Team will be staffed by The Milwaukee Idea office.

THE PROCESS

June/July	Evaluation Team selected
August	Evaluation Team meets with chancellor to review charge and receive action plans
September/October	• Evaluation Team meets to review and discuss Action Plans; develops list of clarifying questions for Action Teams. Questions and comments distributed to Action Team co-leaders for follow up.
	• Evaluation Team, or subcommittee of the Evaluation Team, dialogues with Action Team leaders to review questions and responses.
October/November	Consultation with Schools and Colleges as appropriate.
October	Evaluation Team assesses Action Team responses and formulates recommendations to chancellor on an Idea-by-Idea basis.
November	Chancellor receives reports of Evaluation Team, makes implementation decisions. Governance units and staff take up portions of Idea as appropriate.

THE CHARGE

Review

The Evaluation Team will review—individually and as a group—the written Action Plans submitted by each of The Milwaukee Idea Action Teams. The Action Plans for each First Idea will be rated according to the guidelines of the *Action Team Charge* and *Criteria for Funding* documents.

The Evaluation Team is expected to place particular emphasis on the need for Action Plans to embrace collaboration, interdisciplinary and community partnerships, and diversity. The plans must also be financially realistic and rely on a strong mix of funding options, including UWM, System, private and public support.

Clarify

The Evaluation Team will meet with the leaders of each of the Action Teams to discuss the proposal and to clarify details.

Assess

The Evaluation Team will assess the viability of each First Idea. First Ideas will be evaluated on their own merits and written recommendations for implementation will be given. The Evaluation Team is free to make whatever recommendations it deems appropriate to the chancellor. The following scale is a suggested guideline:

1) *Ready for the chancellor.* The Action Plan is sound and ready for the Chancellor and administration to integrate into UWM budget and staff plans so that the plan can be launched.

2) *Ready for the chancellor, subject to meeting stated conditions.* The Action Plan is sound, but before the chancellor and administration can begin integrating, other independent conditions—such as ratification by a community partner or secured external funding—need to be completed.

3) *Needs further refinement.* The Evaluation Team sees merit in the plan but does not consider it ready for the chancellor to move forward. The Evaluation Team will outline its concerns and make recommendations for how they can be addressed. This may involve requesting the Action Team to do additional work to refine the plan. If needed, the Evaluation Team may also recommend adding or reconfiguring the membership of the Action Team.

4) *Proposal delayed.* Due to unforeseen conditions or if the Action Plan does not meet the guidelines, the Idea may need to be postponed or reformatted. The Evaluation Team will outline reasons for delaying implementation and proposal alternatives, as appropriate.

Recommend

The Evaluation Team will submit a final report to the chancellor outlining its recommendations for all First Ideas. The chancellor and her administrative team will move forward to provide the financial, staff, and administrative support for the Ideas, in a timely manner. When all details have been finalized, the chancellor will draft Letters of Agreement for each Idea.

EVALUATION SHEET FOR ACTION PLANS

First Idea_____

Strengths:

Weaknesses/questions to be resolved:

Interdisciplinary work:

Community partnership/connection:

Diversity/multiculturalism:

Connecting multiple schools and colleges:

Meaningful community partnerships/involvement:

PRINCIPLES FOR ADMINISTRATION

INITIATIVE LEADERSHIP

In several First Idea initiatives, leaders emerged through existing campus leadership roles related to emerging First Ideas as well as through the Action Team process, allowing The Milwaukee Idea to build upon existing strength and leadership at UWM. In other initiatives, leaders emerged through collaborative, interdisciplinary roles being performed by newly created deputy chancellors. In future rounds and when there is turnover of initiative leadership, leaders will be selected through an open campus recruitment process.

Initiative leaders (other than deputy chancellors) will hold leadership positions equivalent to center directors operating across UWM schools and colleges and will serve annual renewable terms. Center directors will be compensated for their administrative roles in a fashion generally congruent with that given to center directors, including compensation through administrative increments associated with the administrative position and recognizing unique circumstances of individuals with regard to nature of appointment (i.e., nine month, annual) and other factors. For example, many center directors receive 1/9th summer salary and/or an administrative adjustment to their salary.

STRUCTURE AND ADMINISTRATIVE OVERSIGHT

Administering and coordinating interdisciplinary initiatives that cut across schools and colleges requires innovative mechanisms with only limited parallels at UWM and other universities. As the First Ideas are launched, a mechanism for administrative oversight and review will be Deans Councils, composed of a lead dean along with other members of the Academic Deans Council whose responsibilities or faculty, staff, or students are involved (or likely to be involved) in the initiative. (Intent is to be as inclusive as possible of persons with interest in the First Idea.) It is expected that Deans Councils will meet at least once each academic semester.

*Lead dean*s will be responsible for general oversight of administrative issues related to the initiative. Meetings of the Deans Council may be called by any council member. Lead dean designation may be shifted among Deans Council members over time.

Business operations/appointment process. As a general rule, business operations and appointment approval responsibility for individual First Idea initiatives will be vested in the school or college of the lead dean or deputy chancellor. Financial matters will be handled through the unit business manager of the lead dean or deputy chancellor.

The deans council or deputy chancellor for each First Idea initiative will be responsible for:

1) Working with the leaders of individual initiatives to review operational issues and challenges that arise in implementing the interdisciplinary initiatives

2) Reviewing progress toward meeting outcomes identified for the initiative by the Action Team and initiative leaders

3) Reviewing operational plans and budgets for the initiative

4) Working with the initiative, Milwaukee Idea Office and campus administration to promote the initiative

5) Conducting annual reviews of initiative leaders with recommendations made to the chancellor and provost

6) Reporting to the chancellor on the progress of the initiative in meeting its identified outcomes. Progress reports and other relevant information on the operations and accomplishments of initiatives will be shared with the University Committee and Academic Staff Committee

The Deans Council and deputy chancellor mechanisms for administering the interdisciplinary initiatives of The Milwaukee Idea may be reviewed over time in light of their capacity to effectively administer the initiatives.

COMMUNITY INVOLVEMENT AS KEY TO ENGAGEMENT

The Milwaukee Idea will strive to ensure meaningful community participation throughout activities relating to planning, implementation, and assessment. As with the Affinity Group and Action Team phases, community participation will be a critical operating feature of The Milwaukee Idea. Community involvement will be formally manifest in membership on the Strategy Group as well as in Advisory/Partnership Councils that will be formed for each First Idea initiative. Each Advisory Council will have multiple community representatives as members with one such community member designated as the Community Liaison. As in the Action Team phases, the Community Liaison will be the key link between the community and the university, providing frequent input and feedback to the initiative leaders, especially between Advisory Committee meetings.

Campus administration and the Trustee Council may convene the Community Liaisons of the individual initiatives of The Milwaukee Idea to gather community perspectives on implementation of The Milwaukee Idea as well as ideas for enhancing effective UWM-community partnerships.

ASSESSMENT

The Milwaukee Idea will be created with an expectation of regular evaluation of the extent of its achievements in creating meaningful university-community partnerships that contribute to the scholarly and instructional missions of the university as well as to the quality of life of the greater Milwaukee community. At the start of implementation, each initiative will be asked to review the outcomes identified in its Action Plan and to revise them with regard to actual budget allocations so as to create an anticipated set of outcomes for the 1999–2001 start-up phase. The Milwaukee Idea office will collaborate with the Trustee Council, the Strategy Team, the provost, and chancellor to develop a framework for assessment that will be shared with initiative leaders. The assessment reports will be forwarded by the initiative to the appropriate Deans Council for consideration and then to the provost and chancellor. Review of progress in achieving outcomes will be considered as part of decisions regarding allocation of budget resources in future biennia.

RESPONSIBILITIES OF THE FIRST IDEA INITIATIVES

In order for The Milwaukee Idea to maximize its potential, it is important that the First Idea initiatives do NOT operate in isolation. It is important that individual initiatives collaborate with other Milwaukee Idea initiatives and contribute to campus efforts to promote university-community engagement and to the acquisition of resources to provide long-term support. It is also important that the initiatives operate within the established parameters of shared governance.

For these reasons each initiative will be expected to do the following:

- **Governance:** Consult with appropriate governance bodies where appropriate in undertaking component initiatives and obtaining governance approvals where so required by university rules and procedures.

- **Information sharing:** Provide information to The Milwaukee Idea office on initiative events, accomplishments, and community partnerships that will support overall promotion of The Milwaukee Idea.

- **Collaboration:** Consider opportunities for collaboration with other First Idea initiatives and develop, where appropriate, collaborative activities.

The Evaluation Team, University Committee, and Academic Staff Committee will identify areas of connection and potential for collaboration.

- **Provide information:** Share information with the Deans Council and The Milwaukee Idea office concerning accomplishments, challenges in implementing interdisciplinary initiatives, and progress in achieving identified outcomes.

- **Promotion:** Work with campus administration and The Milwaukee Idea office to support efforts to promote The Milwaukee Idea, including UWM's request to UW System, Regents, and state government for new state resources.

"Round Two" Support Materials

Memorandum

To: UWM Community

Re: Round Two of Big Ideas

Last fall, Chancellor Nancy Zimpher announced that UWM would create a second opportunity for major new community partnership initiatives to develop as part of The Milwaukee Idea. We are now ready to start the process for what we are calling "Round Two" of "Big Ideas" within The Milwaukee Idea.

The beginning stage of this second round involves preparation of concept papers, which outline new community-university partnership initiatives that foster interdisciplinary work, meaningful and sustainable community partnership, and diversity.

The chancellor will select a reading group to review the submitted concept papers. They will recommend the strongest proposals to move into the next stage, where an Action Team will be created to develop a strategic plan to create and implement the initiative.

If you are interested in developing a concept paper for a potential Big Idea, please contact The Milwaukee Idea office. We will send you a packet of information that outlines the specific form and structure that concept paper proposals should take.

"ROUND TWO" Concept Paper/Idea Template

1) Idea Name

2) The Idea (in one sentence)

3) Rationale

Describe how the Idea relates generally to the concept of The Milwaukee Idea as well as to the core functions and mission of the University of Wisconsin-Milwaukee. Describe how the Idea will create positive change for the university and the community/region in which it is located, noting expected beneficiaries of the Idea once implemented. If possible, show value of fundamental basic and applied research to Idea. Reference Connectors where relevant.

4) Enablers and Barriers

Outline the likely challenges that will be faced in moving forward with the Idea as well as the shared resources, knowledge, experience, or expertise that can be drawn upon to move the Idea forward. Also, where relevant, discuss capacity to implement the Idea.

5) Guiding Assumptions

Articulate the primary assumptions and perspectives that should be kept in mind as plans are designed to implement the Idea—the guiding philosophy that underlies the Idea. Reference Connectors where relevant.

6) Action Steps

Briefly identify the key actions that will need to be taken and the decisions needed to move the Idea to action. (It is not necessary to outline each step in detail, although advice about process will be welcome. An Action Team will ultimately create the specific plans to implement the Idea.)

7) Process Used to Create Idea

Identify the key players on the team that developed this proposal and any process that was followed (group meetings, surveys, etc.). The evidence suggests the more collaborative and inclusive the planning process, the better. We encourage the participation of faculty, staff, students, and community representatives in the development of the concept paper.

"ROUND TWO" EVALUATION SHEET

Proposal # _____ **Title** _____   **Rating Scale:**
1 = lowest; 10 = highest

Criteria	Comments	Rating
Diversity/ Multiculturalism		
Partnerships/ Collaborations (on and off campus)		
Interdisciplinary work		
Contribute to campus life/culture		
Communication and Support		
Create lasting change at UWM		
Encourage wide participation from all people on campus		
Other comments		

SELECT BIBLIOGRAPHY

MANAGING CHANGE

Abrahamson, Eric. "Change Without Pain." *Harvard Business Review,* July/August 2000.

Austin, James E. *The Collaboration Challenge: How Nonprofits and Businesses Succeed Through Strategic Alliances.* San Francisco: Jossey-Bass, 2000.

Collins, James and Porras, Jerry. *Built to Last: Successful Habits of Visionary Companies.* New York, NY: HarperCollins, 1994.

Collins, James and Porras, Jerry. "Building Your Company's Vision." *Harvard Business Review,* September-October 1996.

Chrislip, David and Larson, Carl. *Collaborative Leadership: How Citizens and Civic Leaders Can Make a Difference.* San Francisco, CA: Jossey-Bass Publishers, 1994.

Drucker, Peter. *Managing in a Time of Great Change.* New York, NY: Truman Talley Books/Dutton, 1995.

Eckel, Peter; Green, Madeleine; Hill, Barbara; and Mallon, Bill. *On Change,* an occasional paper series of the ACE Project on Leadership and Institutional Transformation, in three volumes. Washington, DC: American Council on Education, 1999.

Fullan, Michael. *Change Forces.* New York, NY: The Falmer Press, 1993.

——————-. *Change Forces: The Sequel.* Philadelphia, PA: The Falmer Press, 1999.

Helgesen, Sally. *The Web of Inclusion: A New Architecture for Building Great Organizations.* New York, NY: Currency/Doubleday, 1995.

Holman, Peggy and Devane, Tom, editors. *The Change Handbook: Group Methods for Shaping the Future.* San Francisco, CA: Berrett-Koehler, 1999.

Peters, Tom. *The Pursuit of Wow! Every Person's Guide to Topsy-Turvy Times.* New York, NY: Vintage Books, 1994.

Sarason, Seymour and Lorentz, Elizabeth. *Crossing Boundaries: Collaboration, Coordination, and the Redefinition of Resources.* San Francisco, CA: Jossey-Bass, 1998.

Shenkman, Michael. *The Strategic Heart: Using the New Science to Lead Growing Organizations*. Westport, CT: Praeger, 1996.

Senge, Peter, et al. *The Dance of Change: The Challenges of Sustaining Momentum in Learning Organizations*. New York, NY: Currency/Doubleday, 1999.

CHANGE AND THE UNIVERSITY

Cassell, Frank; Klotsche, J. Martin; and Olson, Frederick, with the assistance of Donald Shea and Bea Bourgeois. *The University of Wisconsin-Milwaukee: A Historical Profile, 1885–1992*. Milwaukee, WI: UWM Foundation, 1992.

Duderstadt, James. *A University for the 21st Century*. Ann Arbor, MI: The University of Michigan Press, 2000.

—————————. "A Choice of Transformations for the 21st-Century University." *The Chronicle of Higher Education*, February 4, 2000.

Hirsch, Werner and Weber, Luc. "The Glion Declaration: The University at the Millennium." *The Presidency*, American Council on Education, Fall 1998.

Johnson, Daniel and Bell, David. *Metropolitan Universities: An Emerging Model in American Higher Education*. Denton, TX: University of North Texas Press, 1995.

Kerr, Clark. "Clark Kerr's Perspective on Leadership Challenges." *Change*, January/Feburary 1998.

Kettl, Donald. "Reinventing The Wisconsin Idea," the La Follette Institute's Sesquicentennial Paper Series, Madison, WI: University of Wisconsin-Madison, February 1999.

Kliewer, Joy Rosenzweig. *The Innovative Campus: Nurturing the Distinctive Learning Environment*. American Council on Education Series on Higher Education. Phoenix, AZ: The Oryx Press, 1999.

Marchese, Ted. "Restructure?! You Bet! An Interview Change Expert with Alan E. Guskin." *AAHE Bulletin,* The American Association for Higher Education, September 1998.

Norquist, John. *The Wealth of Cities: Revitalizing the Centers of American Life*. Reading, MA: Perseus Books, 1998.

Rhodes, Frank H. T. *The Creation of the Future: The Role of the American University*. Ithaca, NY: Cornell University Press, 2001.

—————————. "The Art of the Presidency." *The Presidency*, American Council on Education, Spring 1998.

Severino, Carol. "The Idea of An Urban University: A History and Rhetoric of Ambivalence and Ambiguity." *Urban Education*, September 1996.

Spaights, Ernest. "Toward a Definition of An Urban University." *Urban Education*, October 1980.

van der Werg, Martin. "Urban Universities Try New Ways to Reach Out to Their Communities." *The Chronicle of Higher Education*, April 30, 1999.

Weinstein, Laurence A. *Moving a Battleship with Your Bare Hands: Governing a University System*. Madison, WI: Magna Publications, 1993.

Wingspread Group on Higher Education. *An American Imperative: Higher Expectations for Higher Education*. Racine, WI: The Johnson Foundation, 1993.

Ziegler, Jerome M. "Winds of Change: The University in Search of Itself." *Metropolitan Universities*, Fall/Winter 1990/91.

UNIVERSITY ENGAGEMENT

Bok, Derek. *Beyond the Ivory Tower: Social Responsibilities of the Modern University*. Cambridge, MA: Harvard University Press, 1982.

Boyer, Ernest L. "Creating the New American College." *The Chronicle of Higher Education*, March 9, 1994.

—————————. *Scholarship Reconsidered: Priorities of the Professoriate*. San Francisco, CA: Jossey-Bass, 1990.

Boyer, Ernest and Hechinger, Fred. *Higher Learning in the Nation's Service: A Carnegie Foundation Essay*. Washington, DC: Carnegie Foundation for the Advancement of Teaching, 1981.

Boyte, Harry and Hollander, Elizabeth. "The Wingspread Declaration on Renewing the Civic Mission of the American Research University." The declaration was a product of a series of conferences sponsored by The Johnson Foundation at Wingspread, in Racine, WI, in 1998 and 1999.

Bringle, Robert; Games, Richard; and Malloy, Edward. *Colleges and Universities as Citizens*. Boston, MA: Allyn and Bacon, 1999.

Carr, James H., editor. "It's Not Just Academic: University-Community Partnerships Are Rebuilding Neighborhoods." *Housing Facts & Figures*, Fannie Mae Foundation, Spring 1999.

Dobelle, Evan. "Stepping Down from the Ivory Tower." Remarks delivered to the National Press Club, Washington, DC, February 18, 1999.

Gamson, Zelda. "Higher Education and Rebuilding Civic Life." *Change*, January/February 1997.

Gaudiani, Claire L. "A Call to Social Stewardship." *The Presidency*, American Council on Education, Winter 1999.

Greiner, William R. "The Courage to Lead: Engaging Universities and Colleges in Public Problem-Solving." *Universities and Community Schools*, a publication of the University of Pennsylvania, Fall/Winter 1997.

Harkavy, Ira. "Historical Evolution of University-Community Partnerships." *Community News & Views*, a publication of the Michigan State University Center for Urban Affairs, Summer 2000.

—————————. "School-Community-University Partnerships: Effectively Integrating Community Building and Education Reform," a paper presented to a Joint Forum of the U.S. Department of Education and the U.S. Department of Housing and Urban Development in Washington, DC, January 8, 1998.

Kellogg Commission on the Future of State and Land-Grant Universities. *The Engaged University*. New York, NY: National Association of State Universities and Land-Grant Colleges, 1999.

The Kellogg Commission —————————. *Renewing the Covenant: Learning, Discovery, and Engagement in a New Age and Different World*, 2000.

Klotsche, J. Martin. *The Urban University and the Future of our Cities*. New York, NY: Harper & Row, 1966.

Stark, Jack. "The Wisconsin Idea: The University's Service to the State." *Wisconsin 1995–1996 Blue Book*. Madison, WI: Legislative Reference Bureau, 1995.

Wergin, Jon and Grassadonia, Jane. "The Milwaukee Idea: A Study of Transformative Change." A paper prepared for the Office of University Partnerships, U.S. Department of Housing and Urban Development, 2001.

Zemsky, Robert, senior editor. "Strategic Community Partnerships." *Exemplars*, November 2000, a companion to *Policy Perspectives*, Knight Higher Education Collaborative, Philadelphia, PA.

INDEX